You can purchase large format limited edition and open edition prints at the following art galleries:

Sie können großformatige limitierter Auflage und offene Ausgabe druckt mit den folgenden Galerien erwerben:

Vous pouvez acheter édition grand format limité et imprime édition ouverte aux galeries d'art suivantes:

Вы можете приобрести крупноформатные работы, выпущенные ограниченным и открытым тиражом в следующих арт галереях:

http://vasiliadis.portfolio.artlimited.net

http://www.250pictures.com/Igor-Vasiliadis.html

http://www.yellowkorner.com/artistes/170/Igor-Vasiliadis.aspx

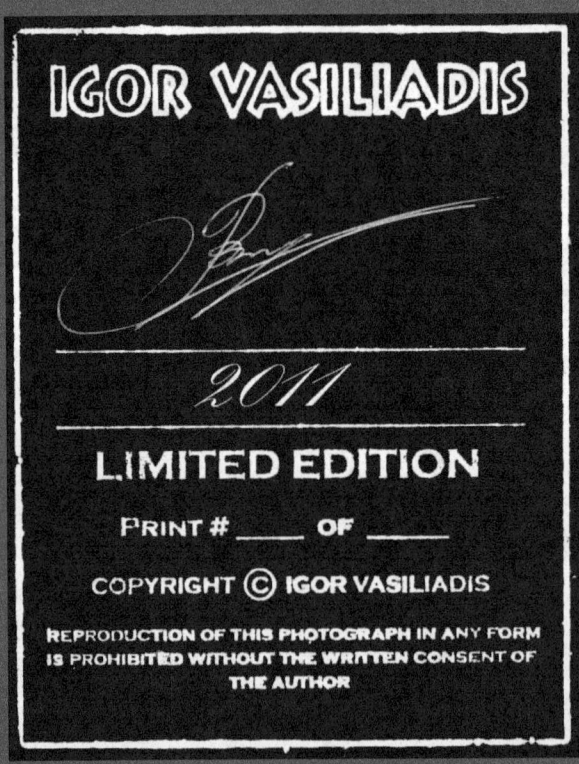

IGOR VASILIADIS

SILVER MAGIC

IGOR VASILIADIS

IGOR VASILIADIS

I always have an inner conflict between the contemporary and the eternal in my art. Fashion, motion and emotion are quite temporal and changing. Composition and the clear sculptural beauty of art nudes are perpetual.

I love old techniques and equipment with long exposures of up to one minute, because this gives time for the soul of my models to come out from deep inside.

Dark tonality, artefacts of drying emulsion and all the mysticism brought by silver and cyanides create the world of mystery, hidden from our eyes in the temporary and momentary world. They can be seen only during rare momentary lapses of reason, when we drop out of reality.

Poisonous vapours of substances used in the process of developing and emulsion ether change your consciousness to the stage when you see things in a different way. The future and the past are visible and are parts of the same. Each thing of beauty uncovers itself as a particular implication of eternal great substance, driving our civilisation forward and caring about it at the same time…

I shoot directly on blackened silver plates 8x10" activated with cadmium salts contained in emulsion. The techniques are similar to the wet plates used in the mid-nineteenth century with some minor improvements and differences.

I also use ambrotypes sometimes, then scan plates for large-format prints or make contact prints on albumen paper.

Ich habe immer einen inneren Konflikt zwischen dem Zeitgenössischen und dem Ewigen in meiner Kunst.

Mode, Bewegung und Emotion sind recht temporär und veränderlich. Komposition und die klare skulpturale Schönheit von künstlerischem

Akt sind unendlich. Ich liebe alte Techniken und Gerätschaften, bei denen oft Belichtunszeiten von bis zu einer Minute entstehen. In dieser Zeit kann die Seele meiner Modelle von tief drinnen heraus aufsteigen.

Dunkle Tonwerte, Artefakte von trocknender Emulsion und all die Geheimnisse, die Silber und Cyanide mitbringen, erzeugen eine Welt der Mystik, die unseren Augen in der temporären und momentanen Welt verborgen bleibt.

Sie können nur während seltener Augenblicke wahrgenommen werden.

Giftige Dämpfe von Substanzen bei der Entwick lung und dem Auftragen der Emulsion ändern unser Bewußtsein und lassen uns Dinge anders sehen. Die Zukunft und die Vergangenheit werden sichtbar und sind Teile desselben.

Ich fotografiere direkt auf geschwärzten Silberplatten im Format 8x10", die mit in der Emulsion enthaltenen Kadmiumsalzen sensibilisiert sind. Die Techniken sind ähnlich denen der Naß platten aus der Mitte des 19. Jahrhunderts mit einigen geringfügigen Verbesserungen und Unterschieden.

Gelegentlich mache ich auch Ambrotypien, die ich entweder für großformatige Ausdrucke scanne oder im Kontakt auf Albuminpapier übertrage.

IGOR VASILIADIS

IGOR VASILIADIS

Я всегда испытывал внутренний конфликт между мгновением и вечностью в моём творчестве.

Мода, движение и эмоция проходящи и изменчивы. Композиционное решение и чистая первозданная скульптурная красота вечны.

Мне близки технологии и оборудование из эпохи зарождения фотографии как искусства, длящиеся бесконечно экспозиции, дающие возможность душе модели вырваться наружу из глубин бессознательного.

Полные загадки тени, созданные сохнущей эмульсией артефакты и мистицизм, возникший из магии серебра и цианидов, рисуют мистерию, скрытую от наших глаз в мире сиюминутного и мгновенного. То, что мы видим, на мгновение выпадая из окружающей реальности, чудесным образом остается с нами навсегда.

Ядовитые испарения веществ, используемых в процессах создания эмульсии и ее обработки изменяют сознание, образы оживают, а свет и тень переплетаются и взаимодействуют. Настоящее и прошлое становятся видны сквозь призрачную завесу настоящего и сливаются воедино. Каждый штрих находит своё место в изумительной гармонии общего и вечного, движущего наш мир и охраняющего его...

Я снимаю на пластины из черненого серебра 20х25 см, активированные солями кадмия, как делали в середине 19-го века, изменив под себя в технологии лишь немногое. Чаще всего я сканирую пластины для печати крупноформатных изображений или использую аутентичную, созданную по старинным рецептам альбуменовую фотобумагу для контактной печати.

J'ai toujours eu un conflit interne entre le présent et l'éternel concernant mon art. La mode, le mouvement et l'émotion sont basés sur le changement et la temporalité, alors que la composition et l'évidente beauté sculpturale des nus artistiques sont perpétuelles.

J'apprécie les anciennes techniques et les équipements avec de longues expositions allant jusqu'à une minute, donnant le temps à l'âme de mes modèles de s'exprimer.

Les tonalités sombres, les artéfacts de séchage de l'émulsion et tout le côté mystique apportés par l'argentique et les cyanures créent un univers de mystère, caché à nos yeux dans le monde instantané.

Ils peuvent être alors aperçus durant les rares défaillances de la raison, lorsque la réalité nous échappe.

Les vapeurs toxiques des substances utilisées dans le processus de développement de l'émulsion semblent changer ma conscience de la scène et un nouveau monde se révèle alors. L'avenir et le passé deviennent visibles et paraissent indissociables.

Chaque partie de la beauté se dévoile comme une implication particulière de la substance éternelle, la conduite de notre civilisation vers l'avant tout en la respectant ...

Je tire directement sur les plaques d'argent 8x10" noircies et activées avec les sels de cadmium contenus dans l'émulsion. Les techniques sont similaires aux plaques humides utilisées dans le milieu du XIXe siècle, avec quelques différences et améliorations.

J'utilise aussi parfois des ambrotypes, puis numérise les plaques pour des tirages grand format, ou réalise des tirages directs par contact sur papier albuminé.

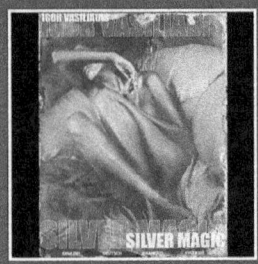
090726-0001
Cover

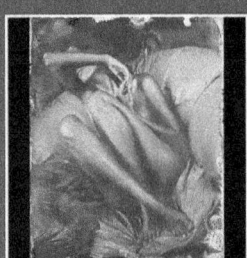
090726-0001
11

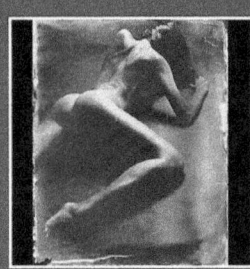
100815-0001
13

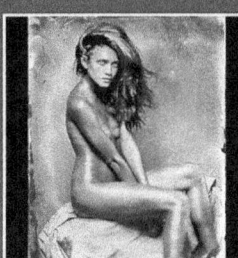
100729-0002
15

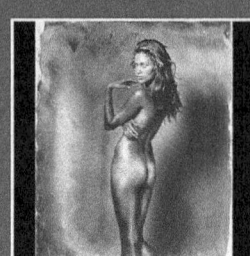
100729-0001
17

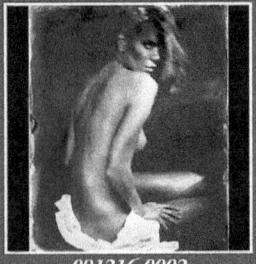
091216-0002
19

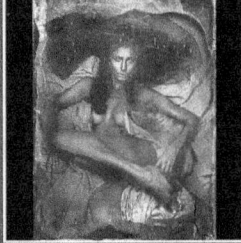
080805-0001
21

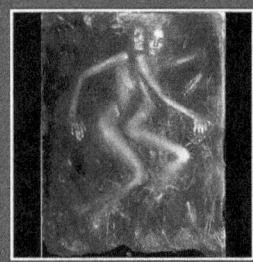
080807-0002
22

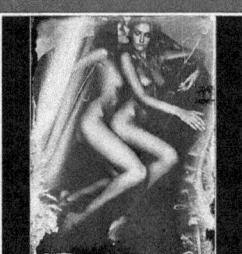
080807-0001
23

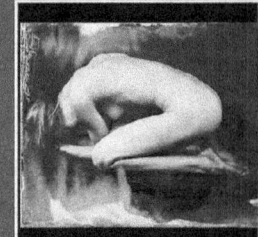
090620-0001
24-25

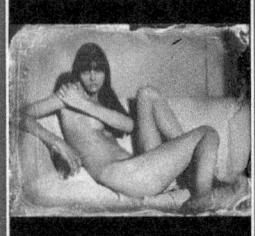
080502-0001
26-27

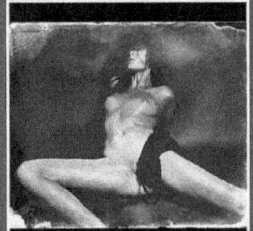
100815-0002
28-29

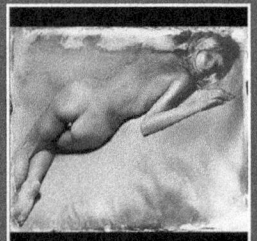
101126-0001
30-31

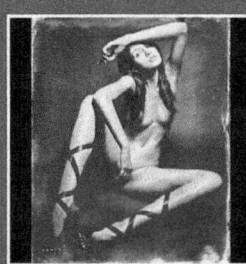
100815-0003
33

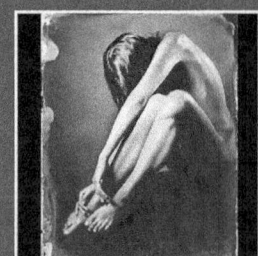
100605-0001
35

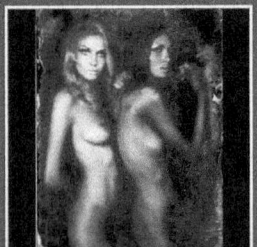
080807-0003
37

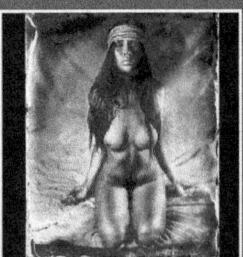
100427-0001
39

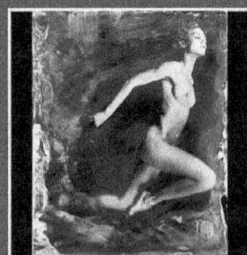
090615-0004
41

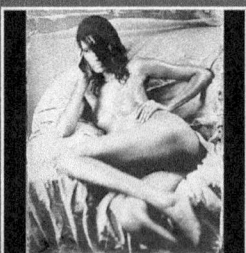
090817-0001
43

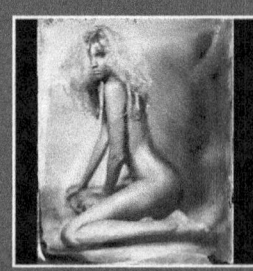
090817-0002
45

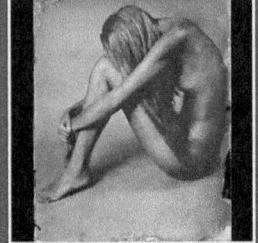
090817-0003
47

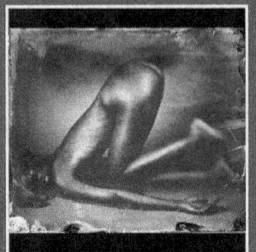
090817-0004
48-49

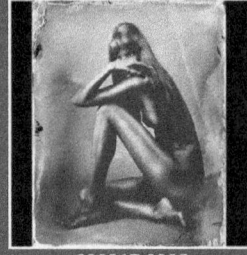
090817-0005
51

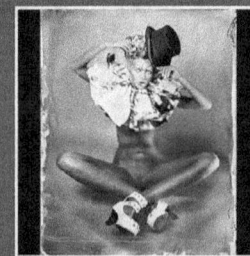
090926-0002
53

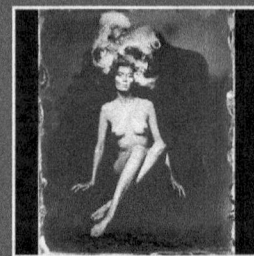
091009-0001
55

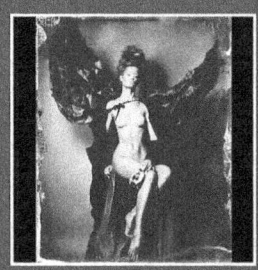

091012-0001
57

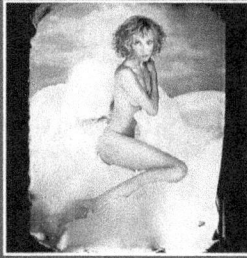

120608-001
59

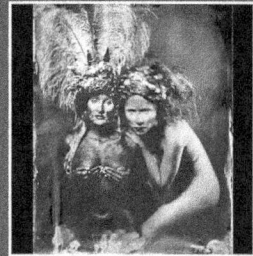

091013-0002
61

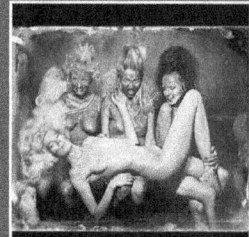

091013-0003
62-63

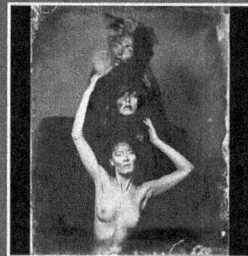

091014-0001
65

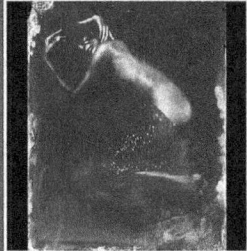

090726-0003
67

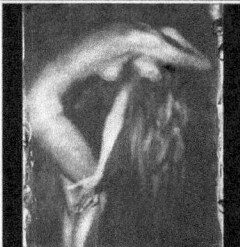

091116-0002
69

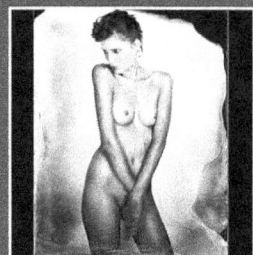

080821-0001
71

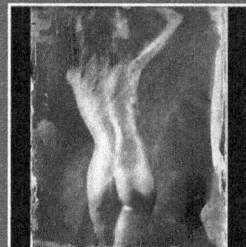

091116-0003
73

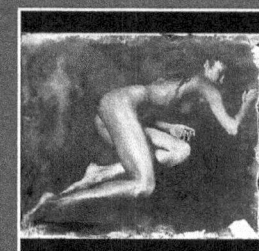

091120-0002
74-75

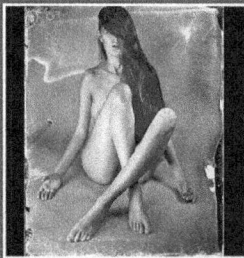

091203-0001
77

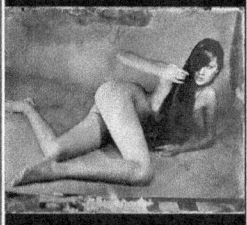

091204-0001
78-79

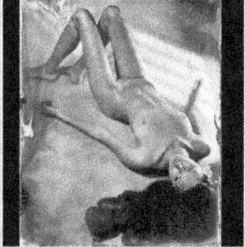

091207-0001
81

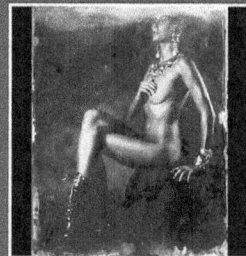

091215-0001
83

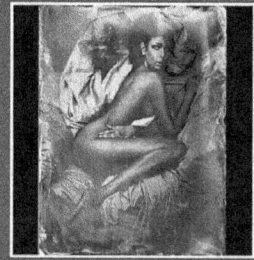

080806-0001
85

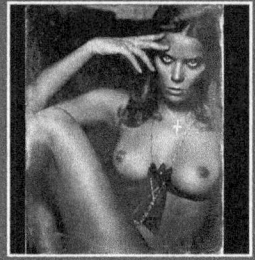

091216-0003
87

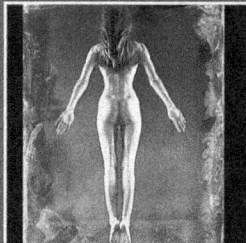

100214-0001
89

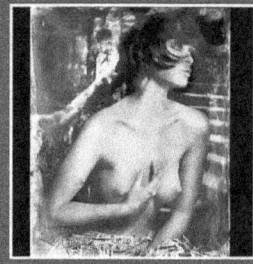

100218-0001
91

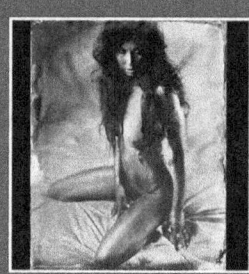

100501-0001
93

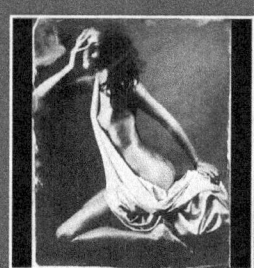

100601-0001
95

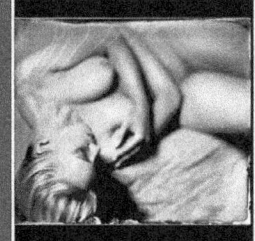

100625-0001
96-97

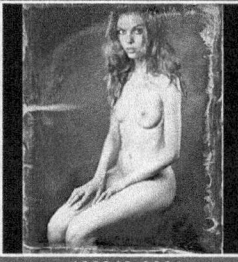

100312-0001
99

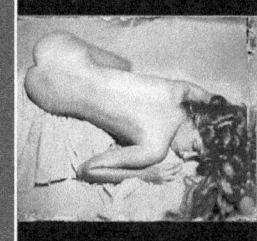

100628-0005
100-101

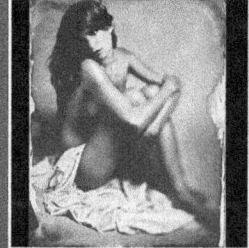

100630-0002
103

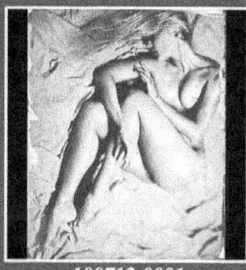

100712-0001
105

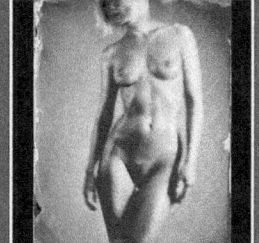

100712-0002
107

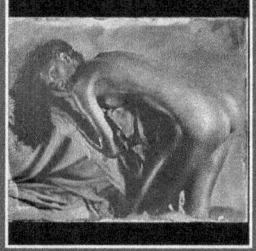

100730-0001
108-109

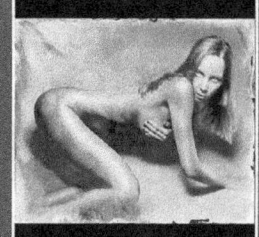

100824-0002
110-111

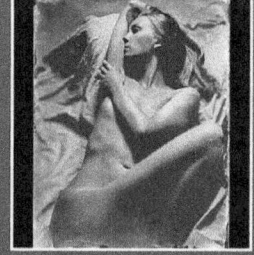

100826-0001
113

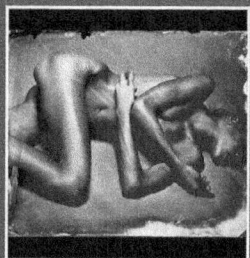

101130-0001
114-115

IGOR VASILIADIS

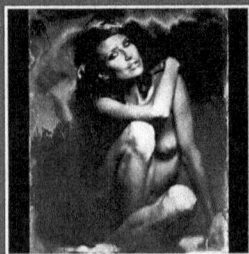

110221-0001
117

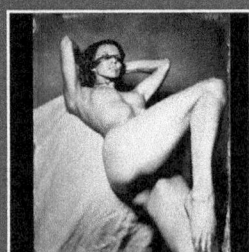

110221-0003
119

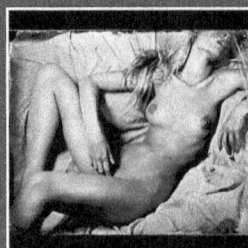

110513-0001
121

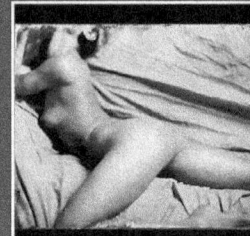

110513-0002
122-123

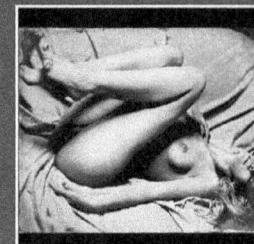

110513-0003
124-125

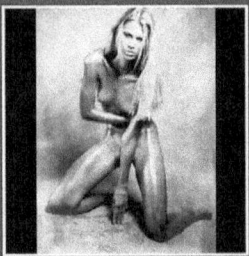

110726-0001
127

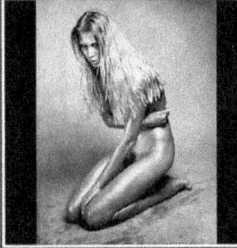

110726-0004
129

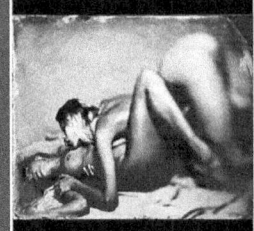

110909-0001
130-131

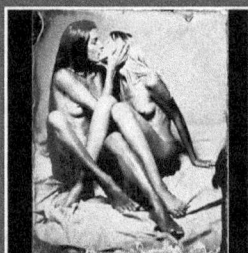

110804-0001
133

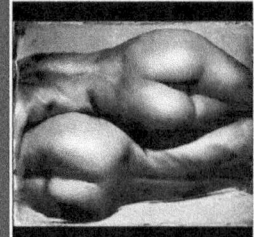

110909-0002
134-135

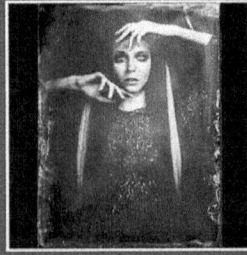

081008-002
139

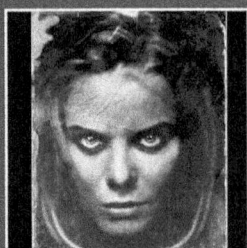

091219-0002
141

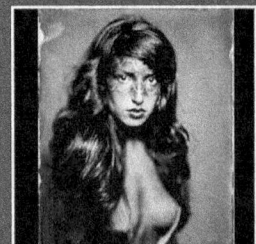

100628-0002
143

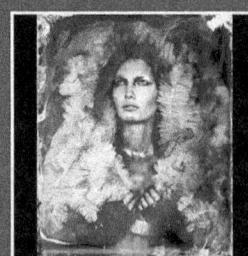

090704-0005
145

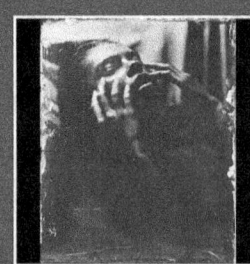

090523-0001
147

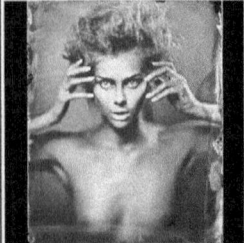

090926-0001
149

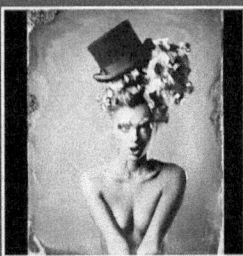

090926-0003
151

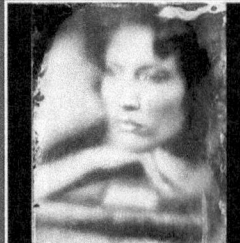

090726-0004
153

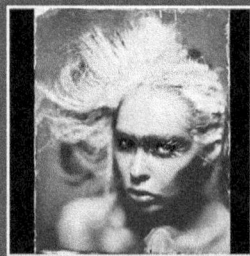

100628-0003
155

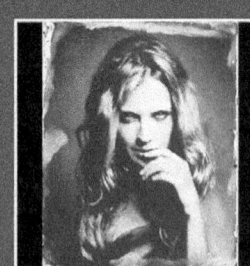

100726-0001
157

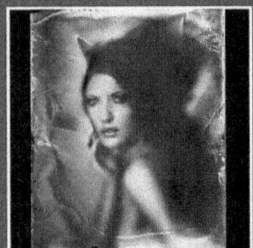

080816-0001
159

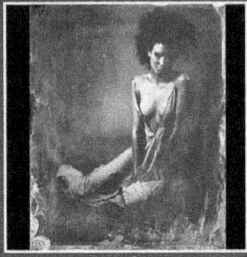

090704-0003
163

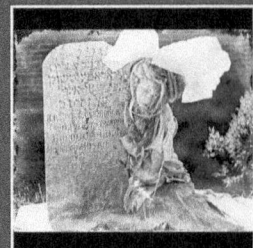

081010-0001
165

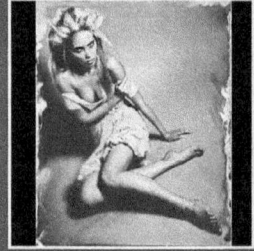

100628-0004
167

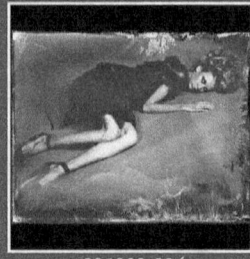

081008-004
168-169

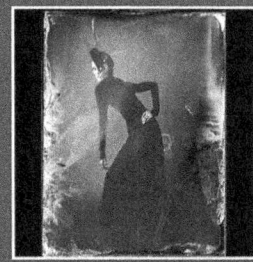

081008-001
171

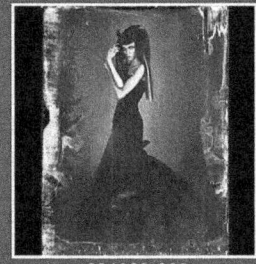

081008-003
173

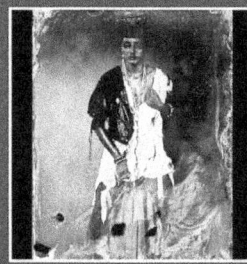

090704-0004
175

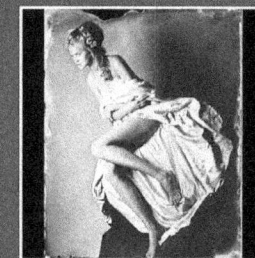

100614-0001
177

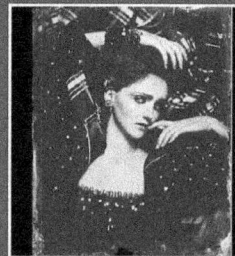

110317-0007
178

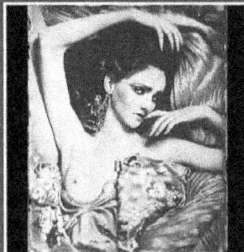

110317-0006
179

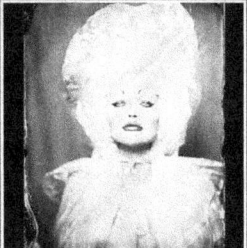

110324-0003
181

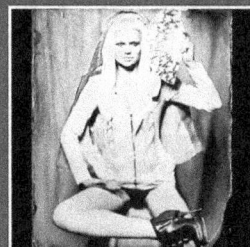

110324-0002
183

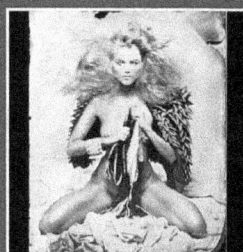

110323-0002
185

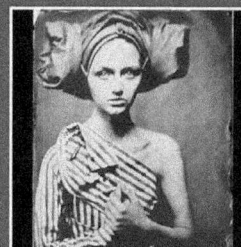

110317-0001
187

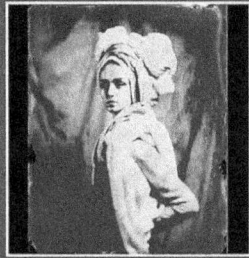

110317-0008
189

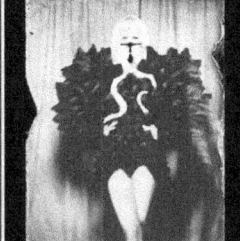

110324-0001
191

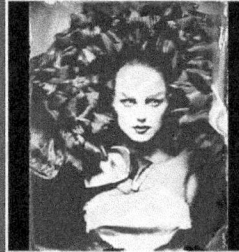

110323-0006
193

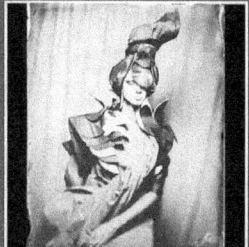

110324-0005
195

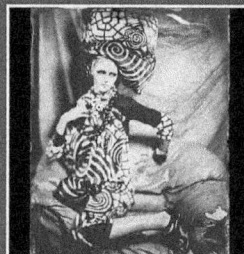

110316-0001
197

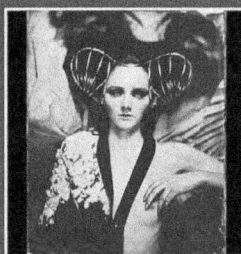

110317-0002
199

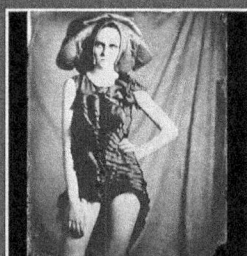

110317-0003
201

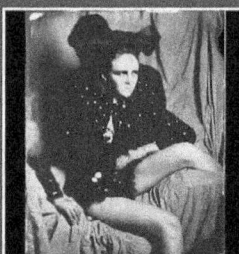

110317-0004
203

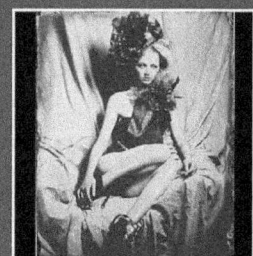

110317-0005
205

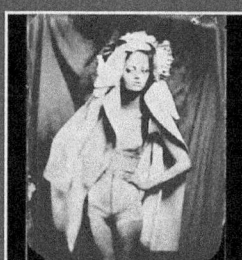

110317-0009
207

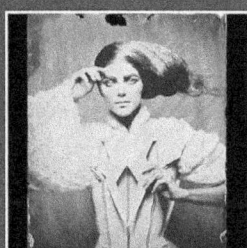

110323-0003
209

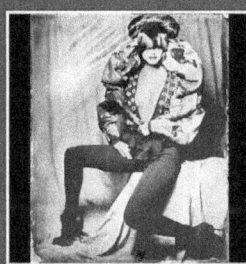

110323-0004
211

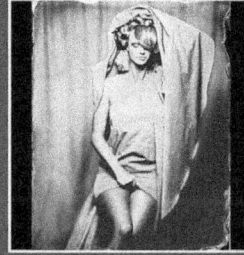

110324-0004
213

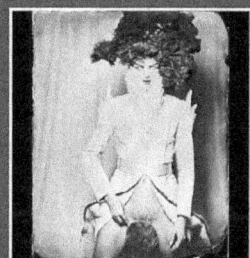

110323-0005
215

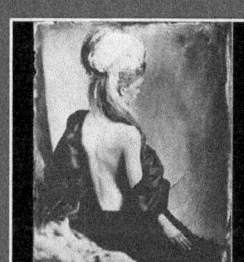

110317-0010
217

IGOR VASILIADIS

Dreams

Expectations

090726-0001

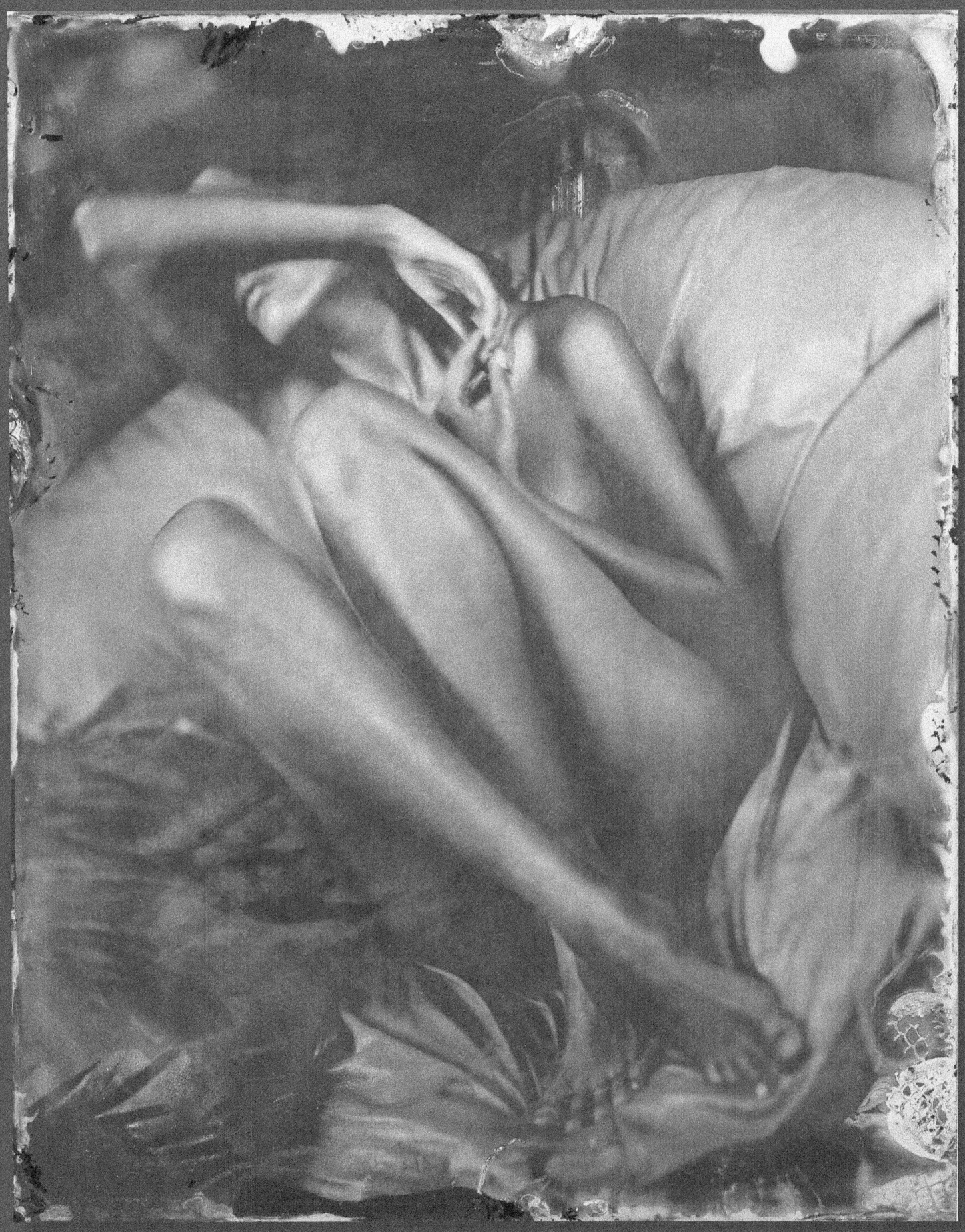

IGOR VASILIADIS

Passion

Obcession

100815-0001

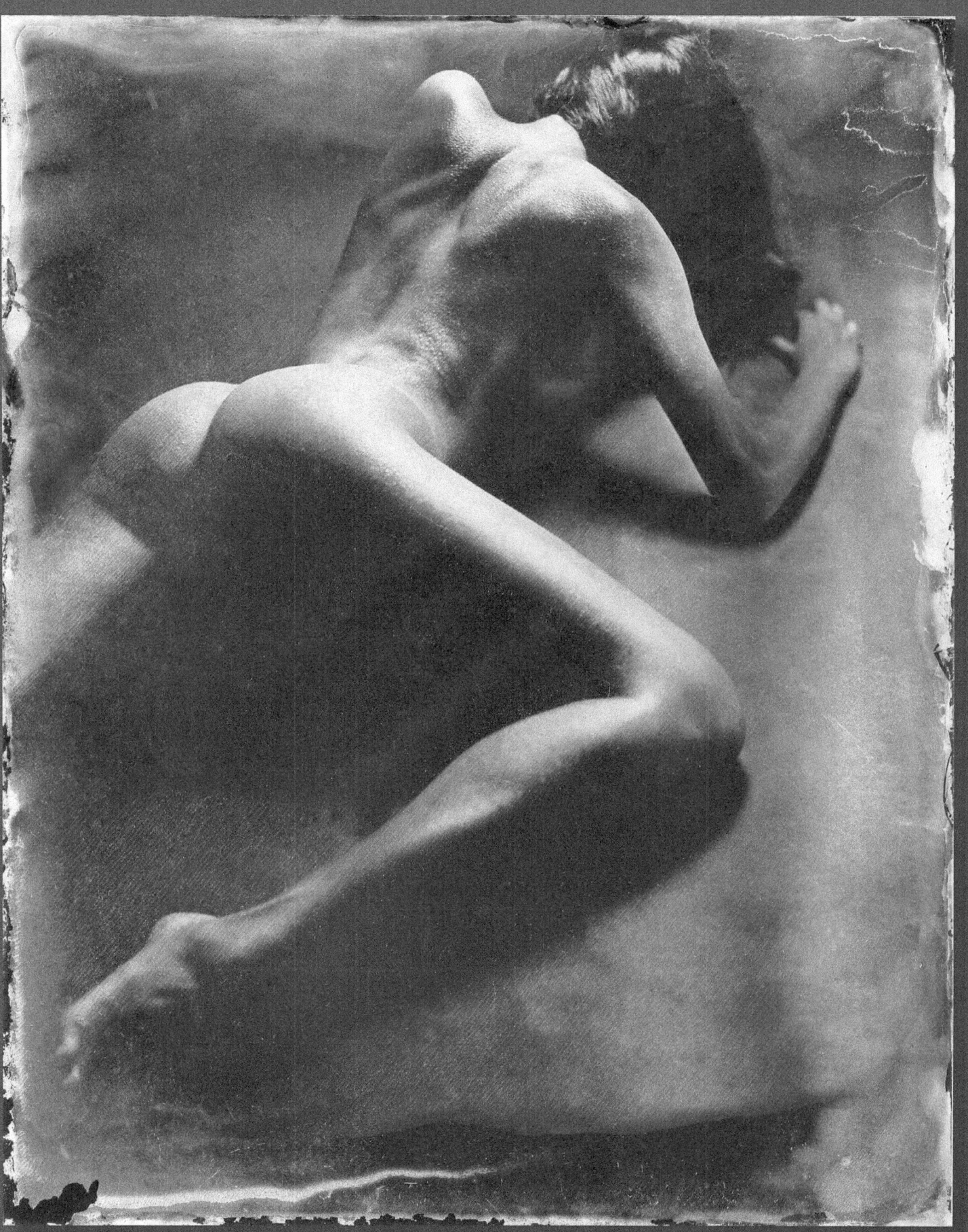

100729-0002

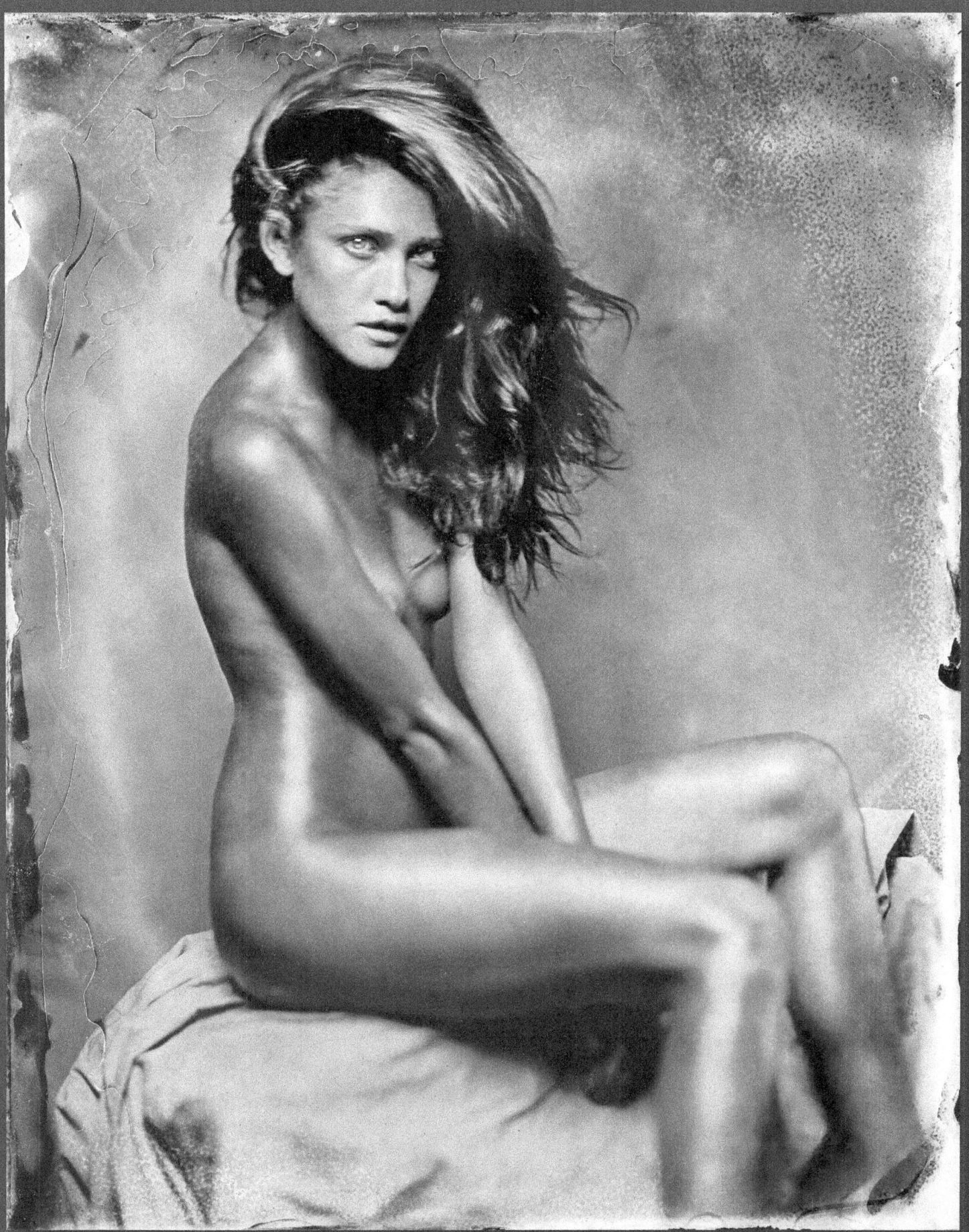

IGOR VASILIADIS

Hopes
Waiting

100729-0001

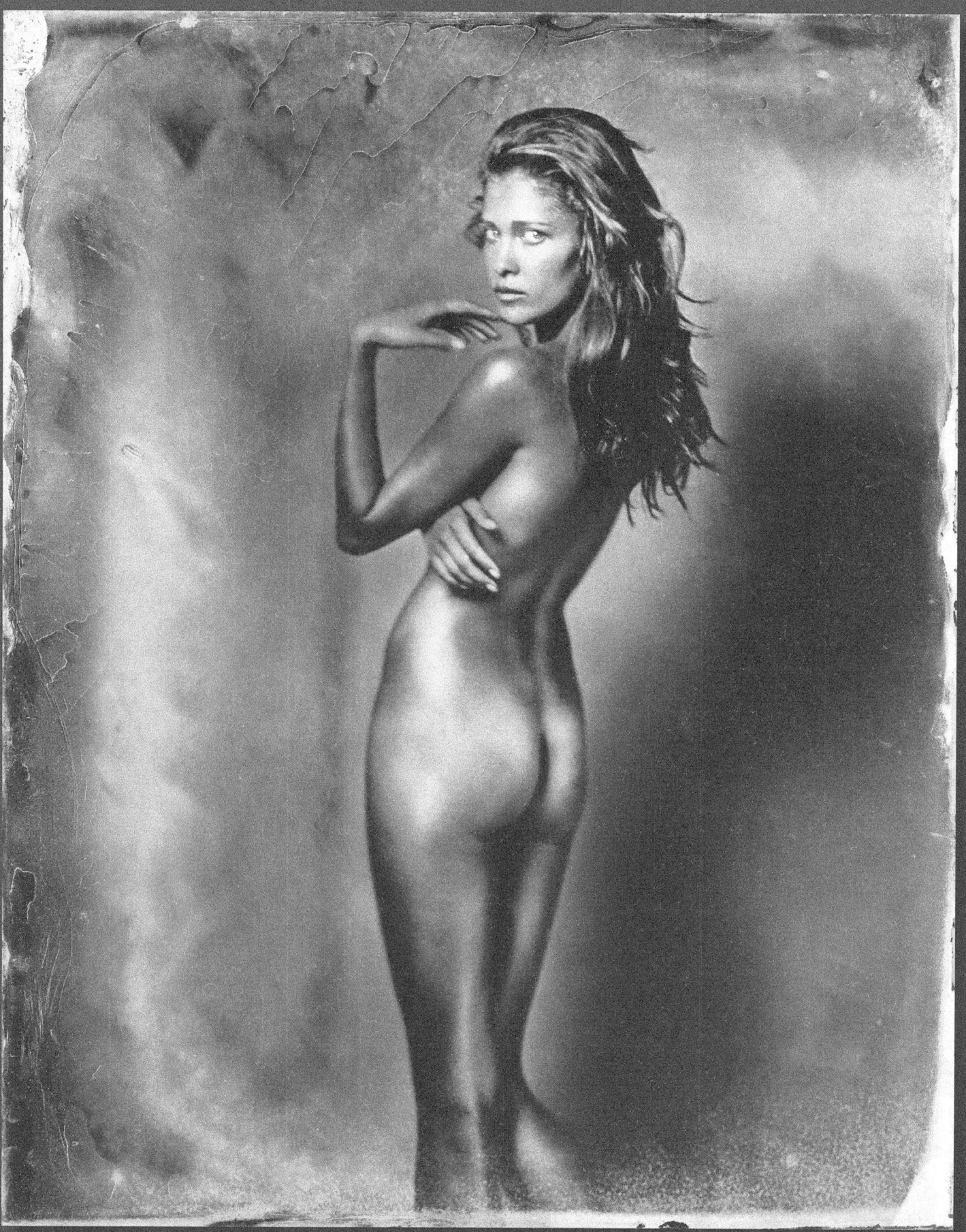

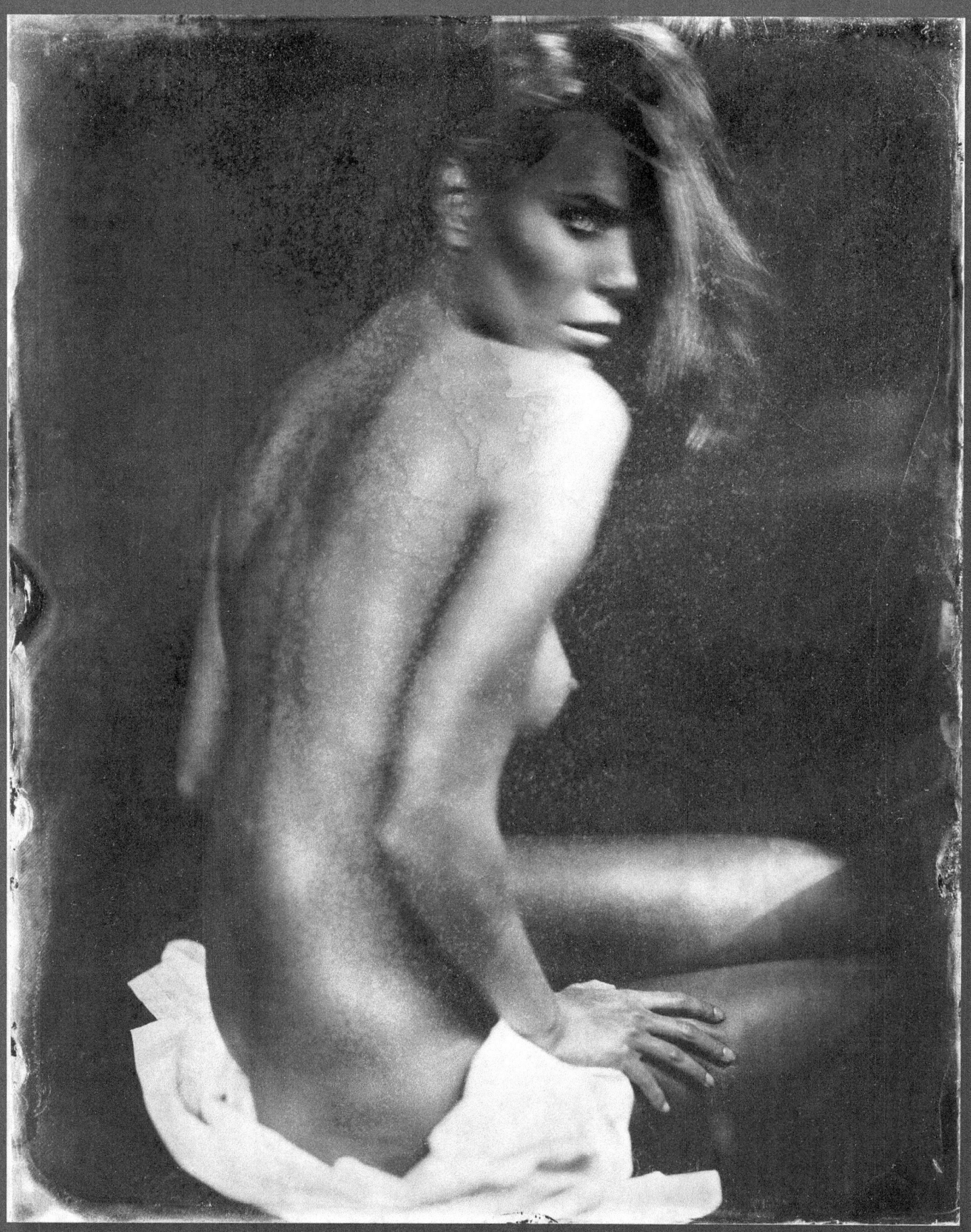

IGOR VASILIADIS

080805-0001

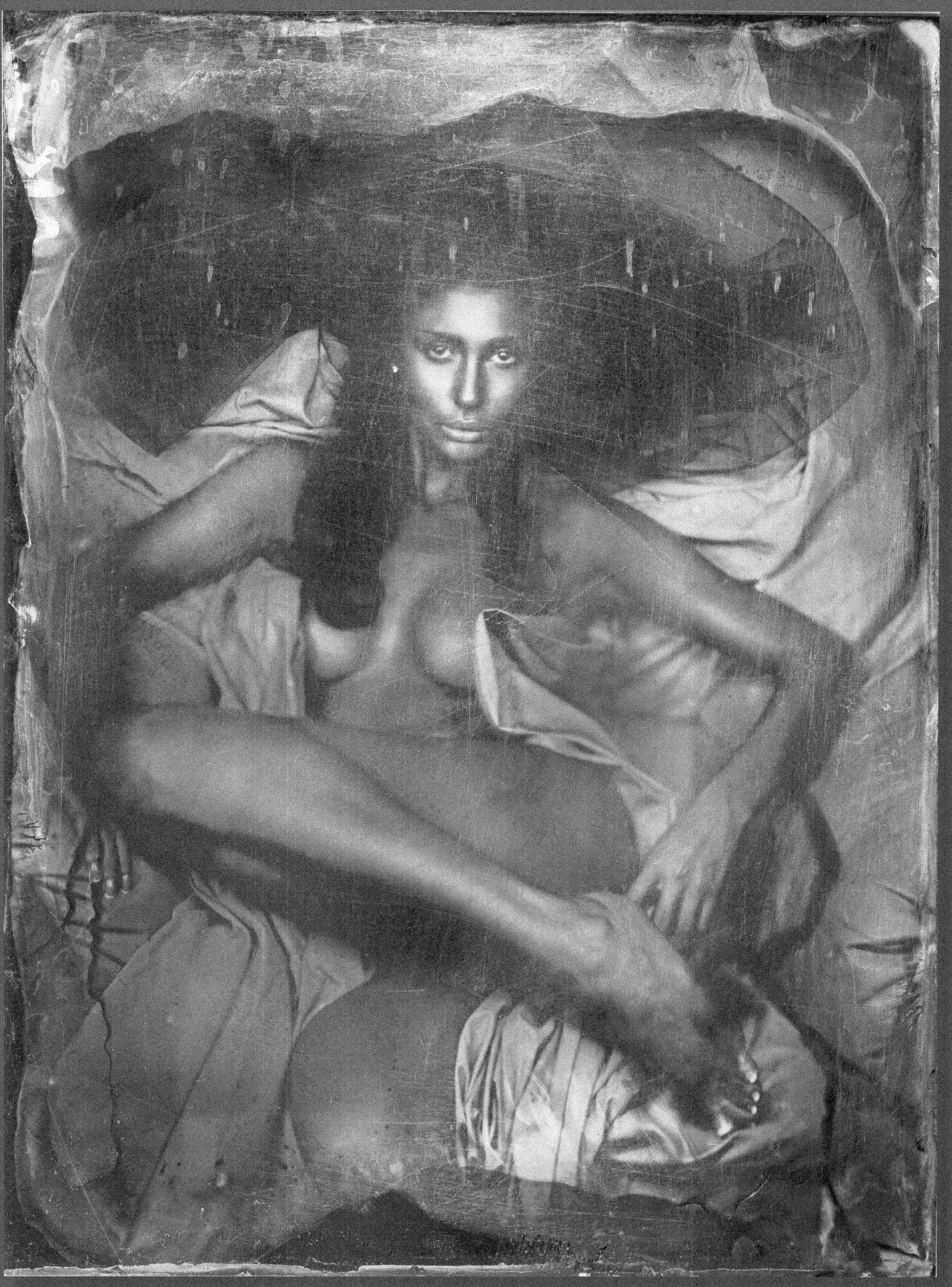

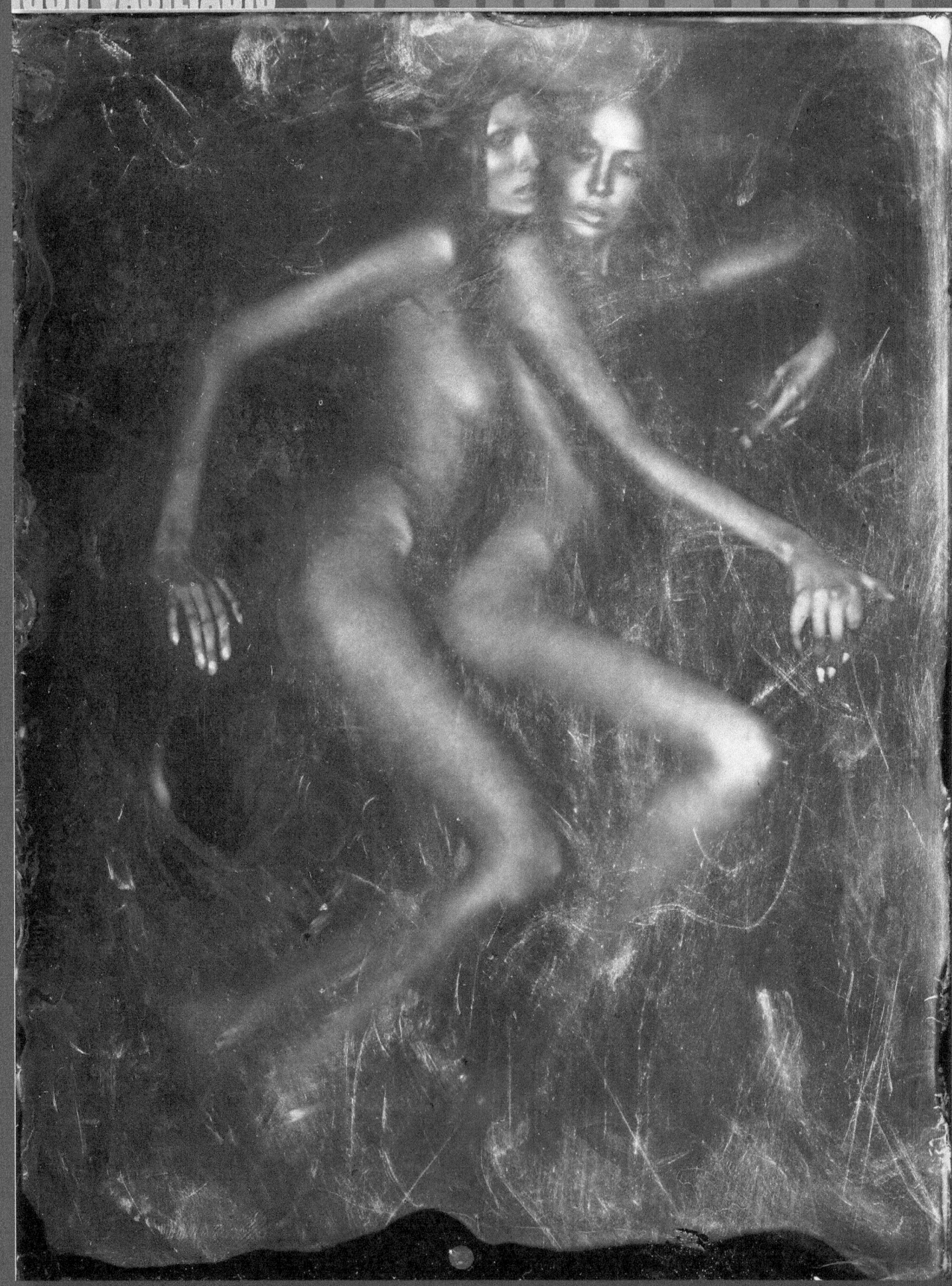

080807-0002

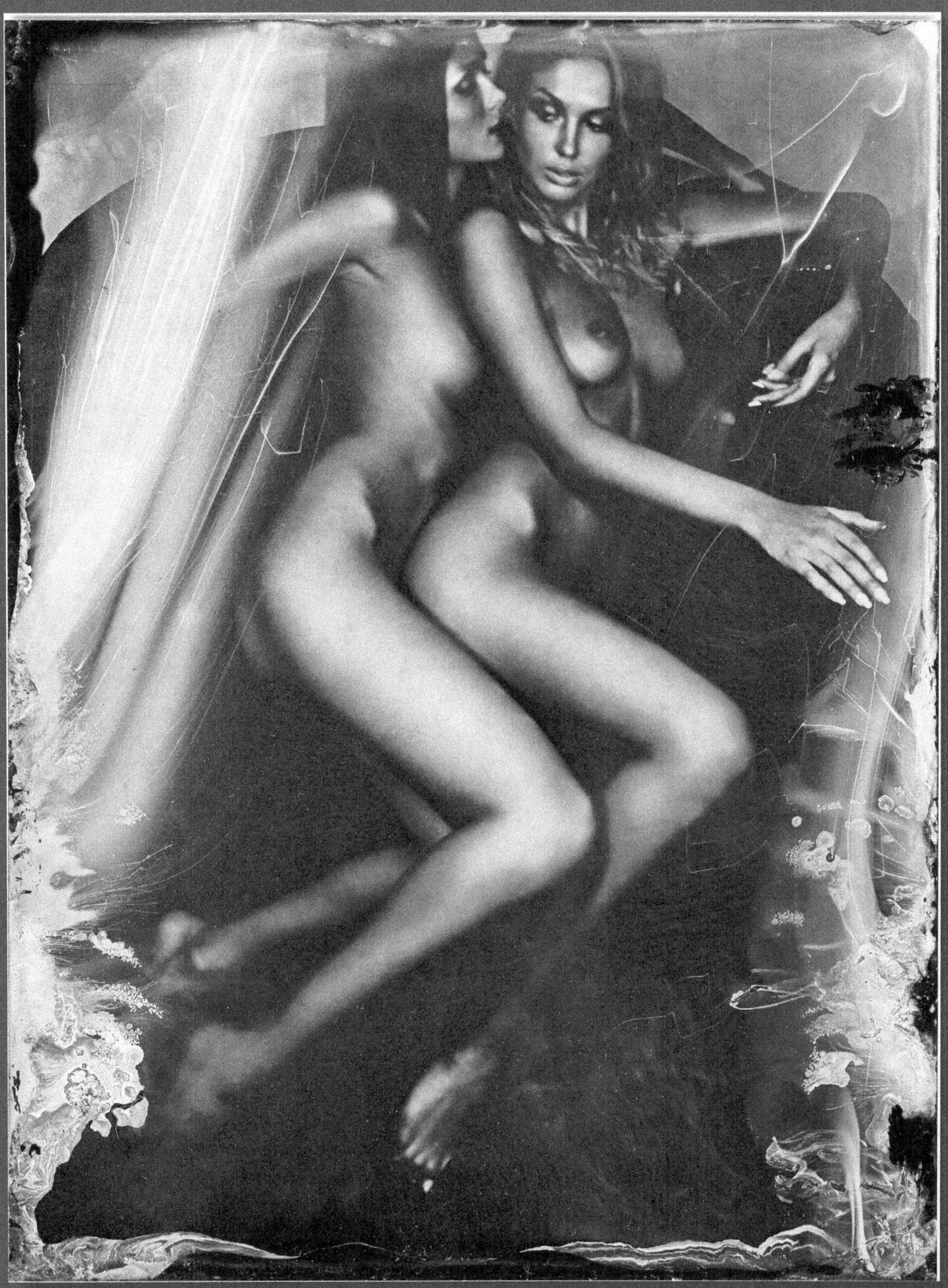

080807-0001

23

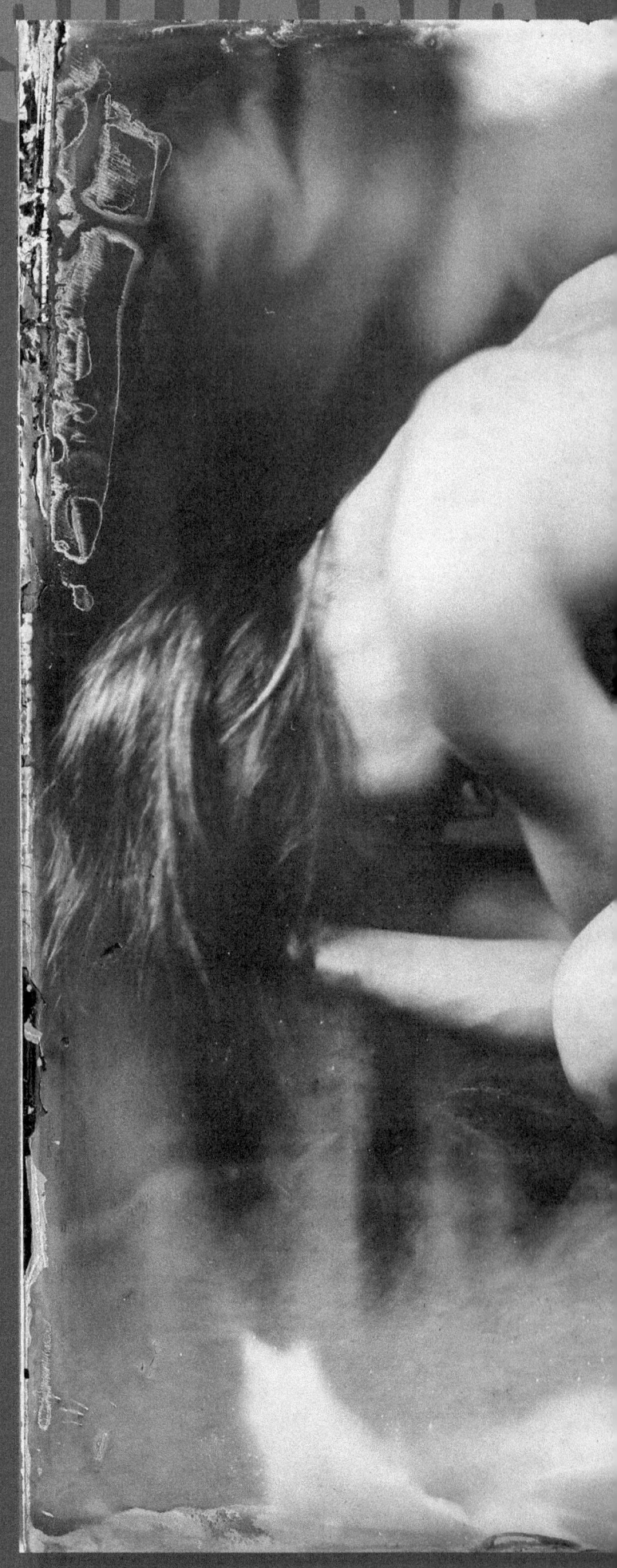

IGOR VASILIADIS

Desire

Aspiration

090620-0001

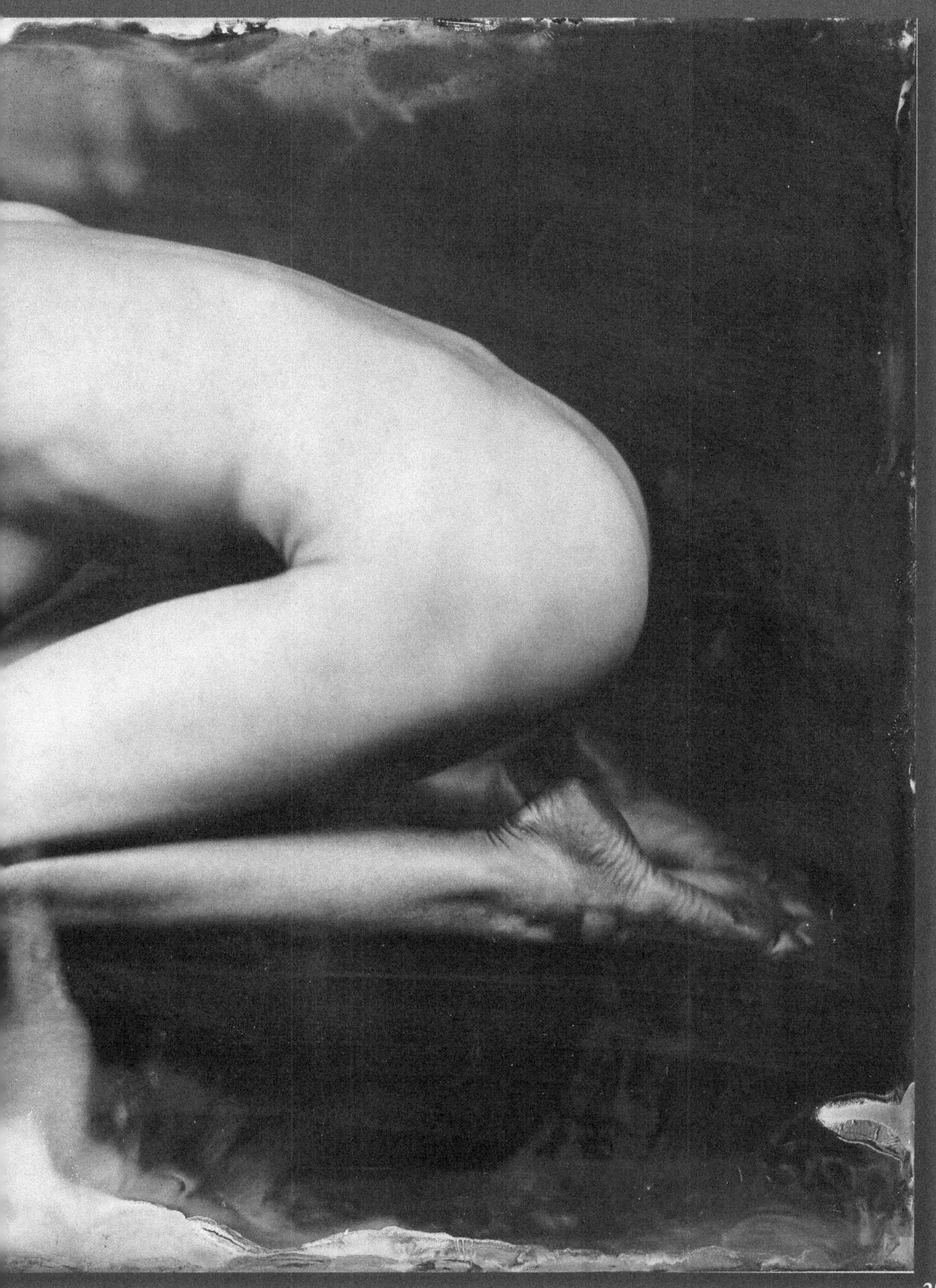

IGOR VASILIADIS

Suspense
Contemplation

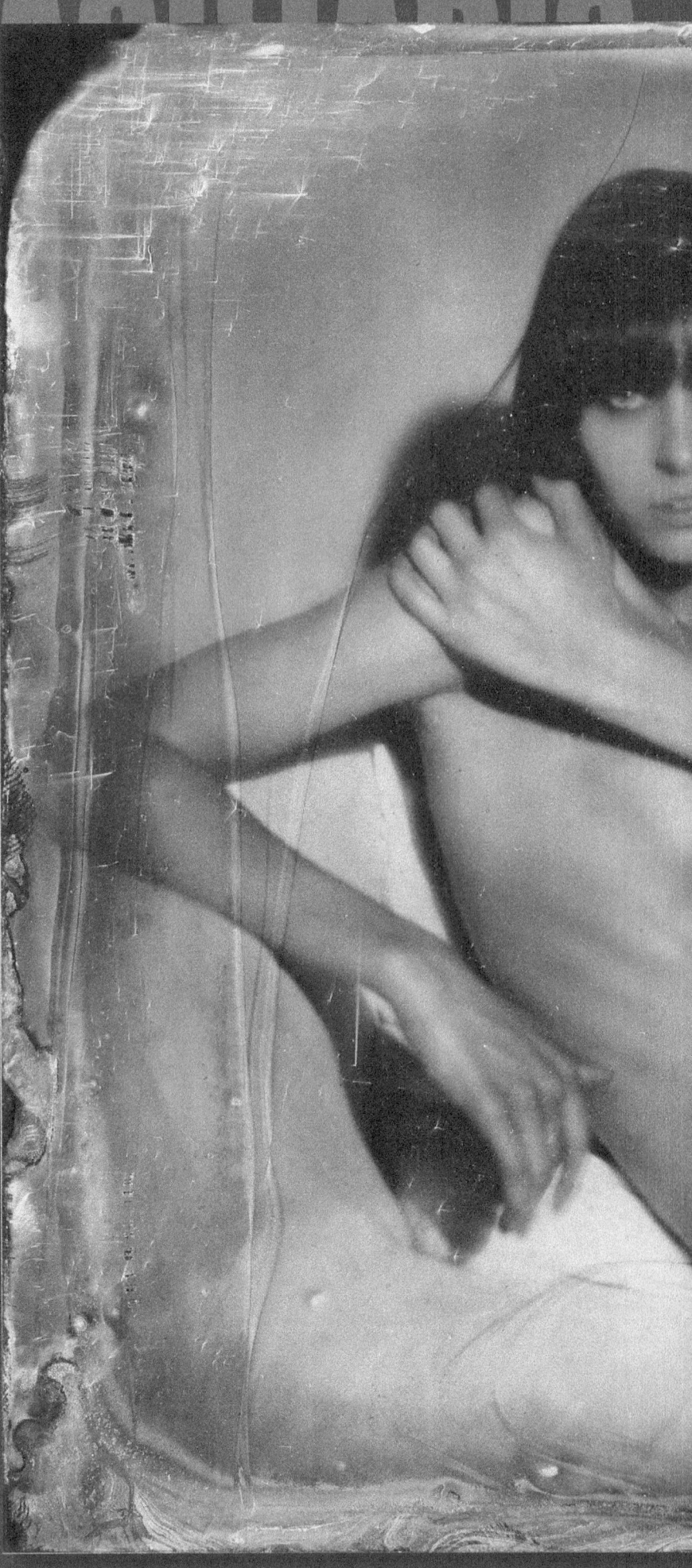

080502-0001

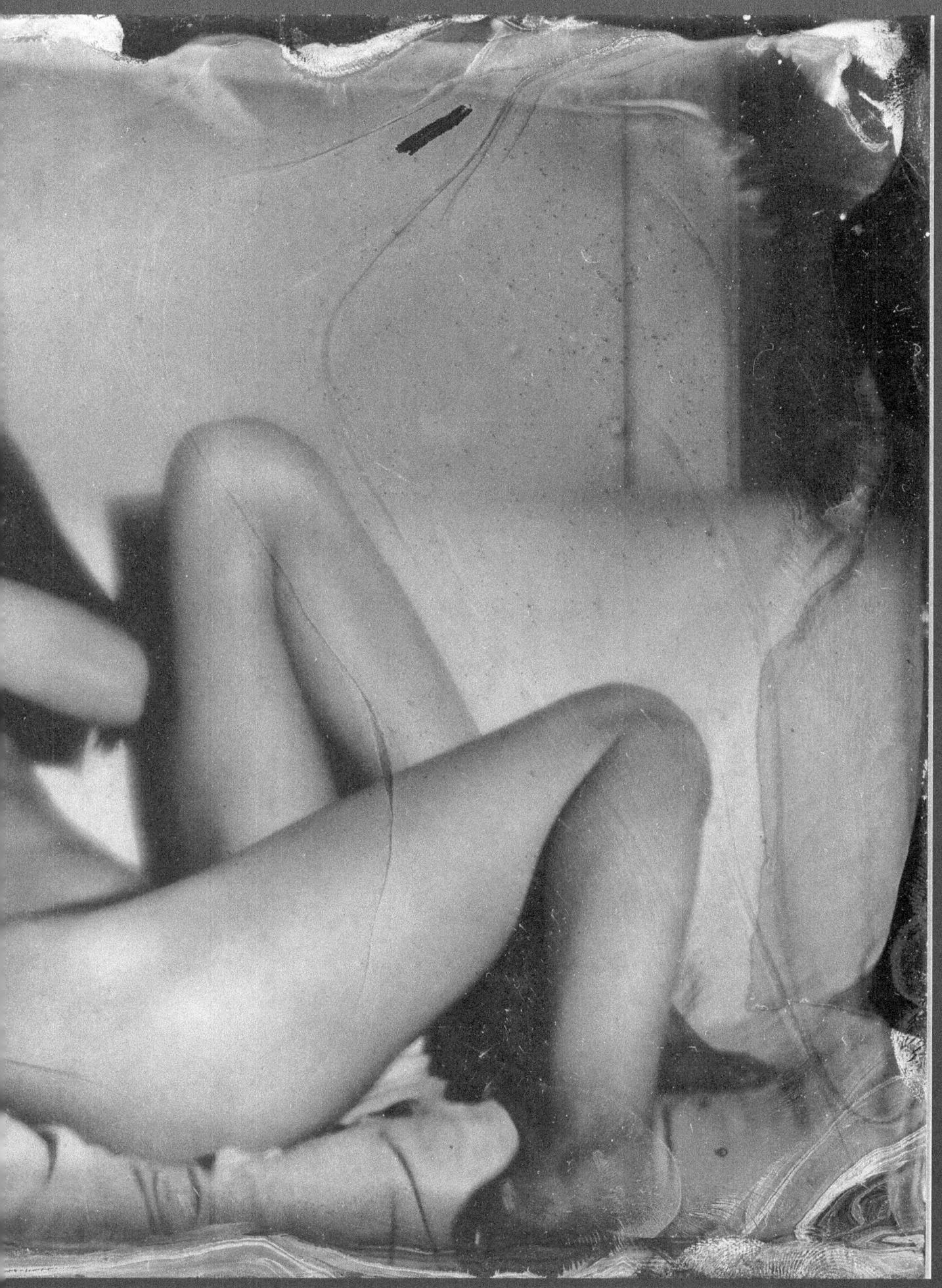

IGOR VASILIADIS

Faith

Desperation

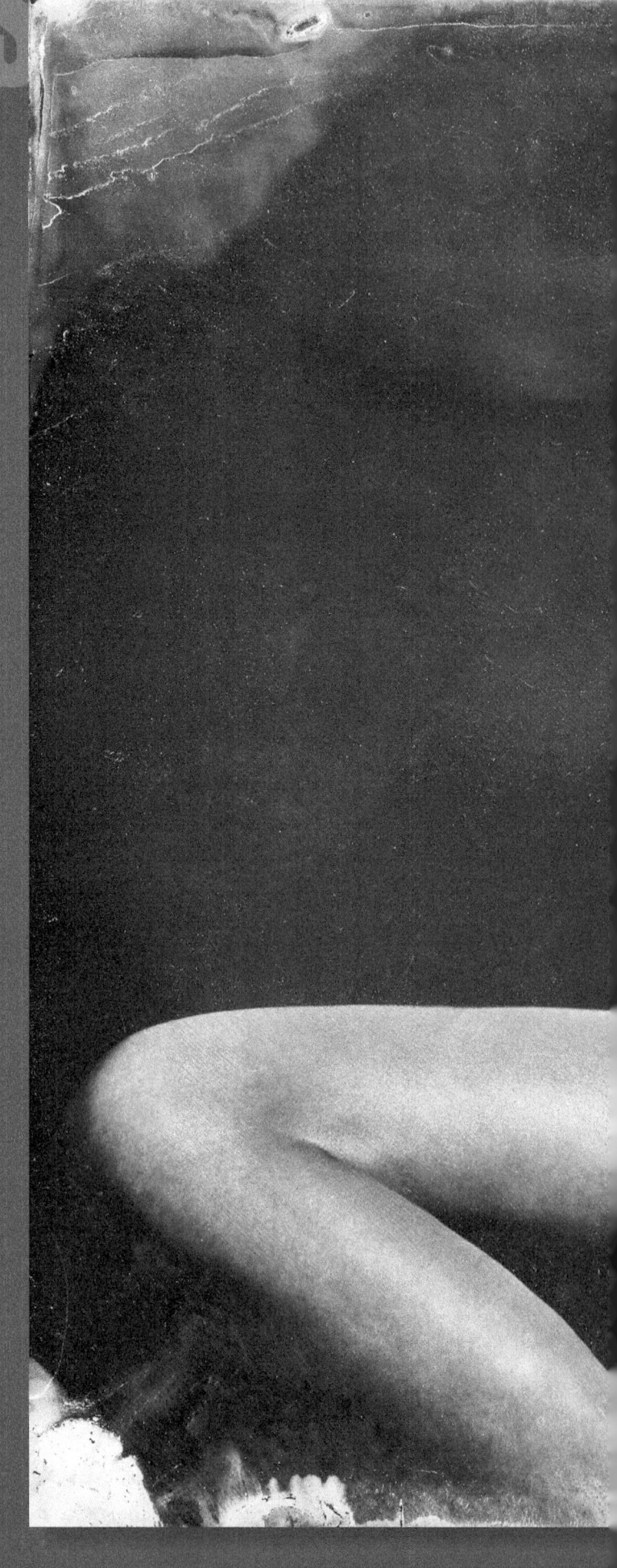

100815-0002

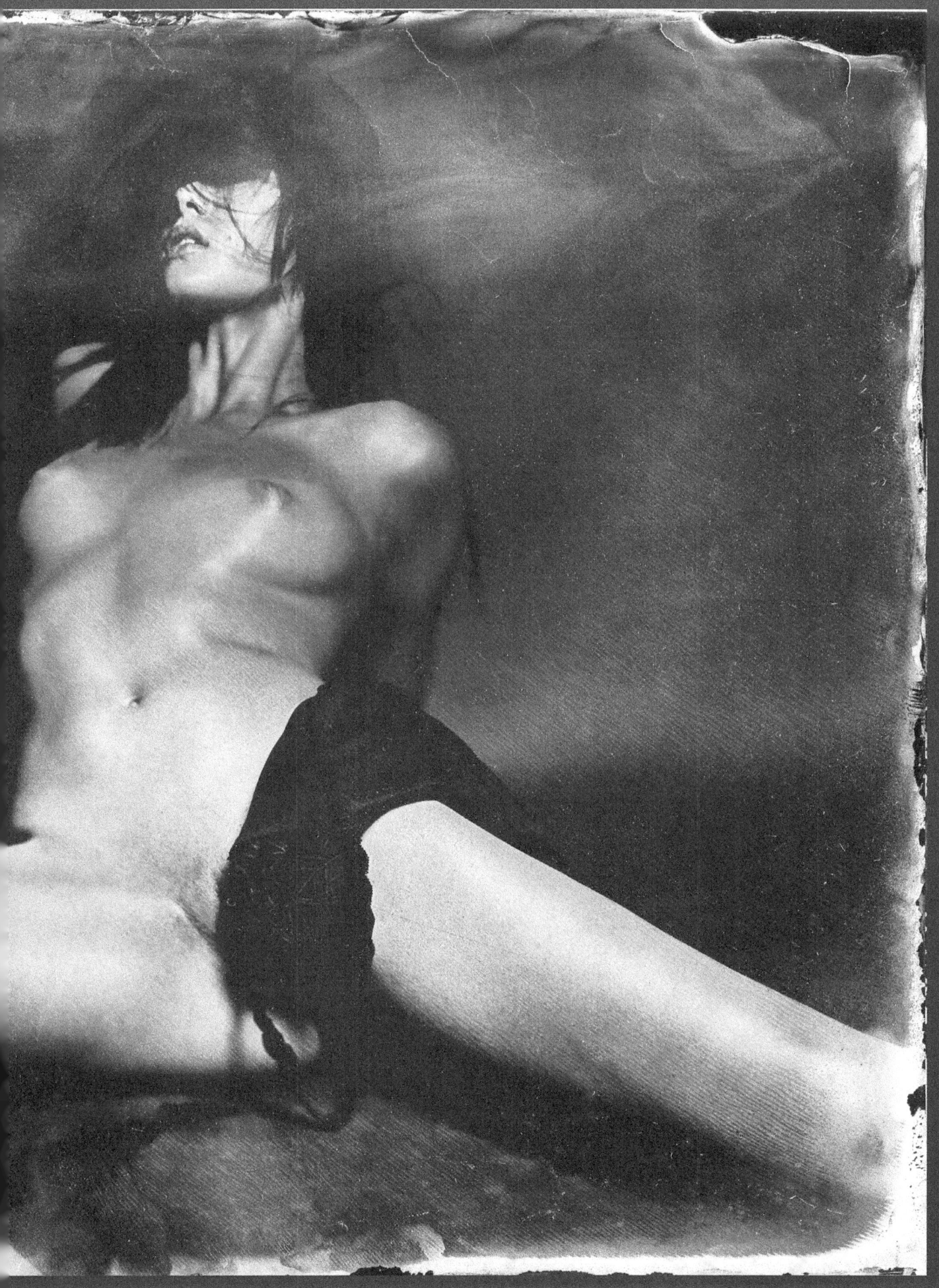

IGOR VASILIADIS

Weariness

Amusement

101126-0001

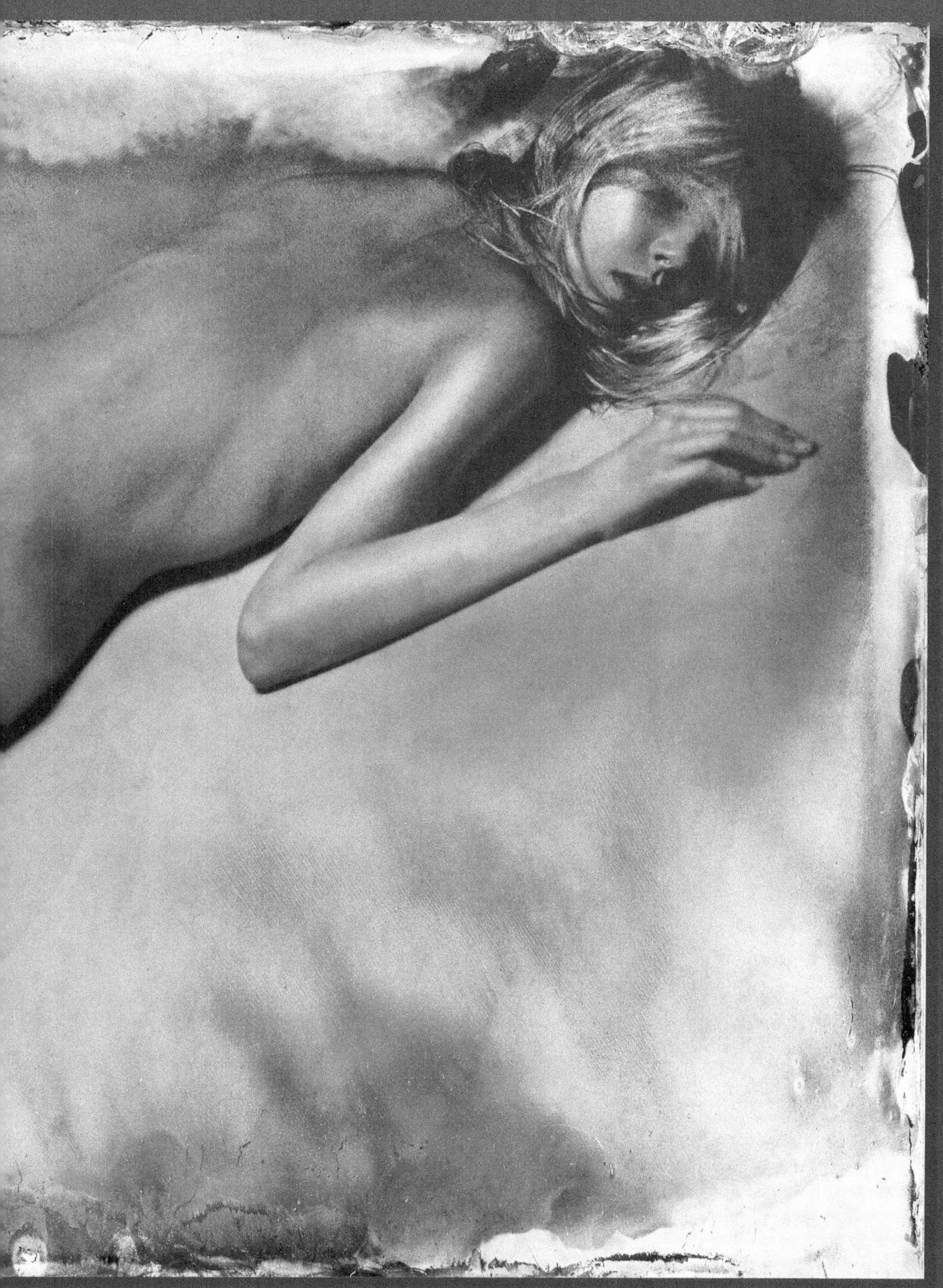

Lightness

Attraction

100815-0003

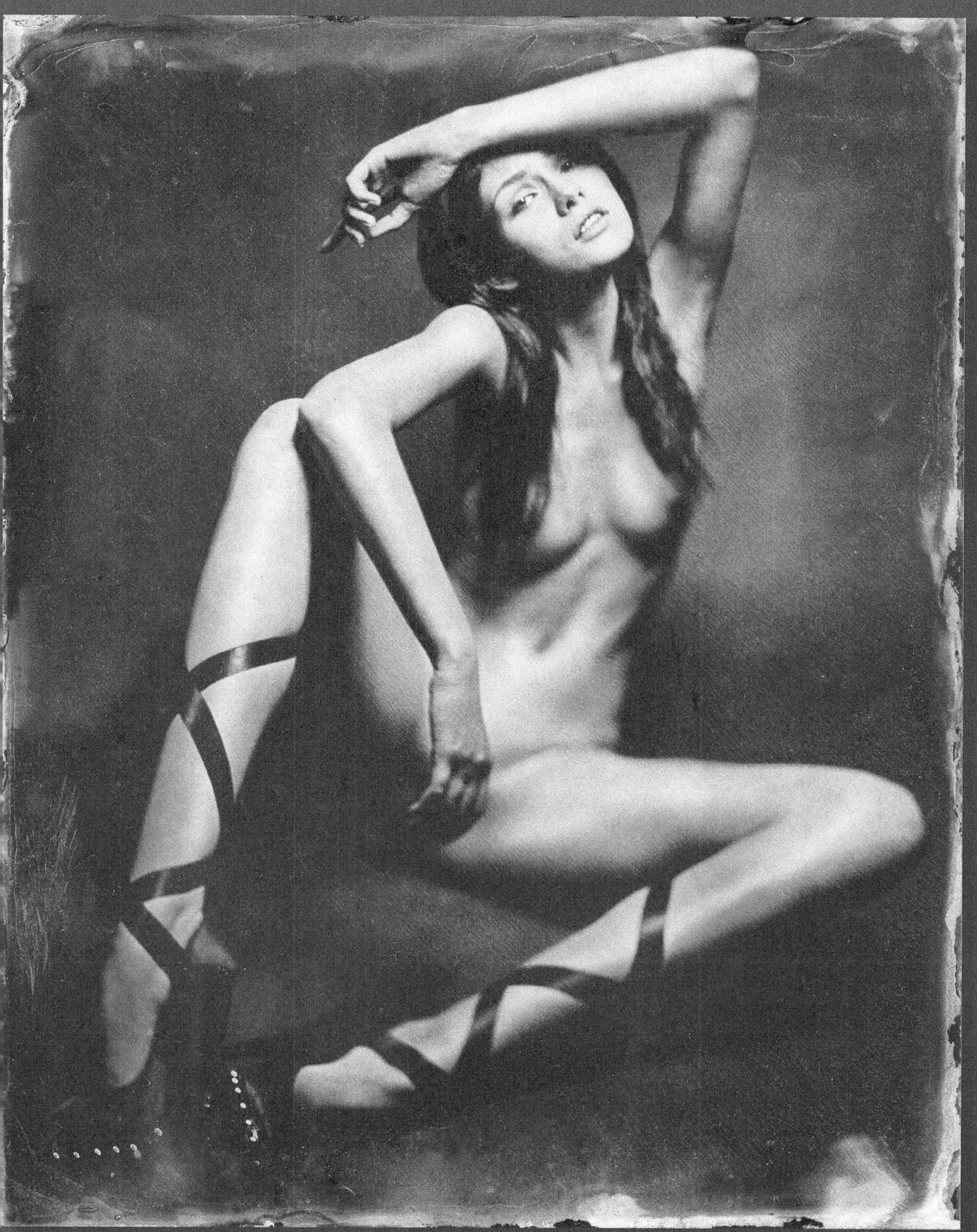

IGOR VASILIADIS

Desire

Demureness

100605-0001

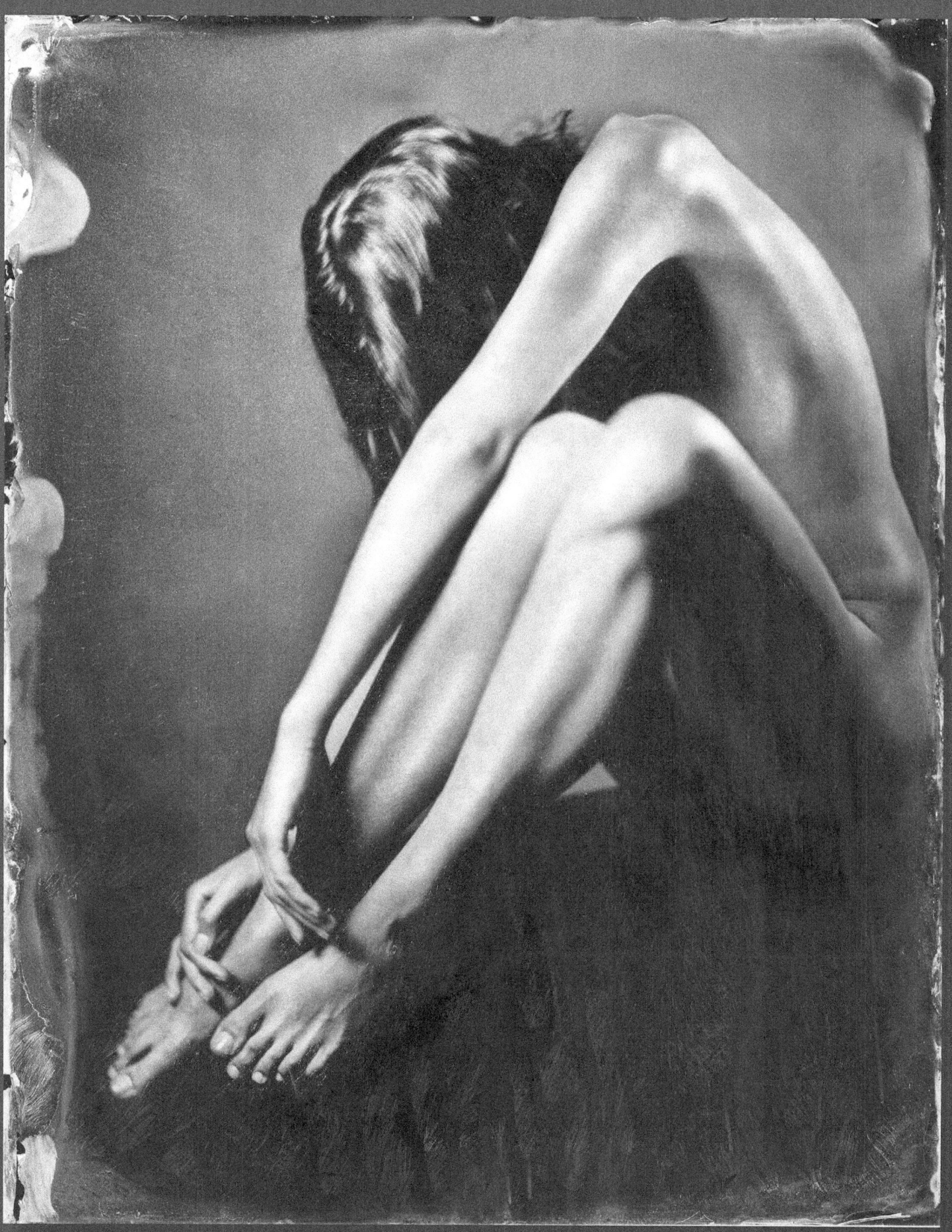

IGOR VASILIADIS

080807-0003

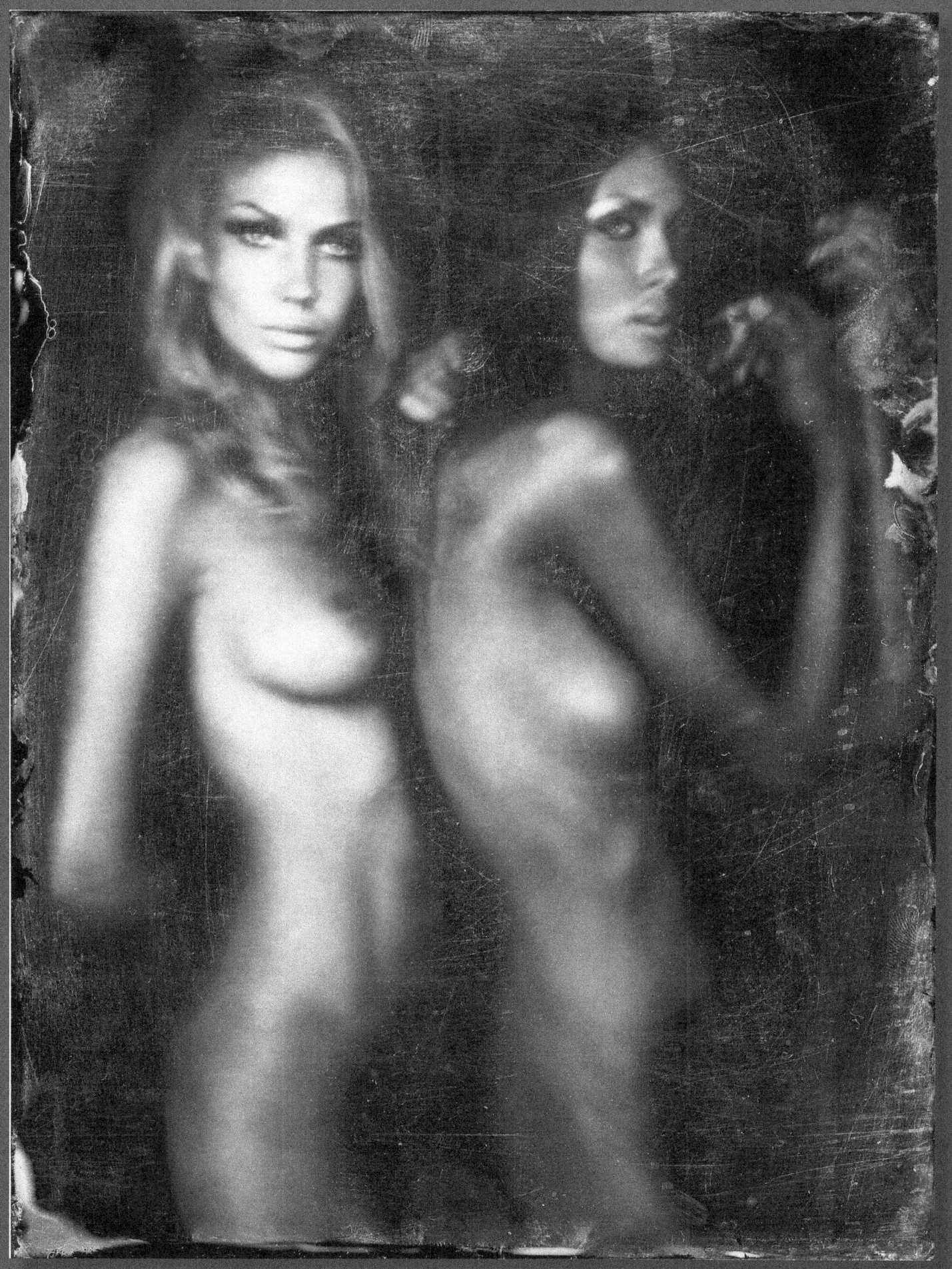

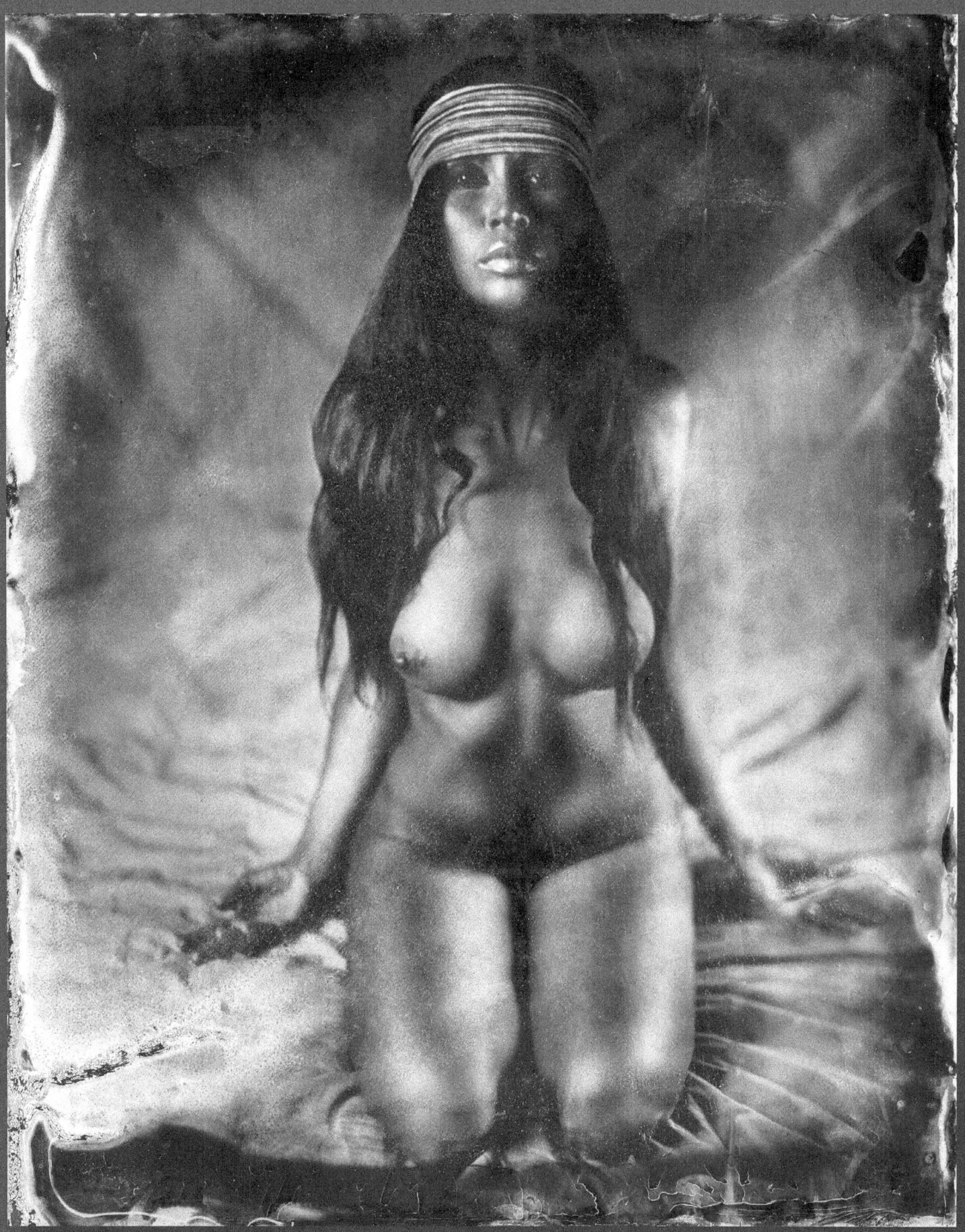

IGOR VASILIADIS

090615-0004

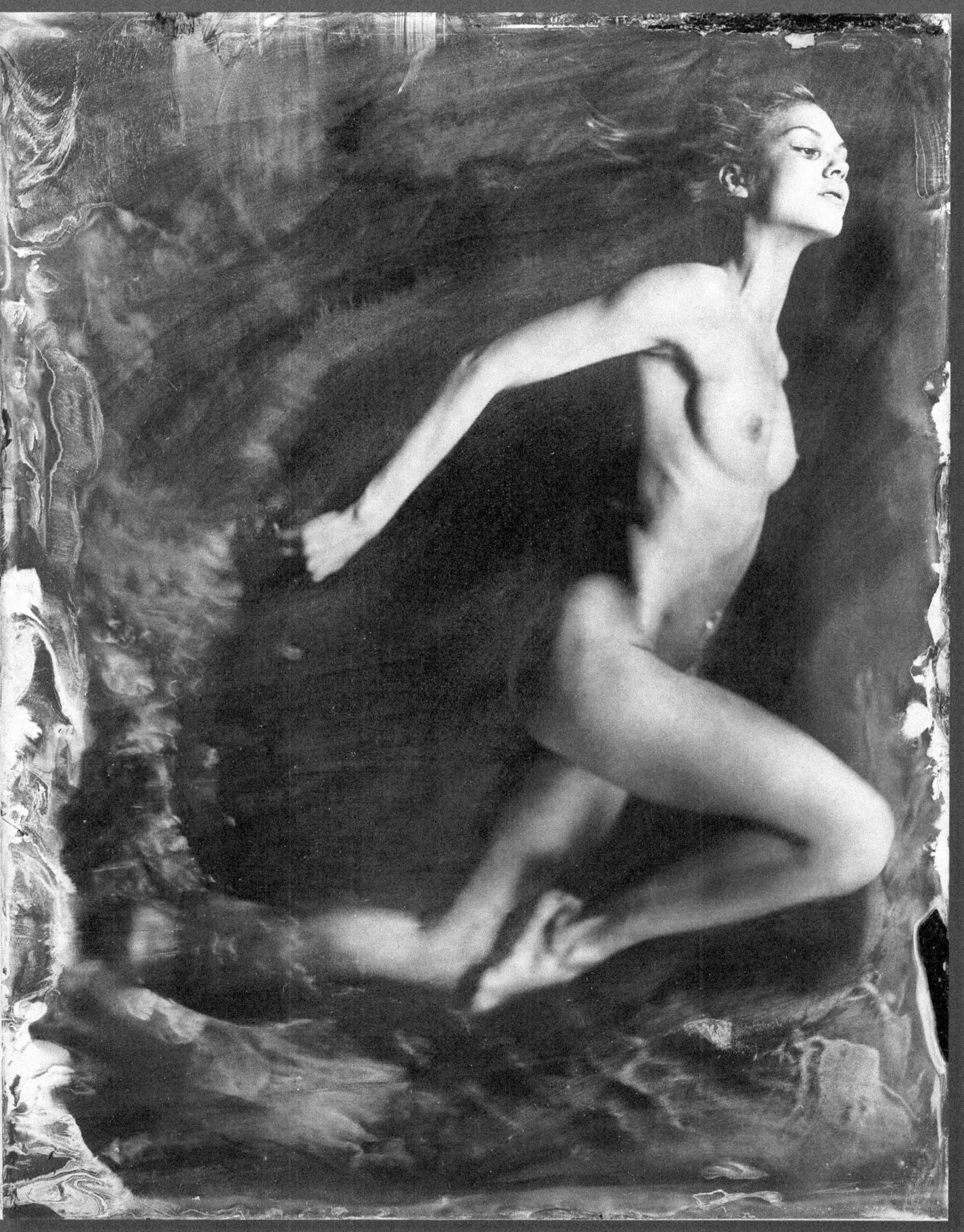

IGOR VASILIADIS

090817-0001

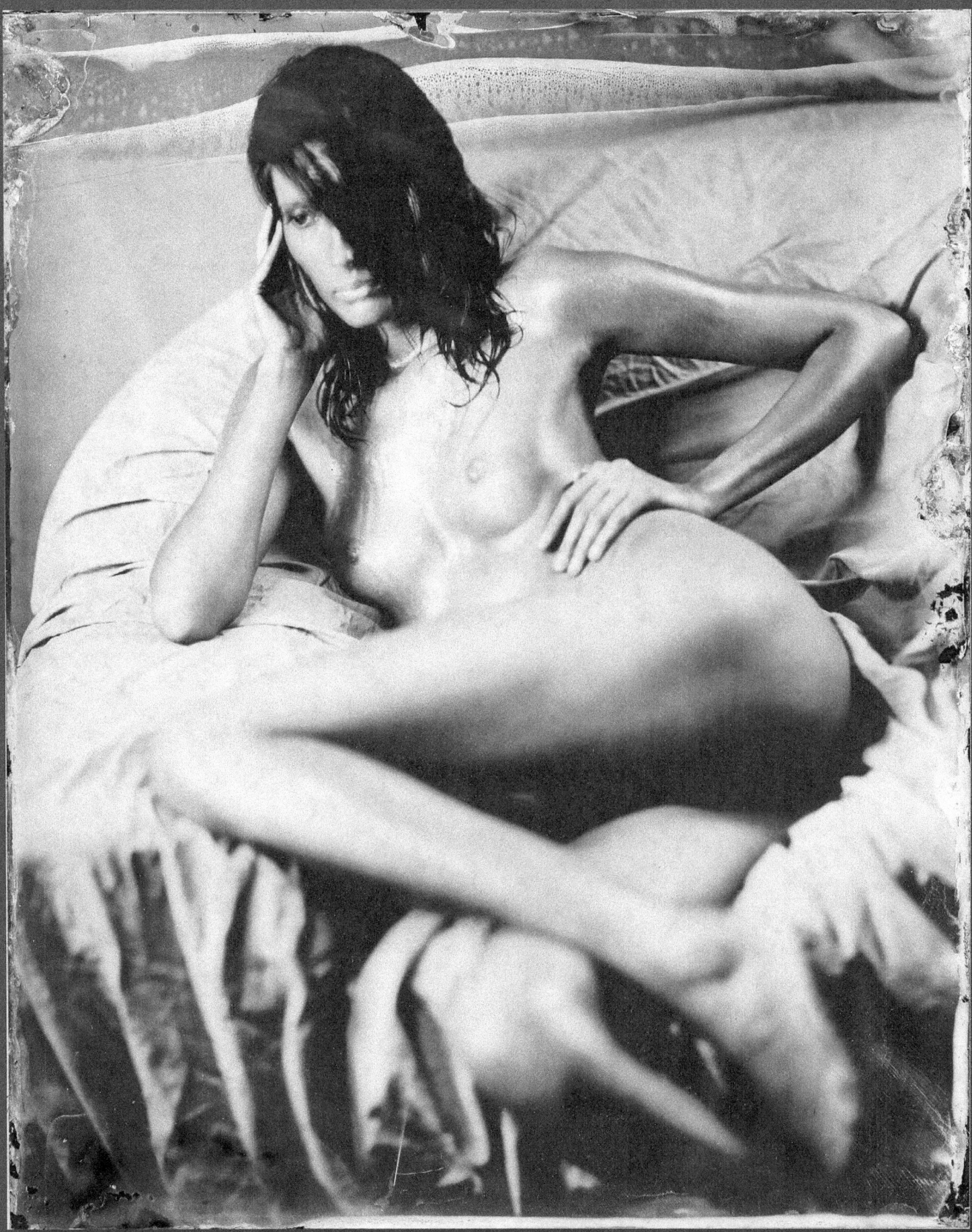

IGOR VASILIADIS

IGOR VASILIADIS

090817-0002

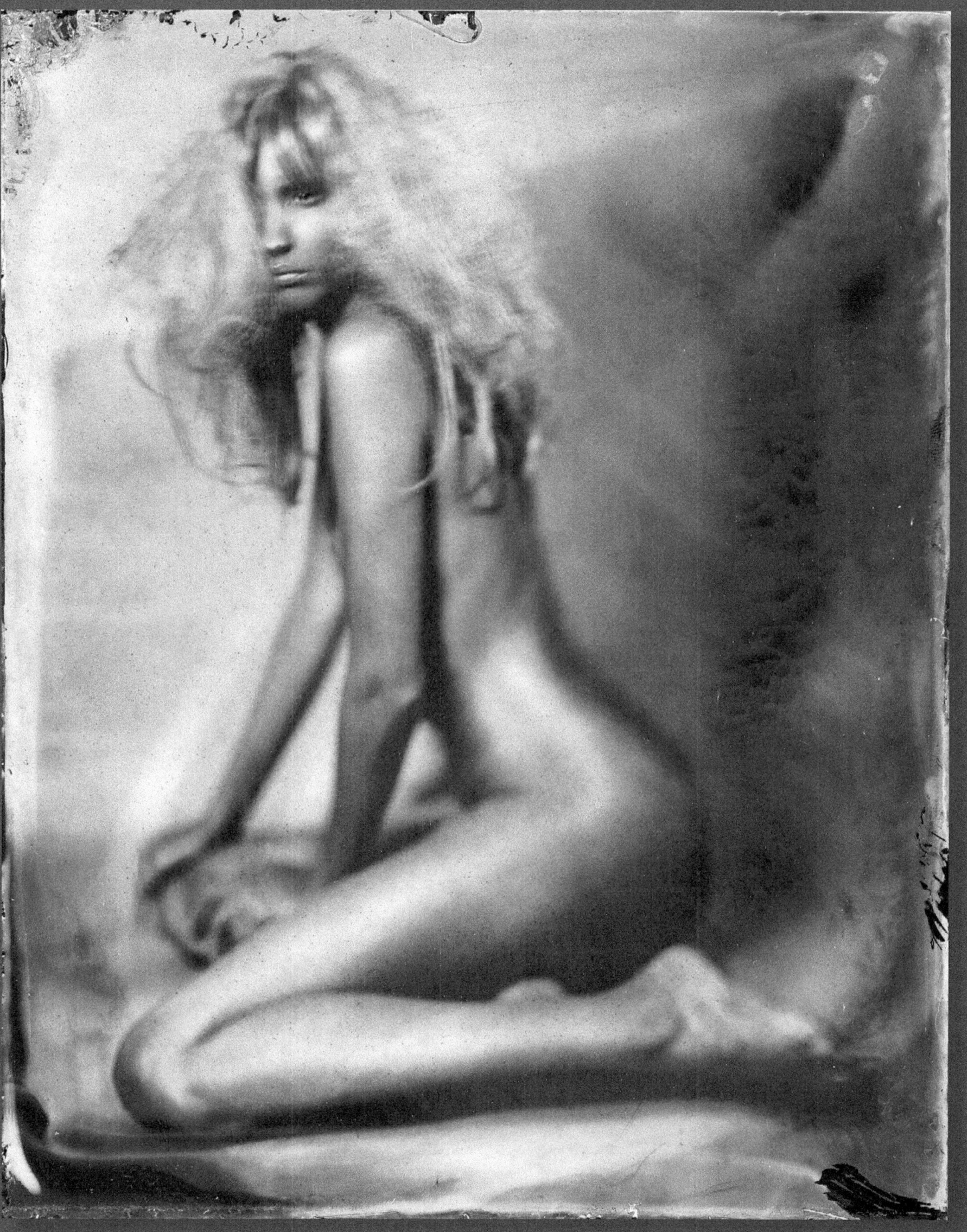

Sadness

Loneliness

090817-0003

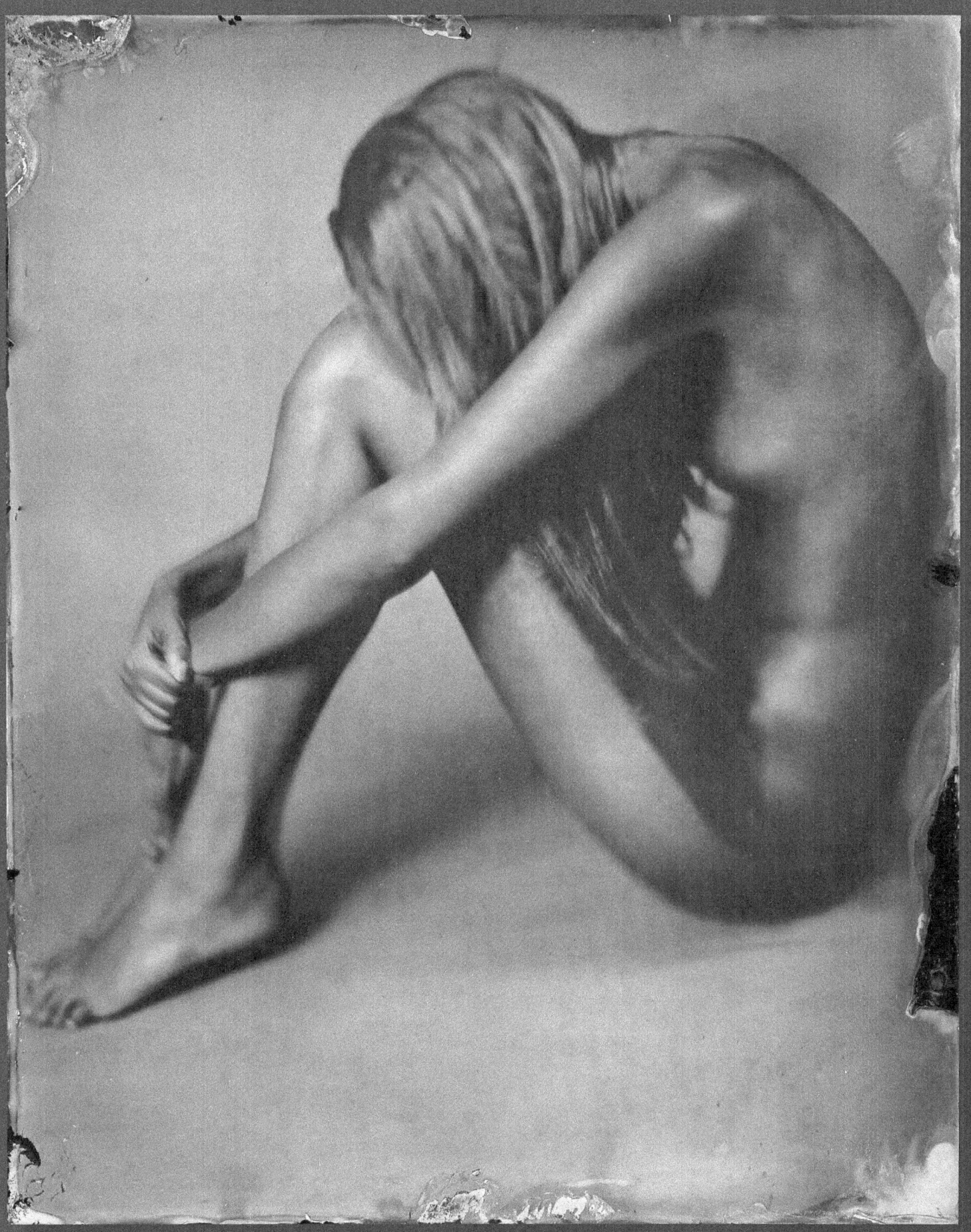

IGOR VASILIADIS

Faith

Desperation

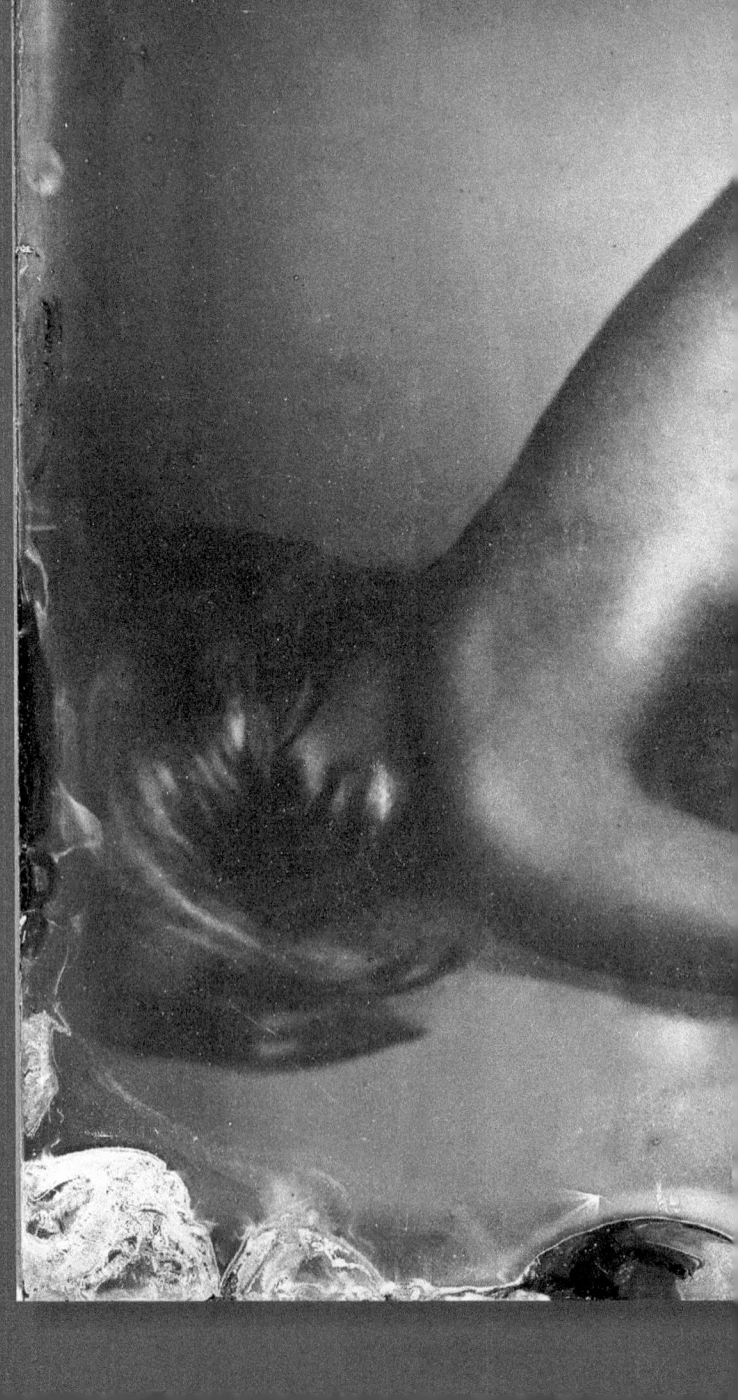

090817-0004

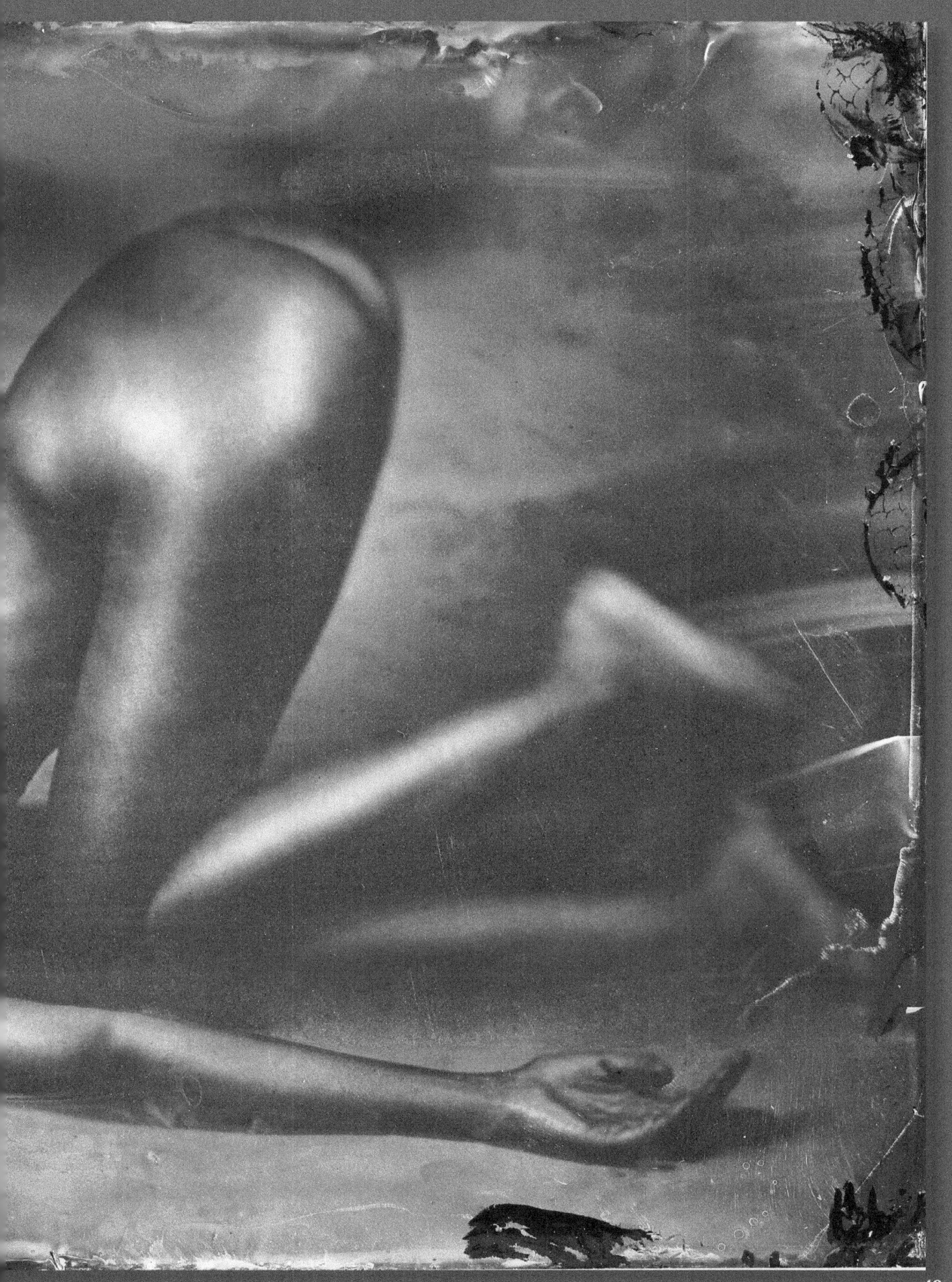

IGOR VASILIADIS

Inscrutability

possession

090817-0005

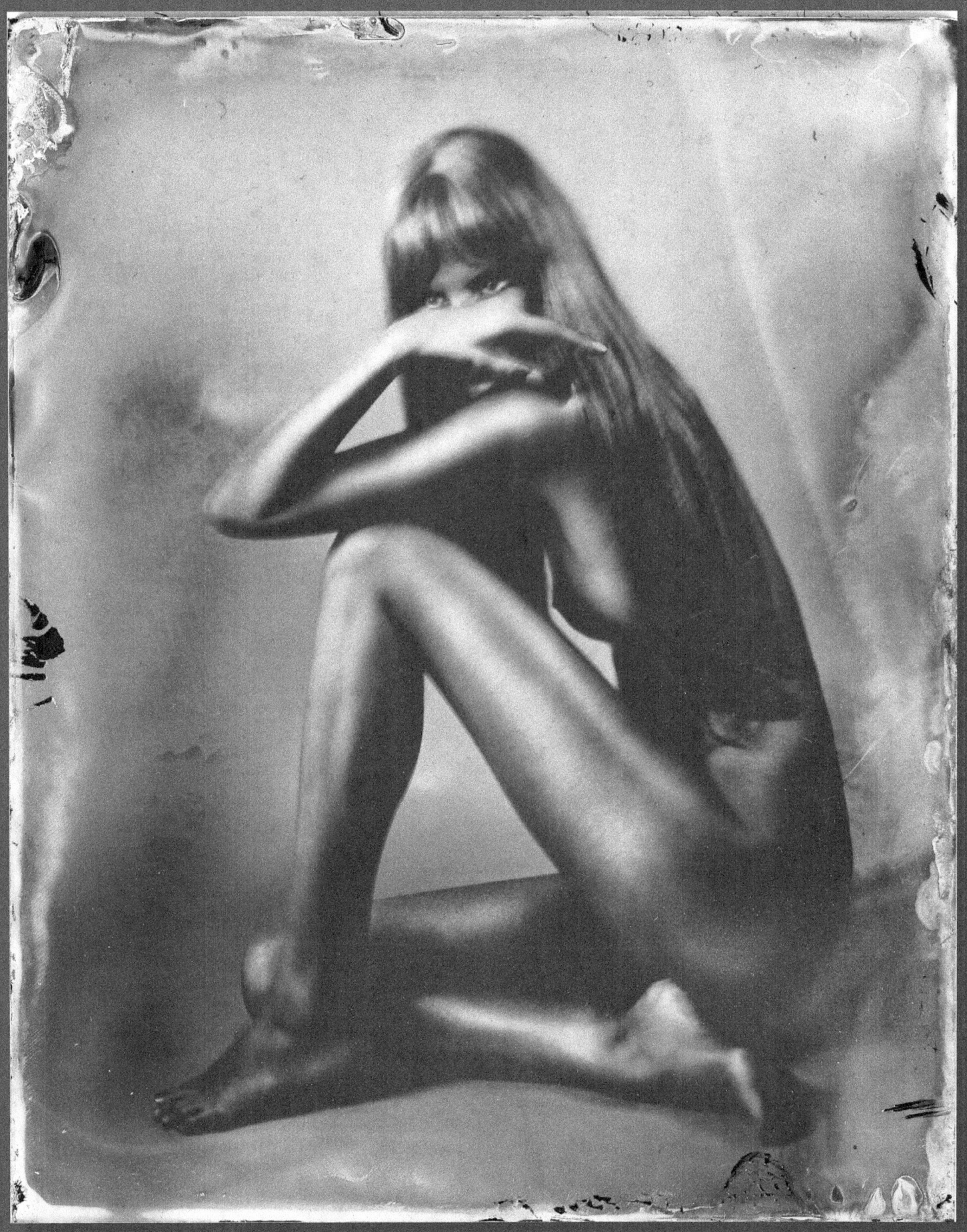

IGOR VASILIADIS

Mummery

Concernment

090926-0002

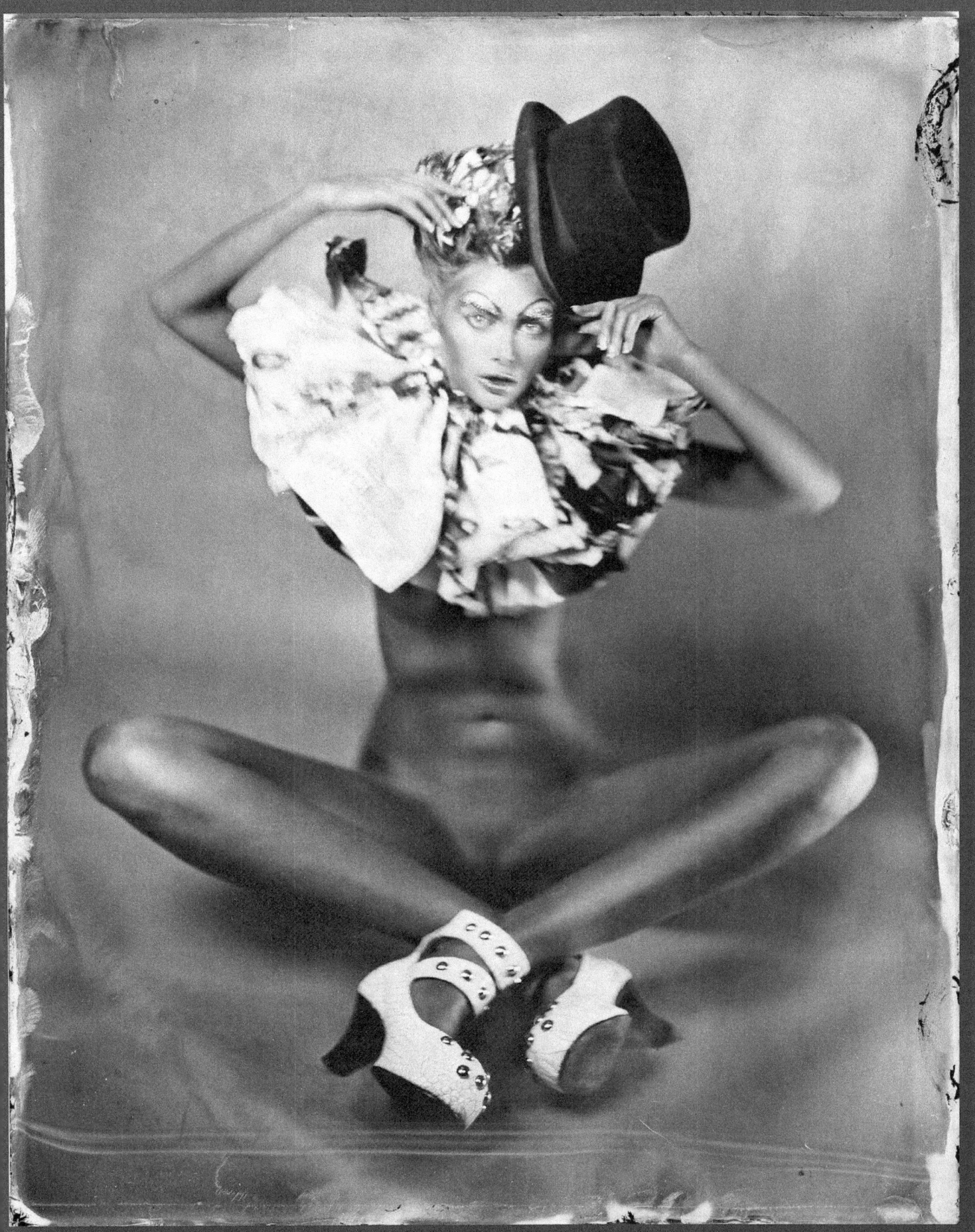

091009-0001

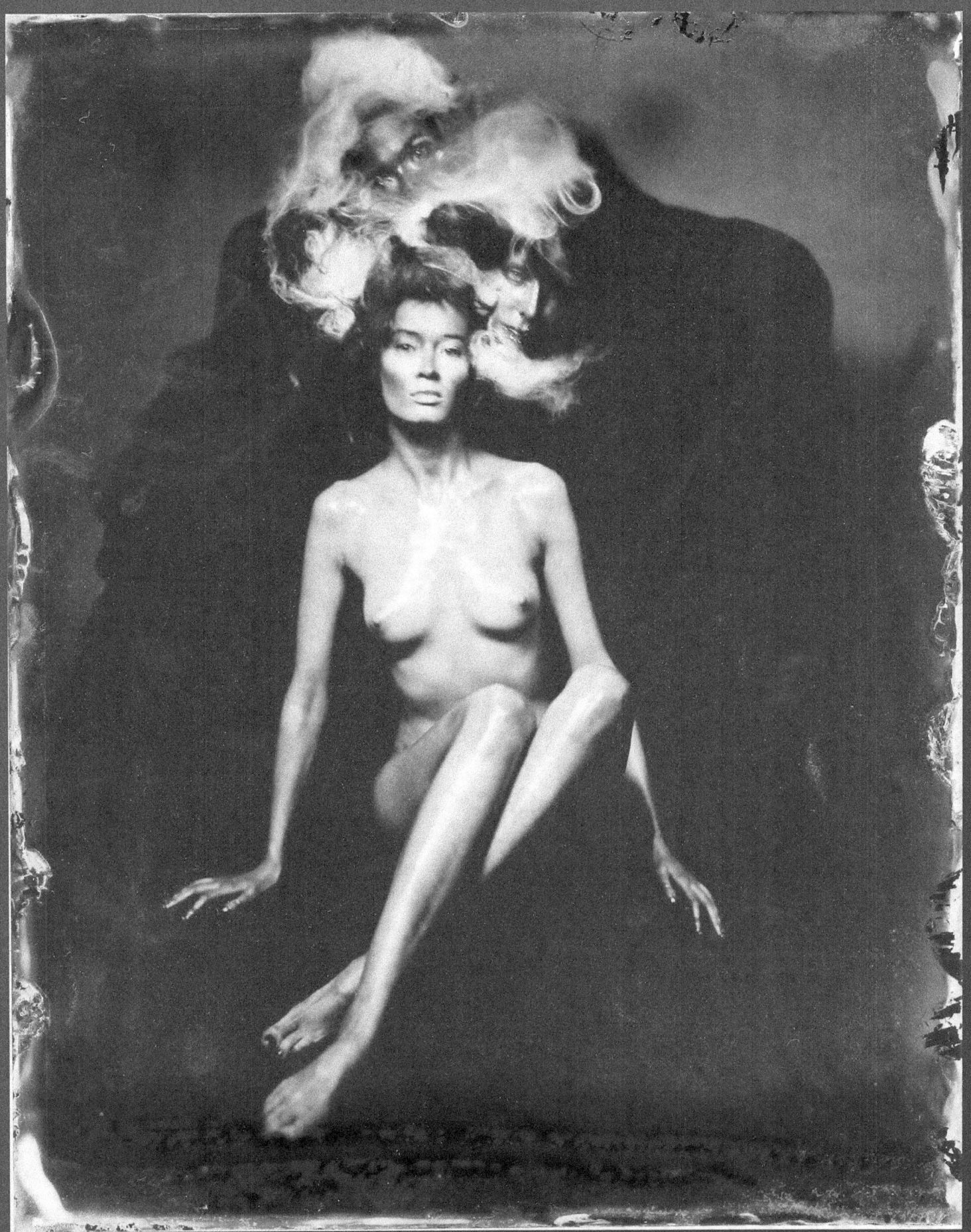

IGOR VASILIADIS

IGOR VASILIADIS

091012-0001

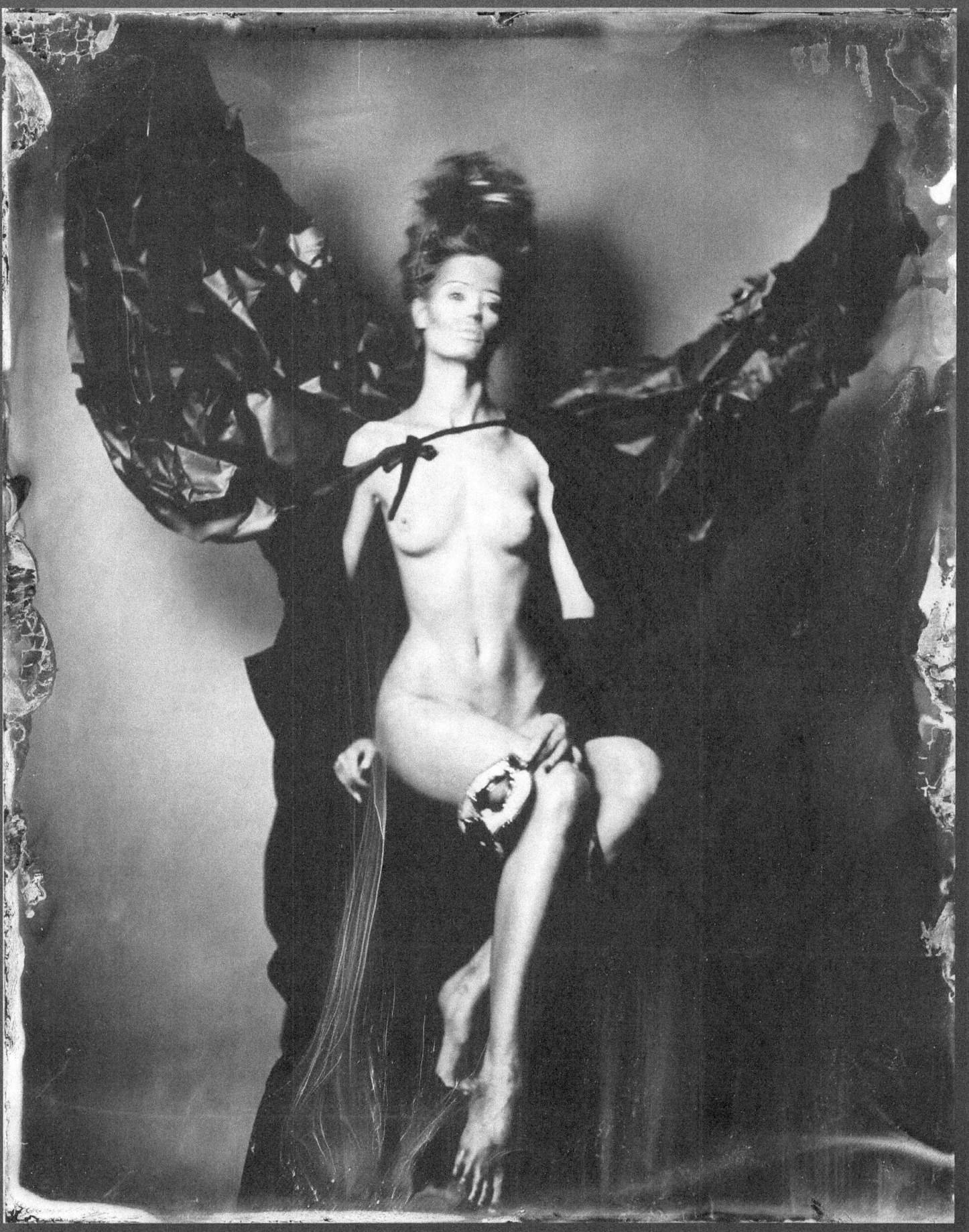

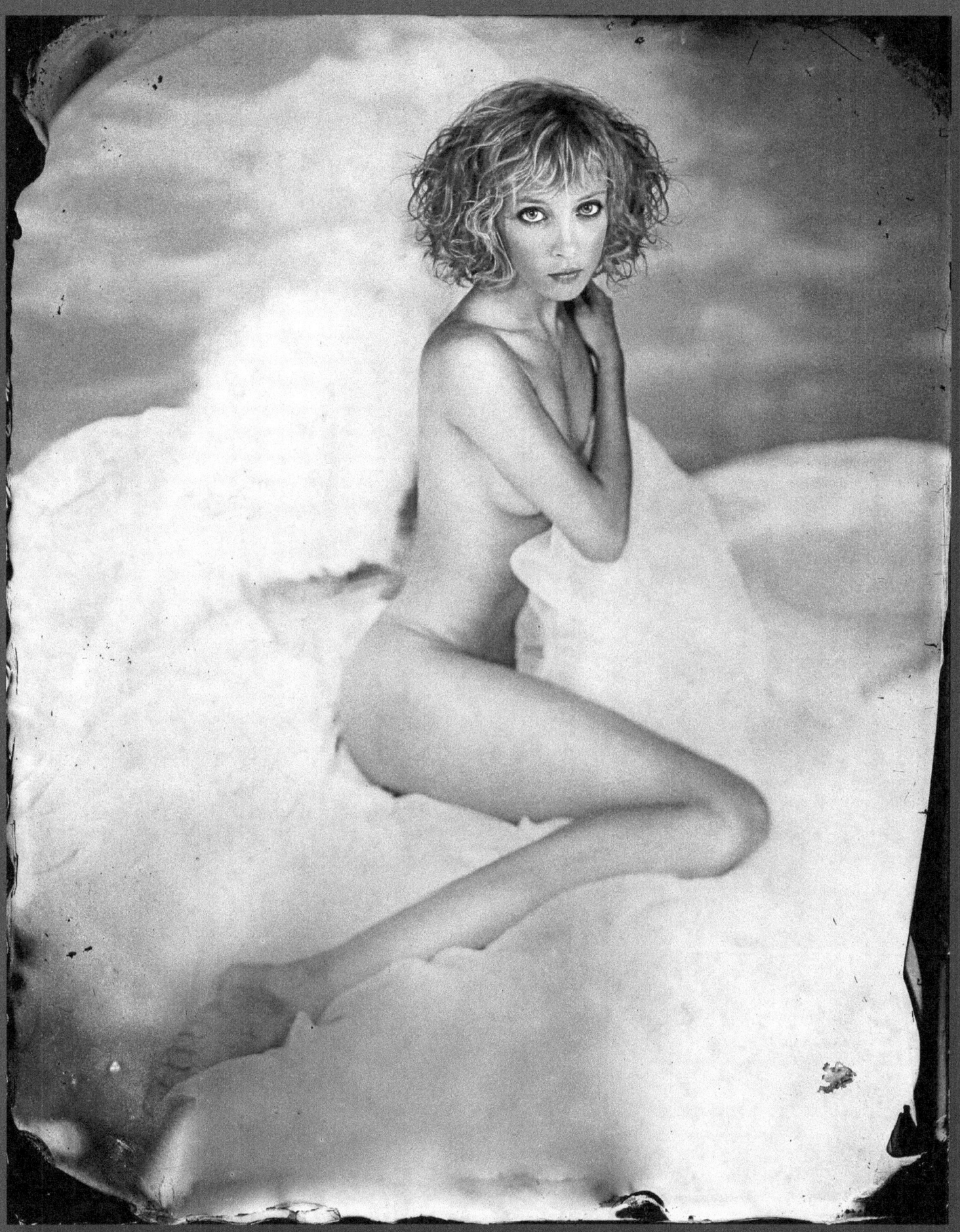

IGOR VASILIADIS

091013-0002

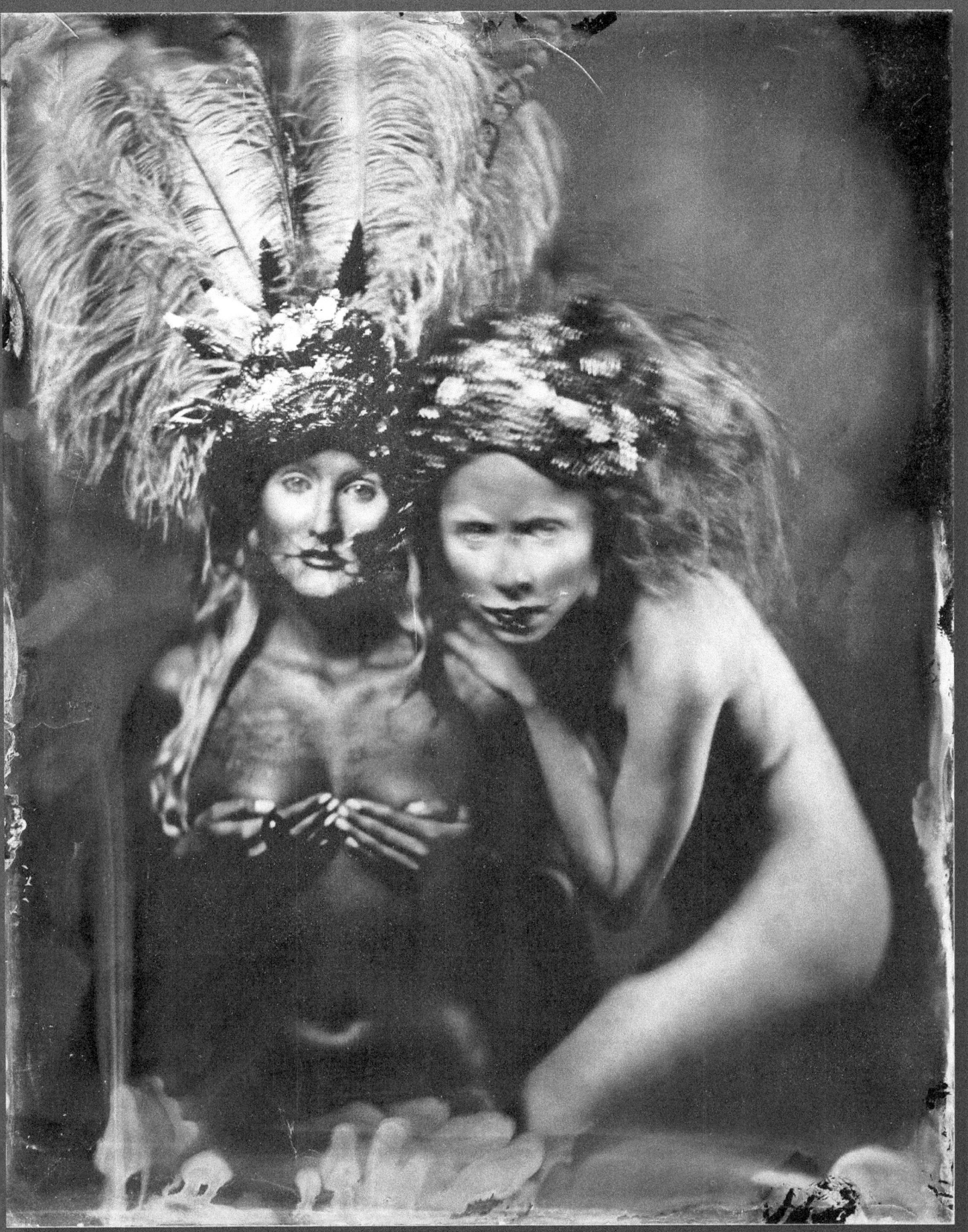

Misticicism
Enchantment

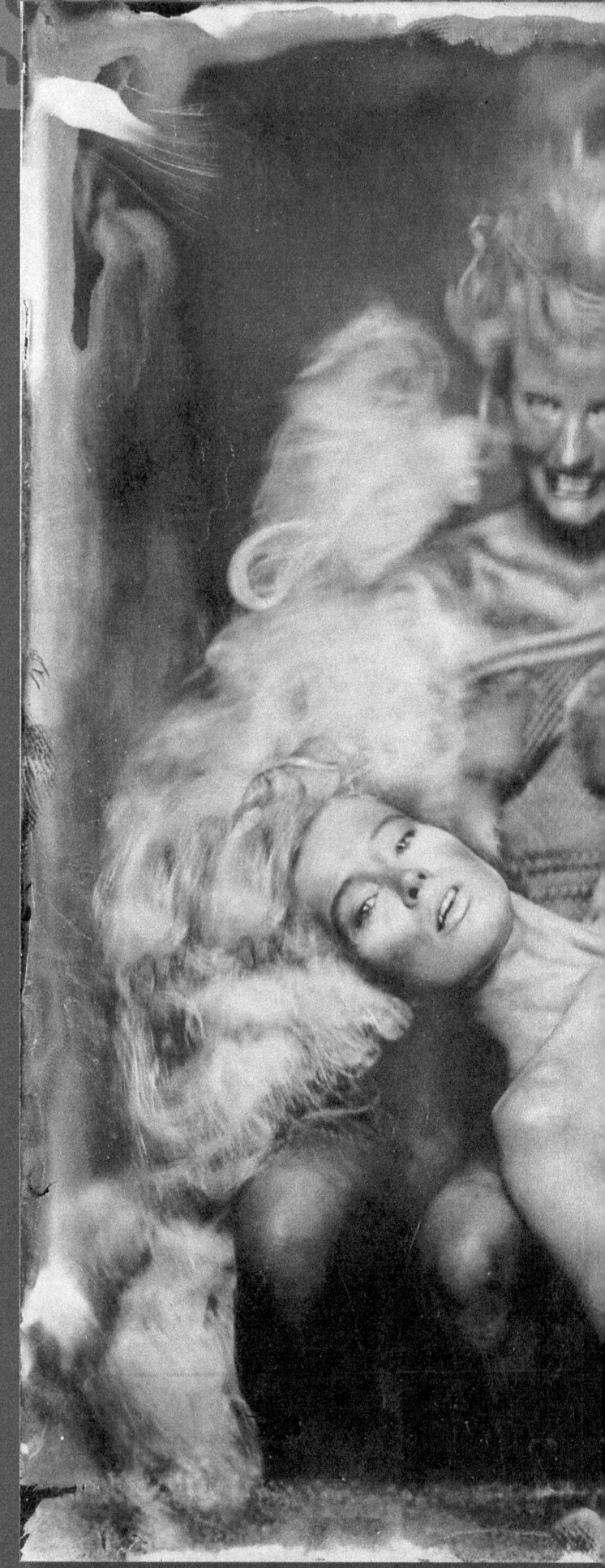

091013-0003

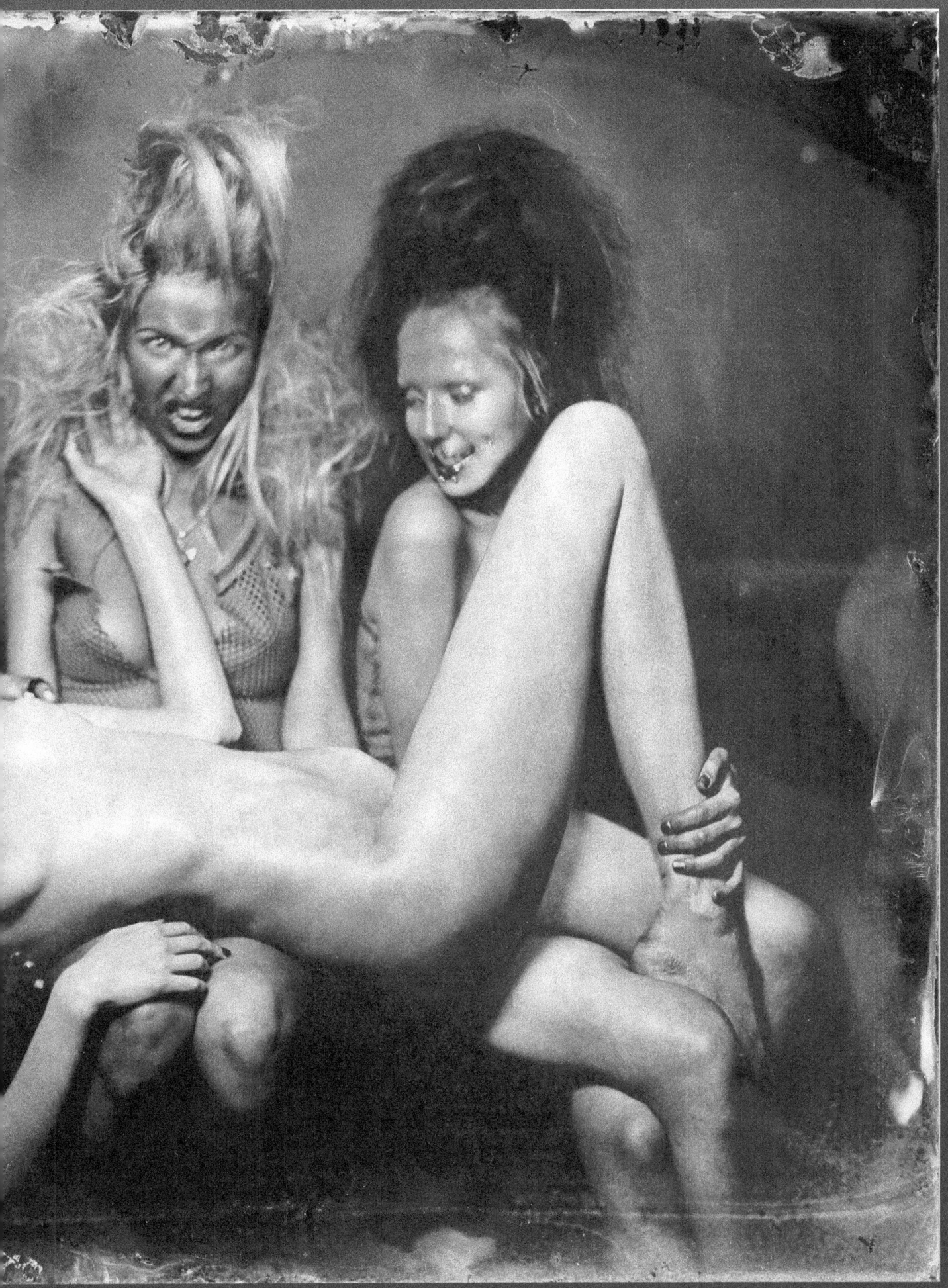

IGOR VASILIADIS

Versatility

Detachment

091014-0001

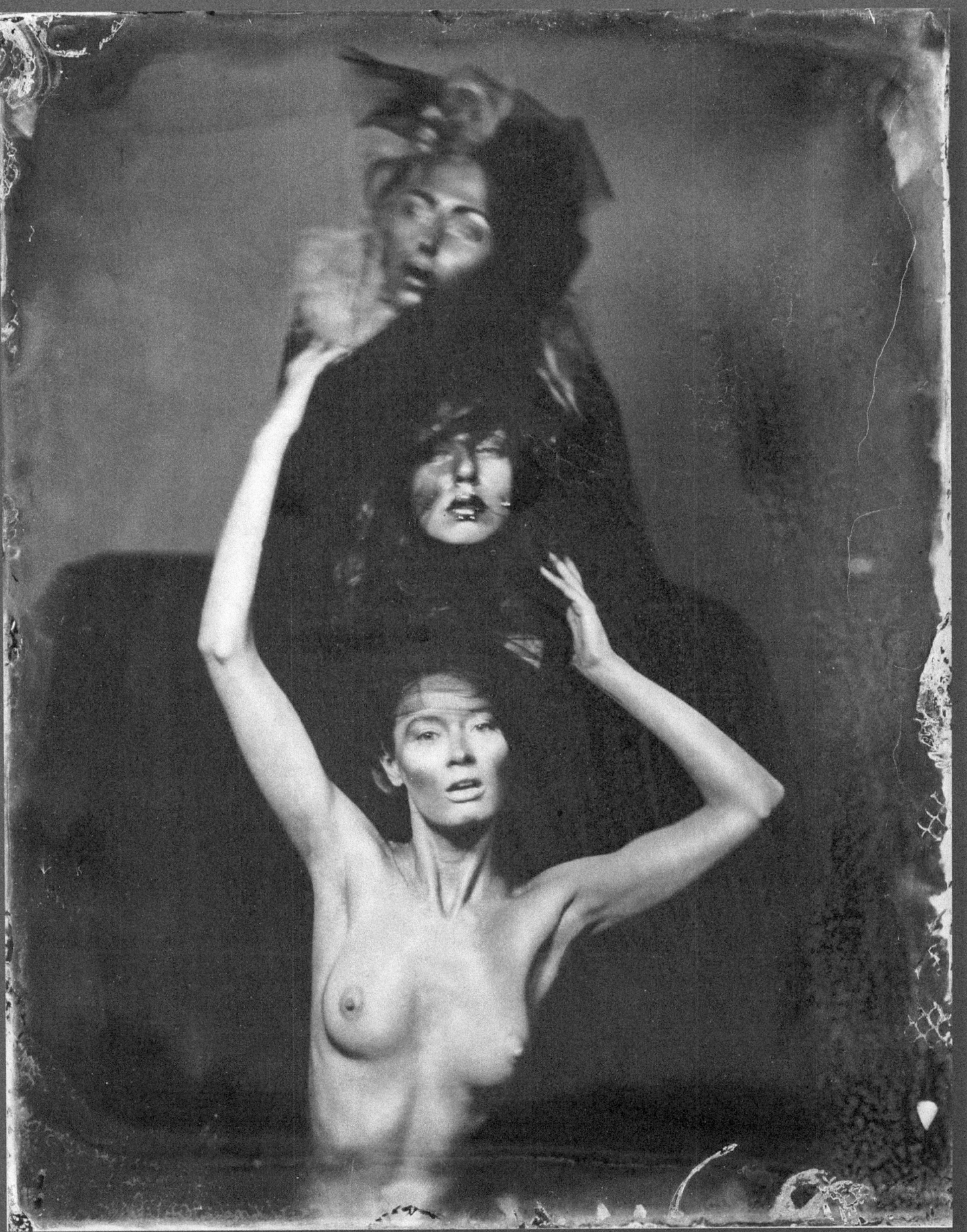

IGOR VASILIADIS

IGOR VASILIADIS

090726-0003

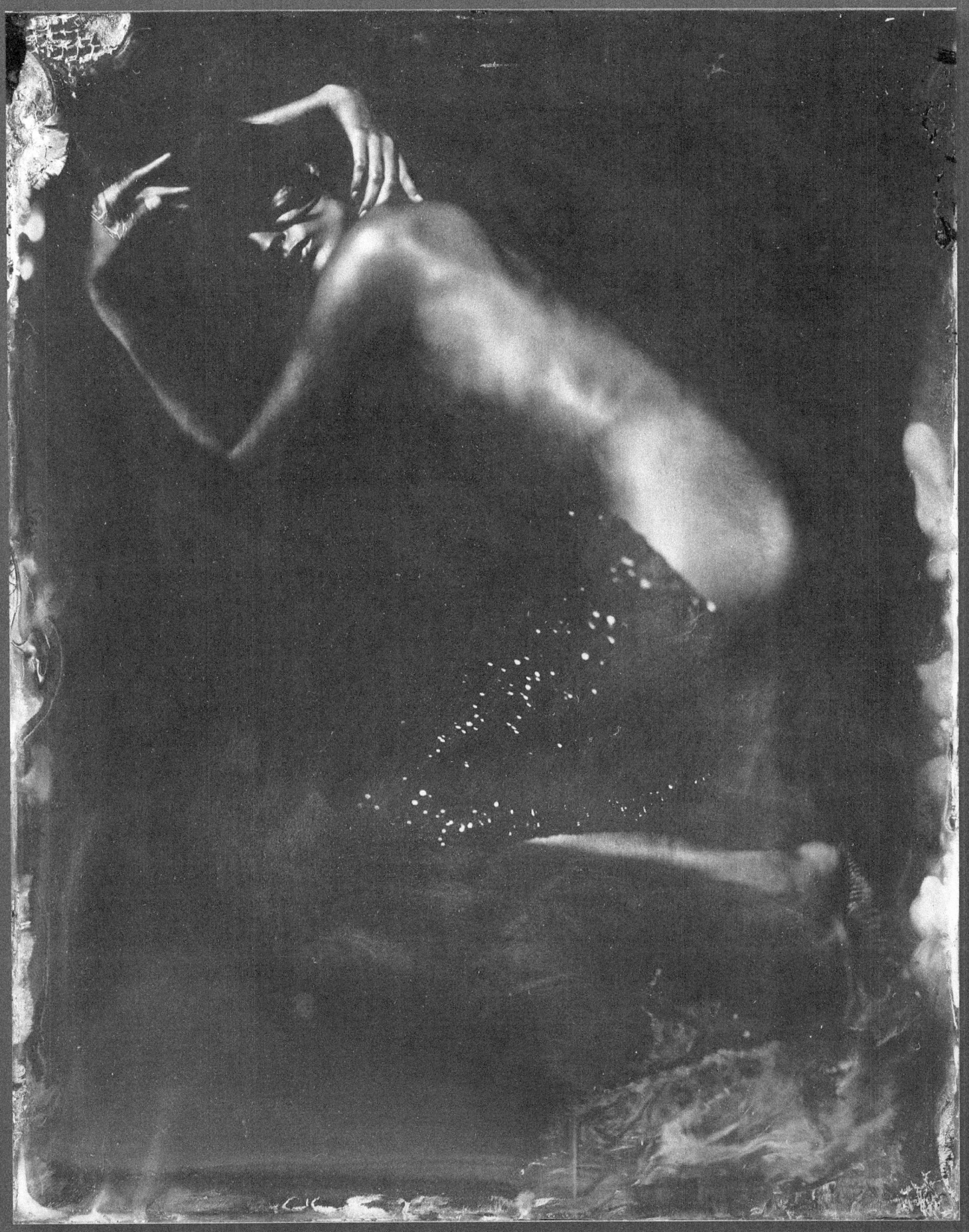

IGOR VASILIADIS

Doubt

Exhaustiveness

091116-0002

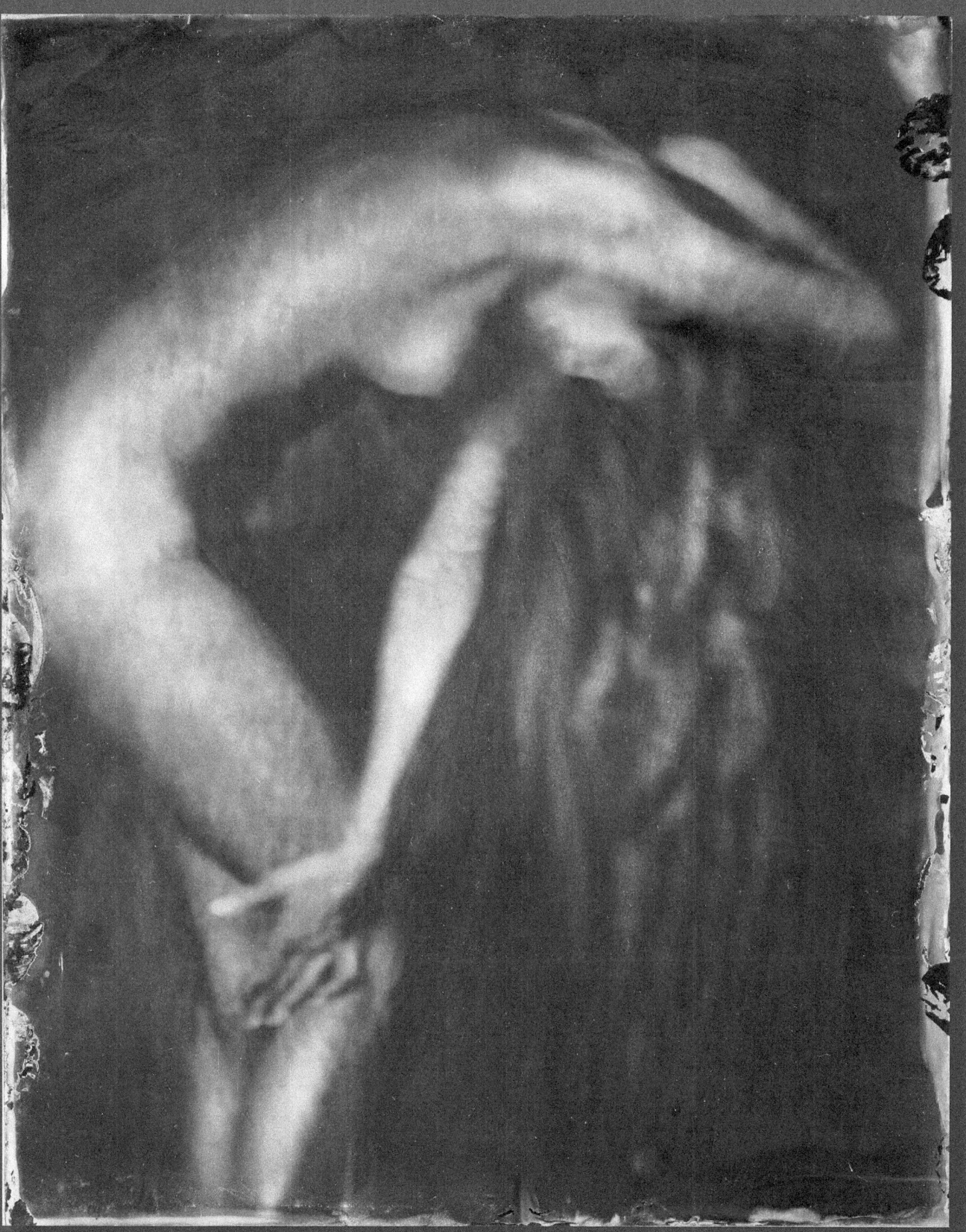

IGOR VASILIADIS

080821-0001

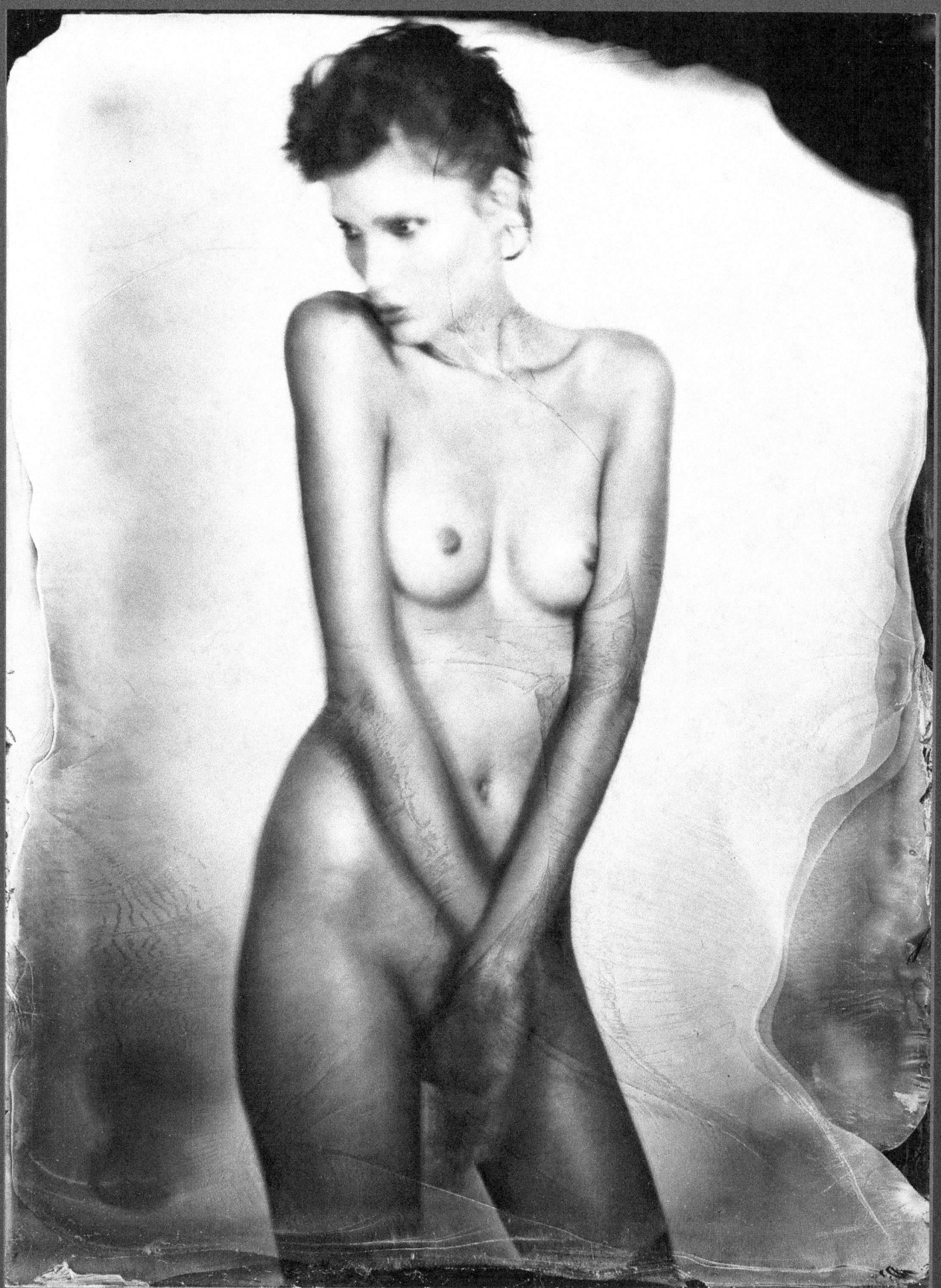

IGOR VASILIADIS

091116-0003

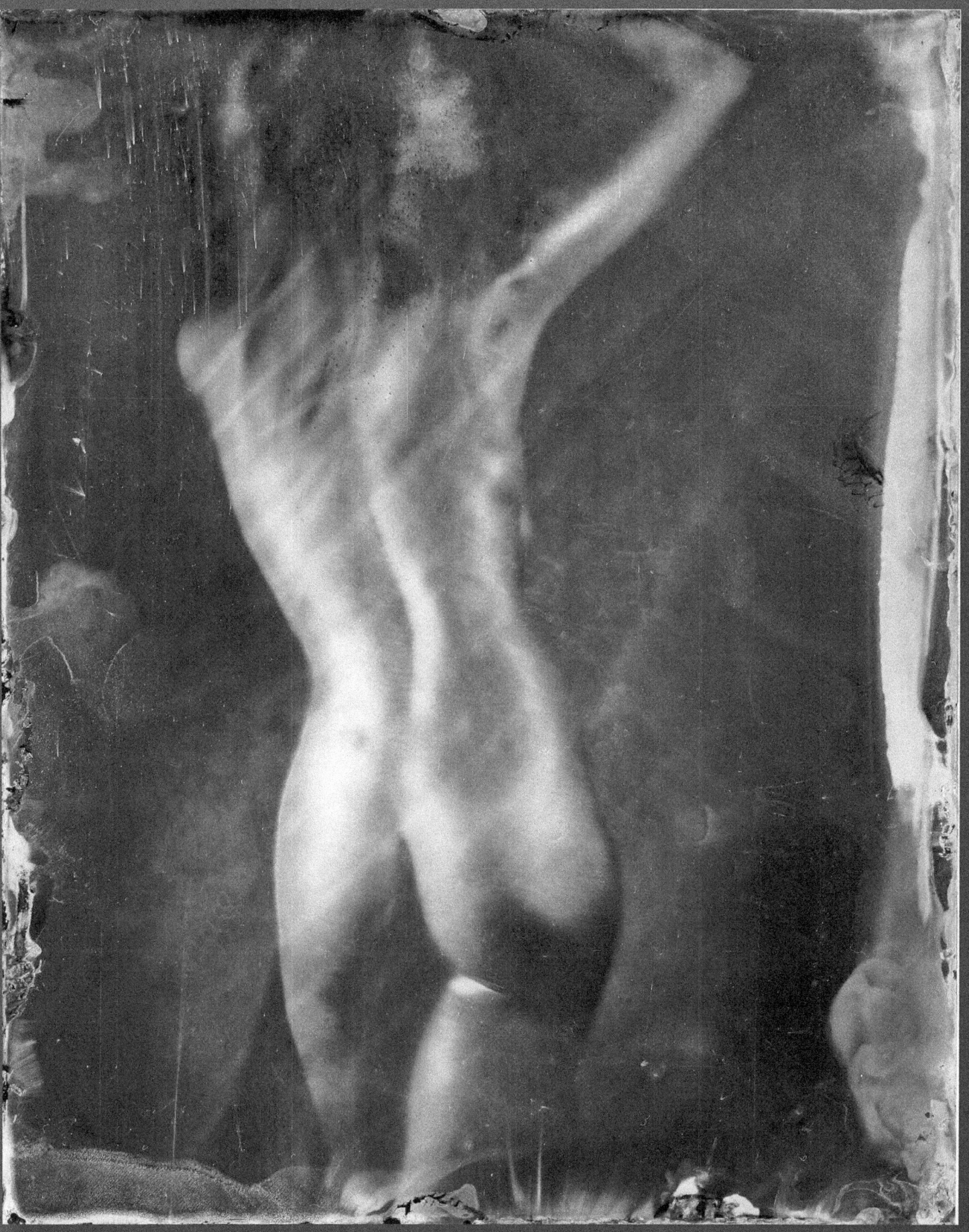

IGOR VASILIADIS

Calmness

Satisfaction

091120-0002

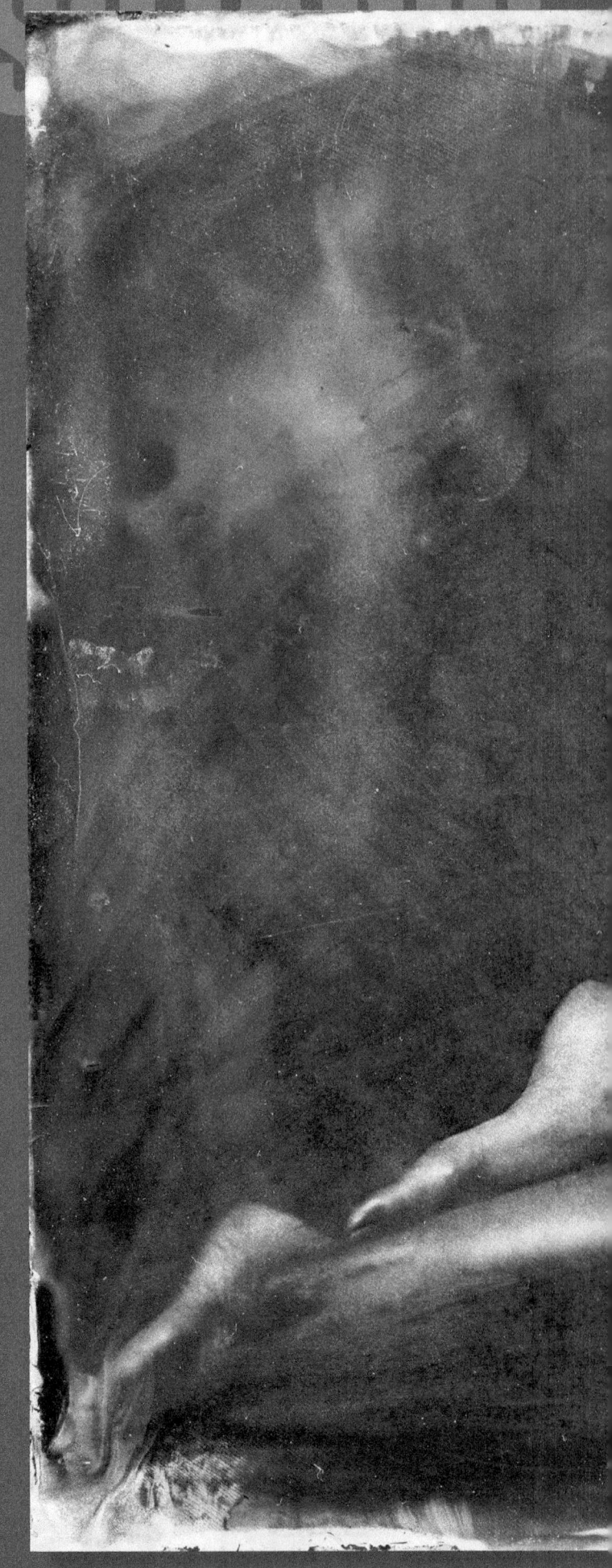

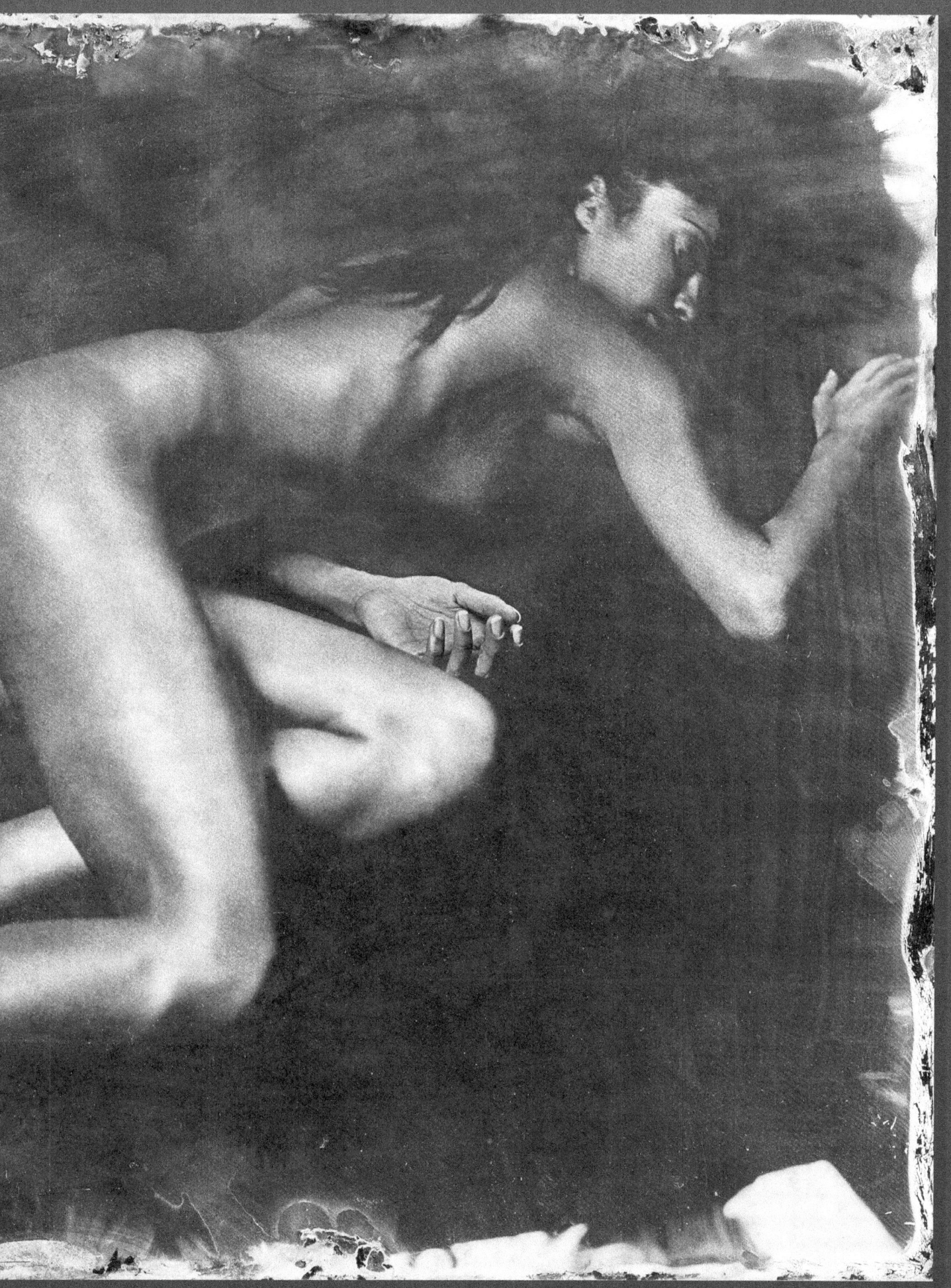

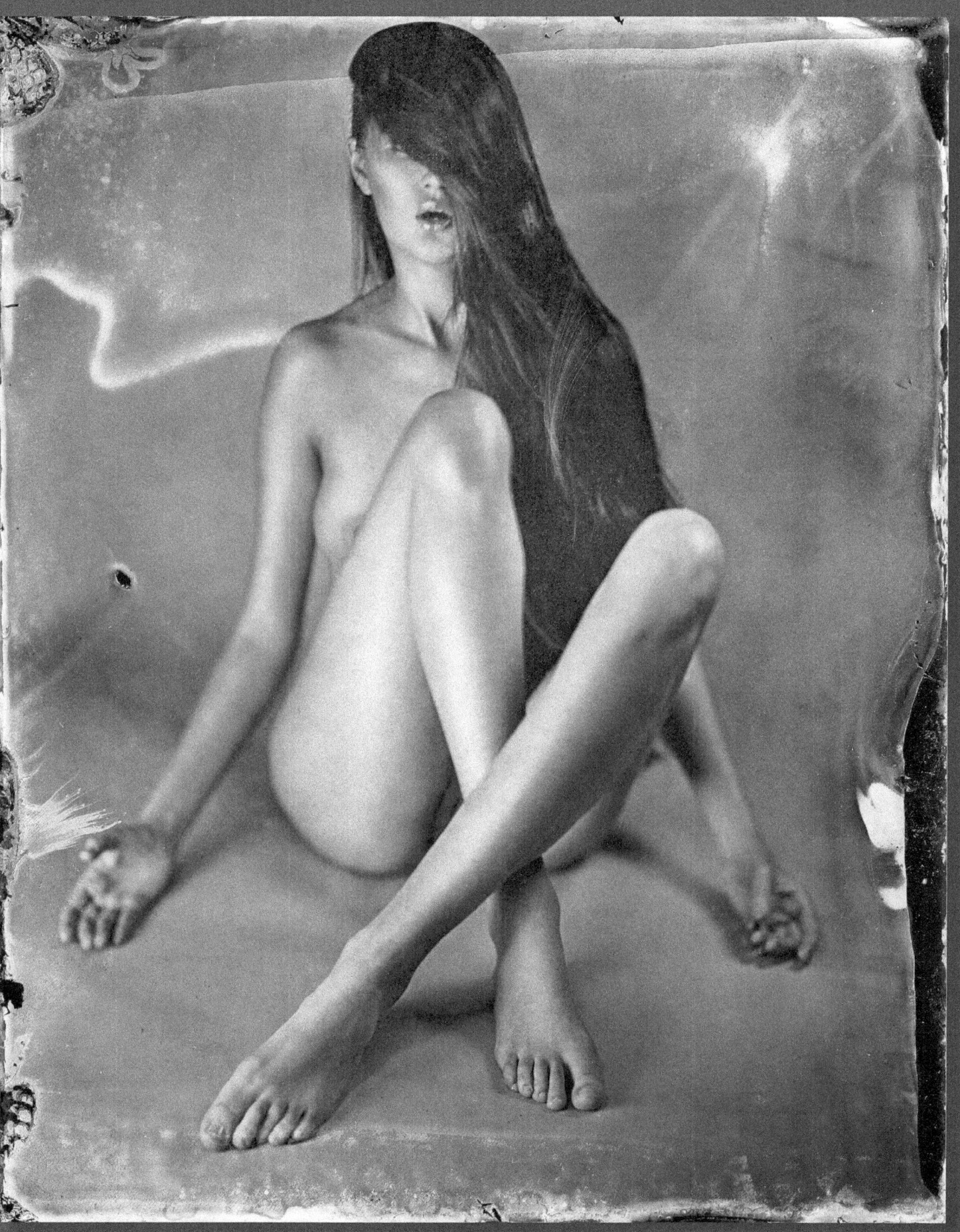

IGOR VASILIADIS

Confidence
Expectation

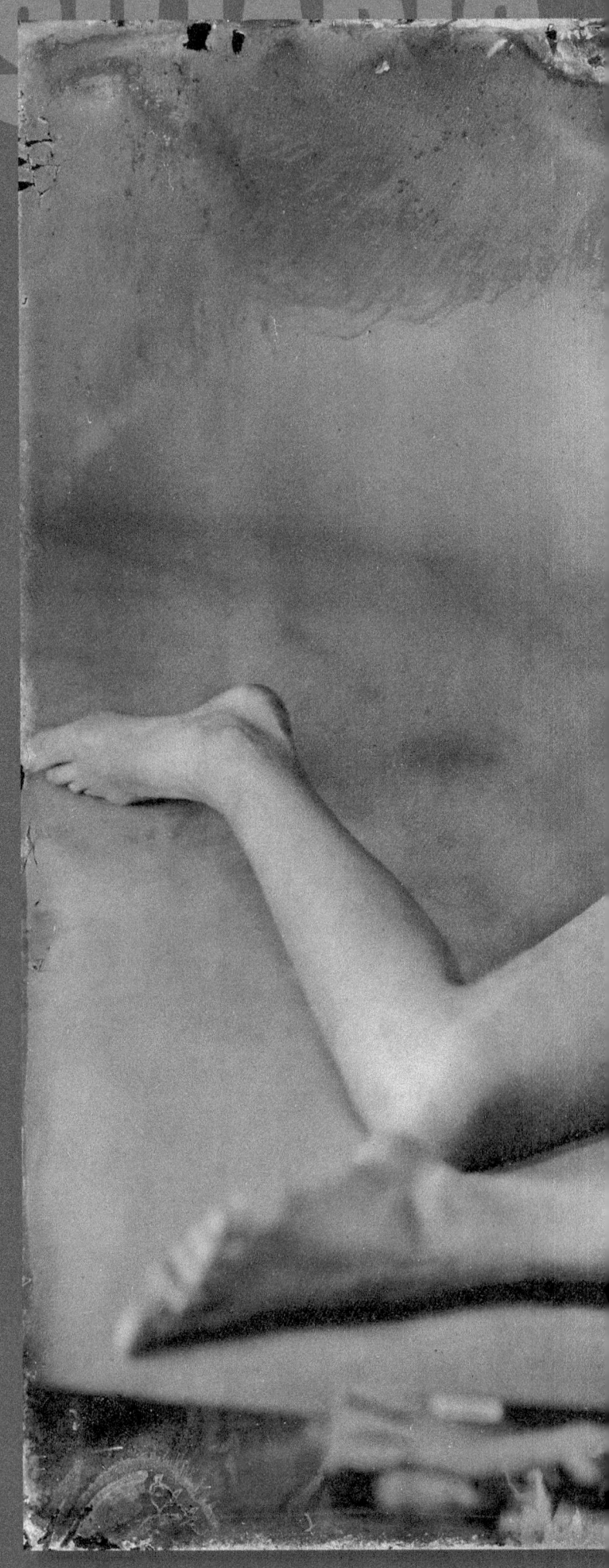

091204-0001

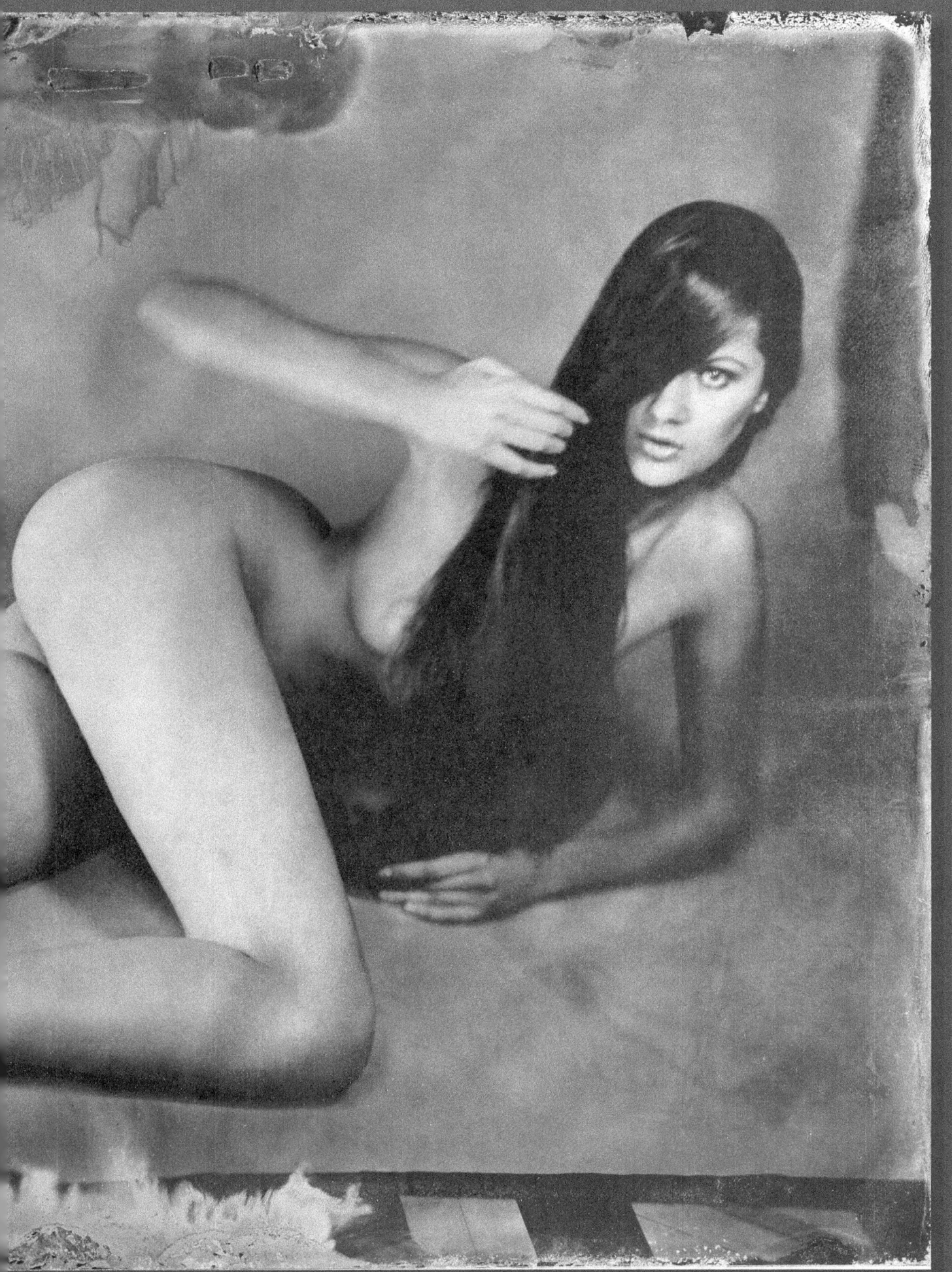

IGOR VASILIADIS

091207-0001

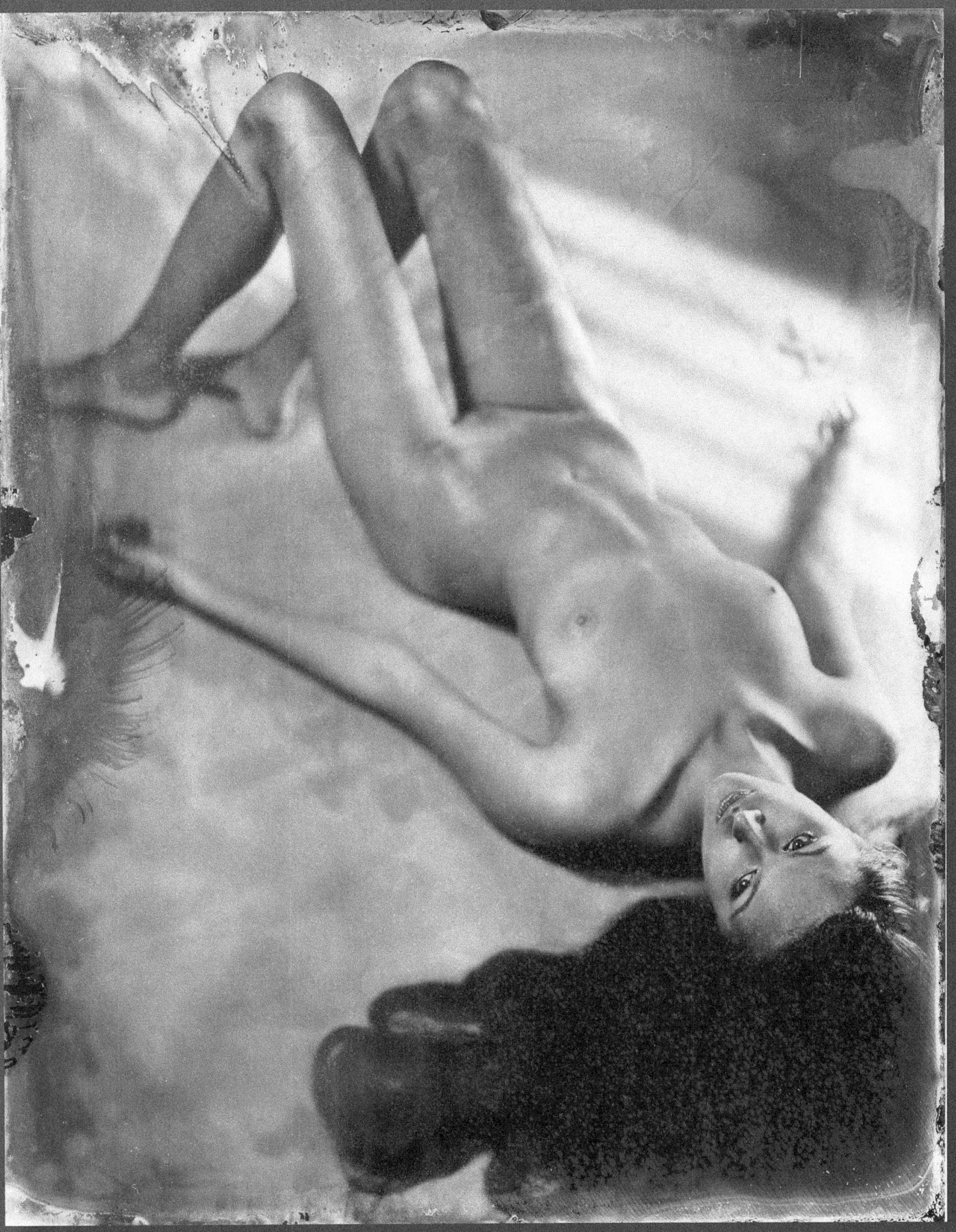

IGOR VASILIADIS

Pride

Dedication

091215-0001

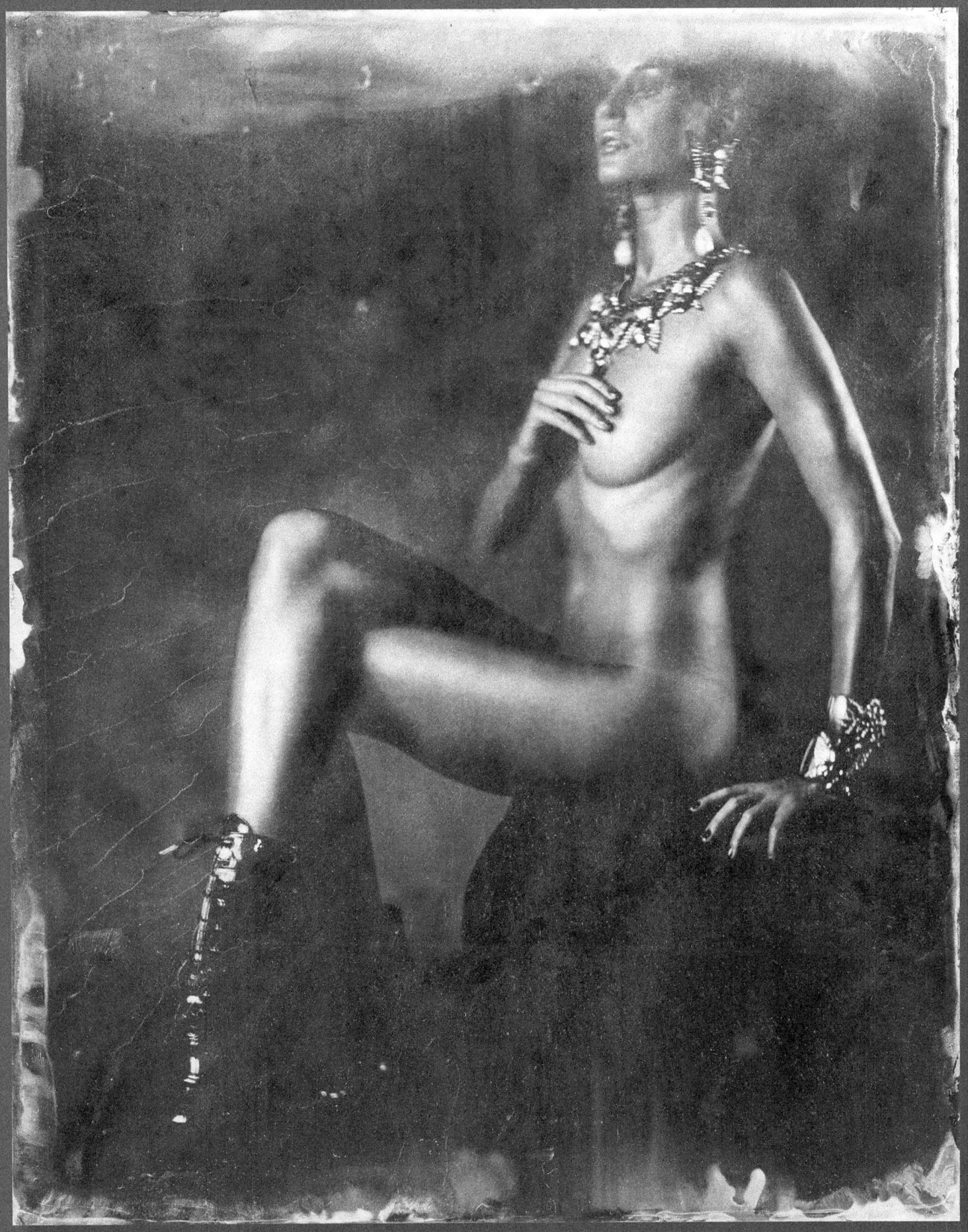

IGOR VASILIADIS

080806-0001

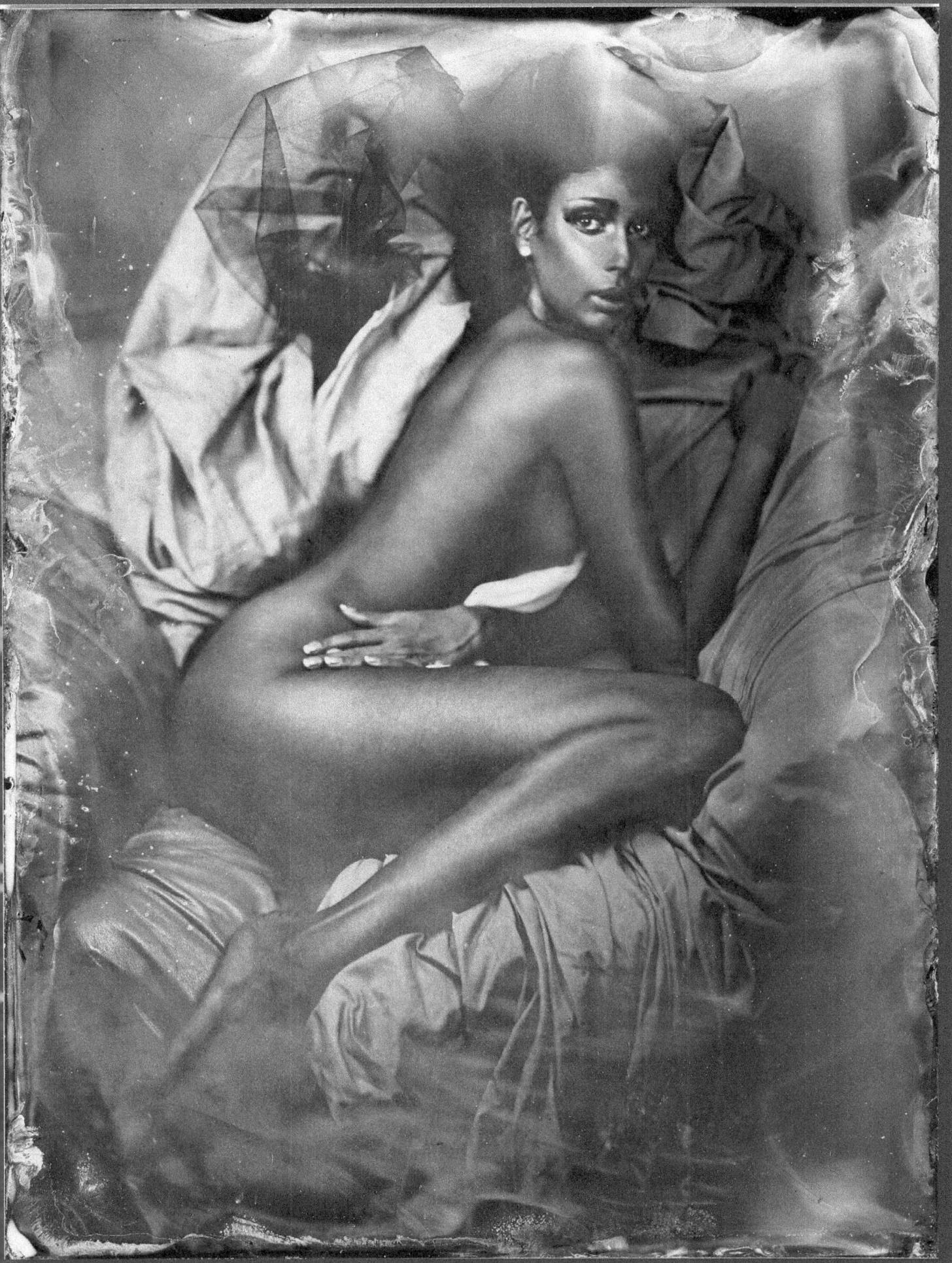

Thinking

Designing

091216-0003

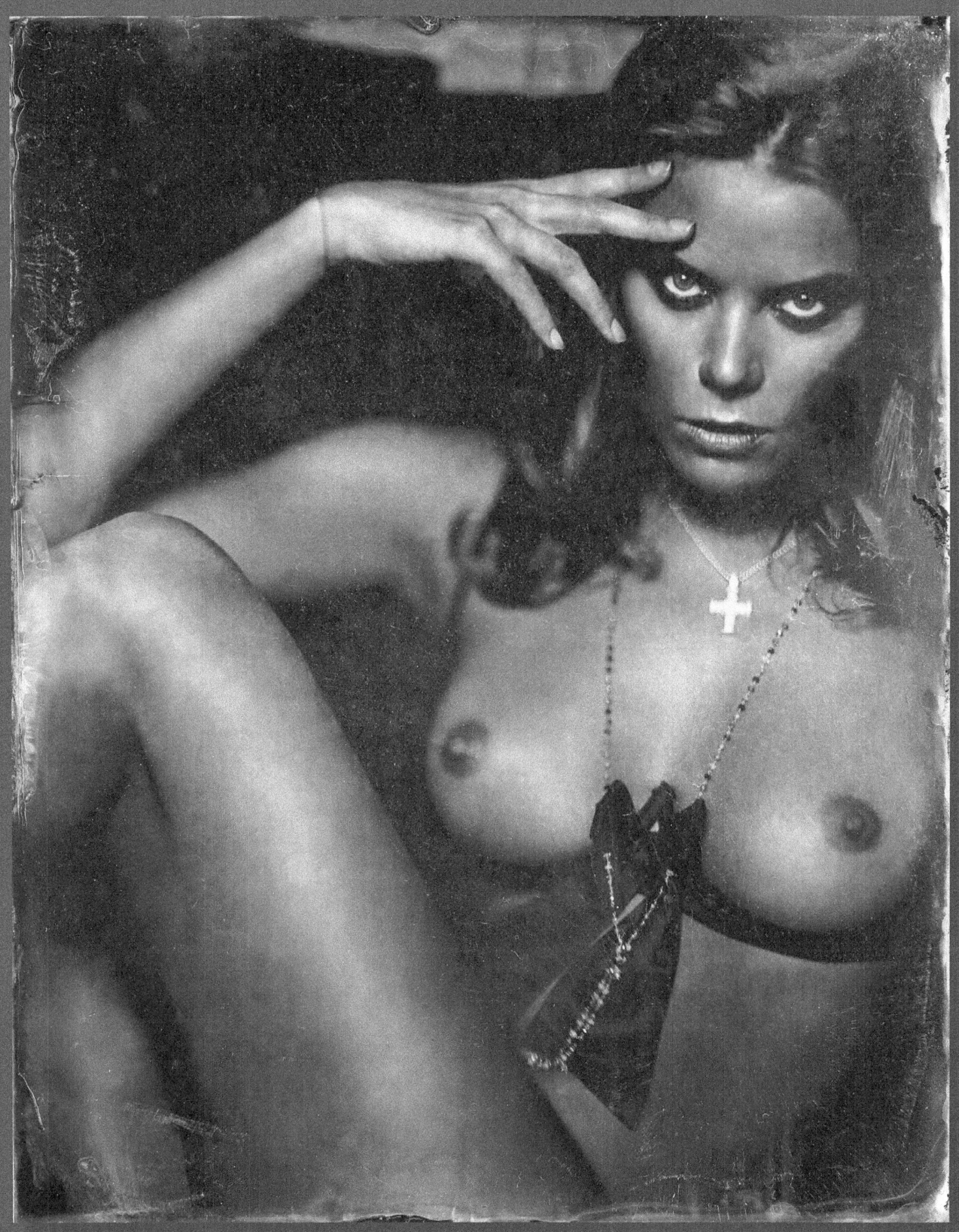

IGOR VASILIADIS

100214-0001

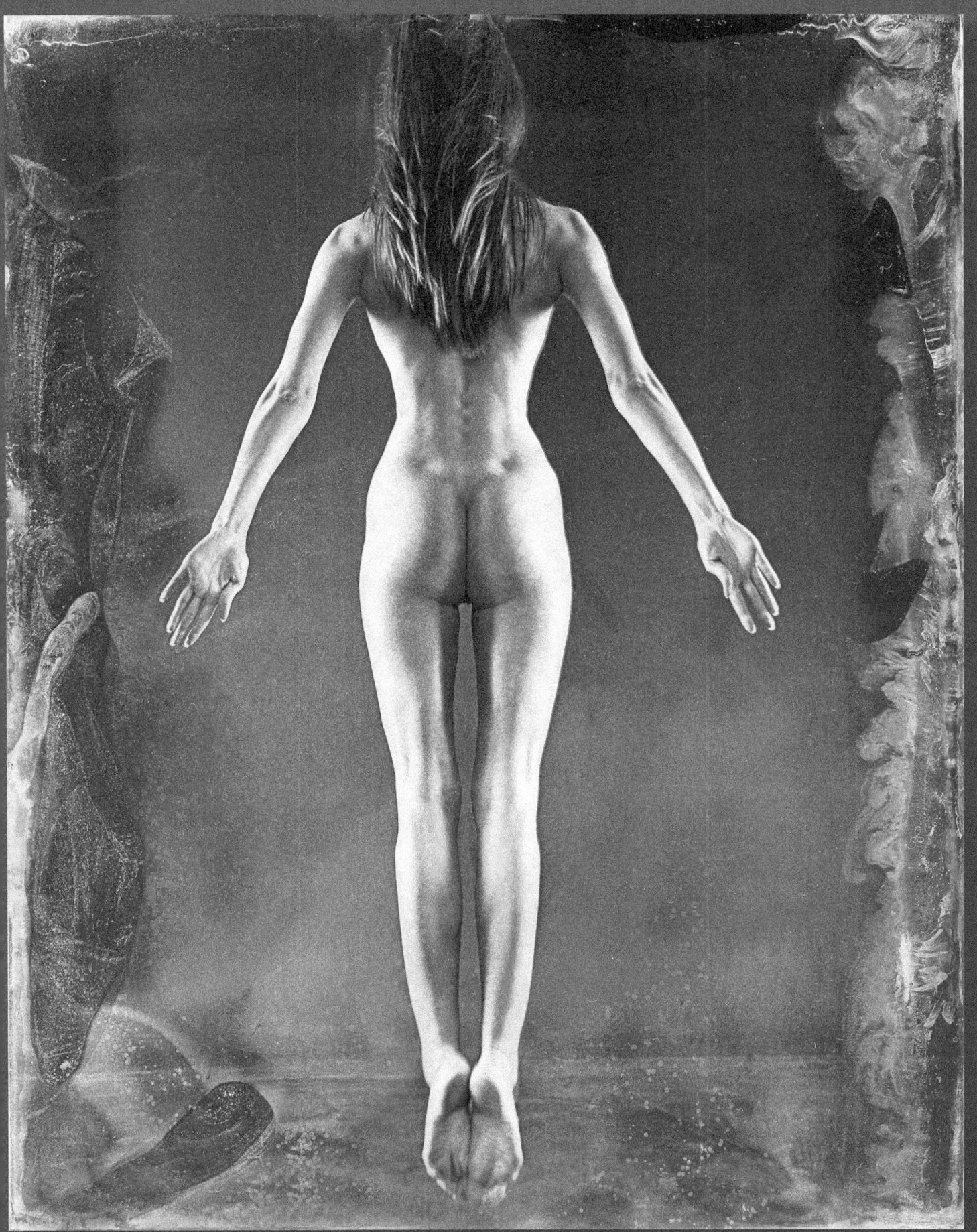

IGOR VASILIADIS

Adoration

Questioning

100218-0001

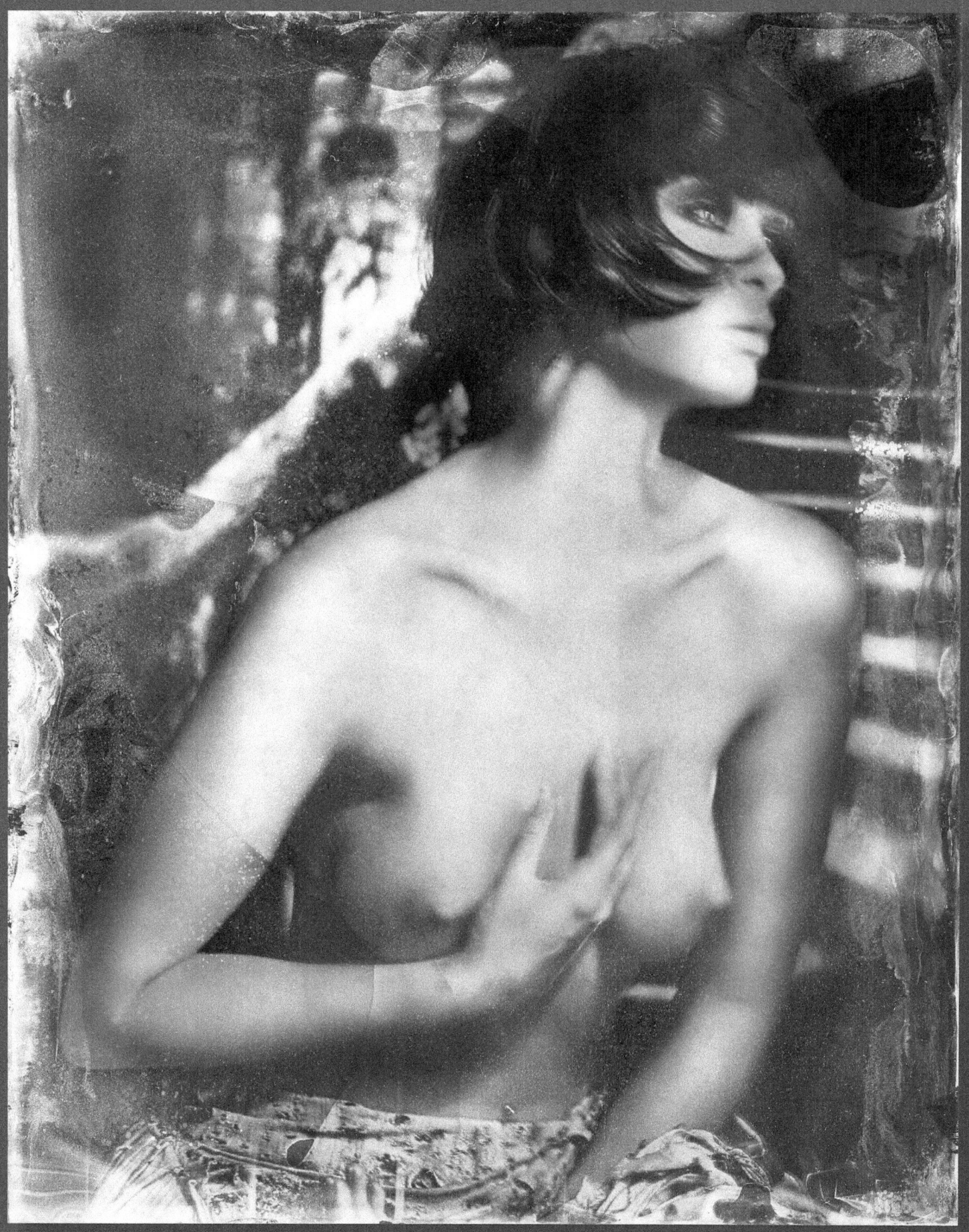

100501-0001

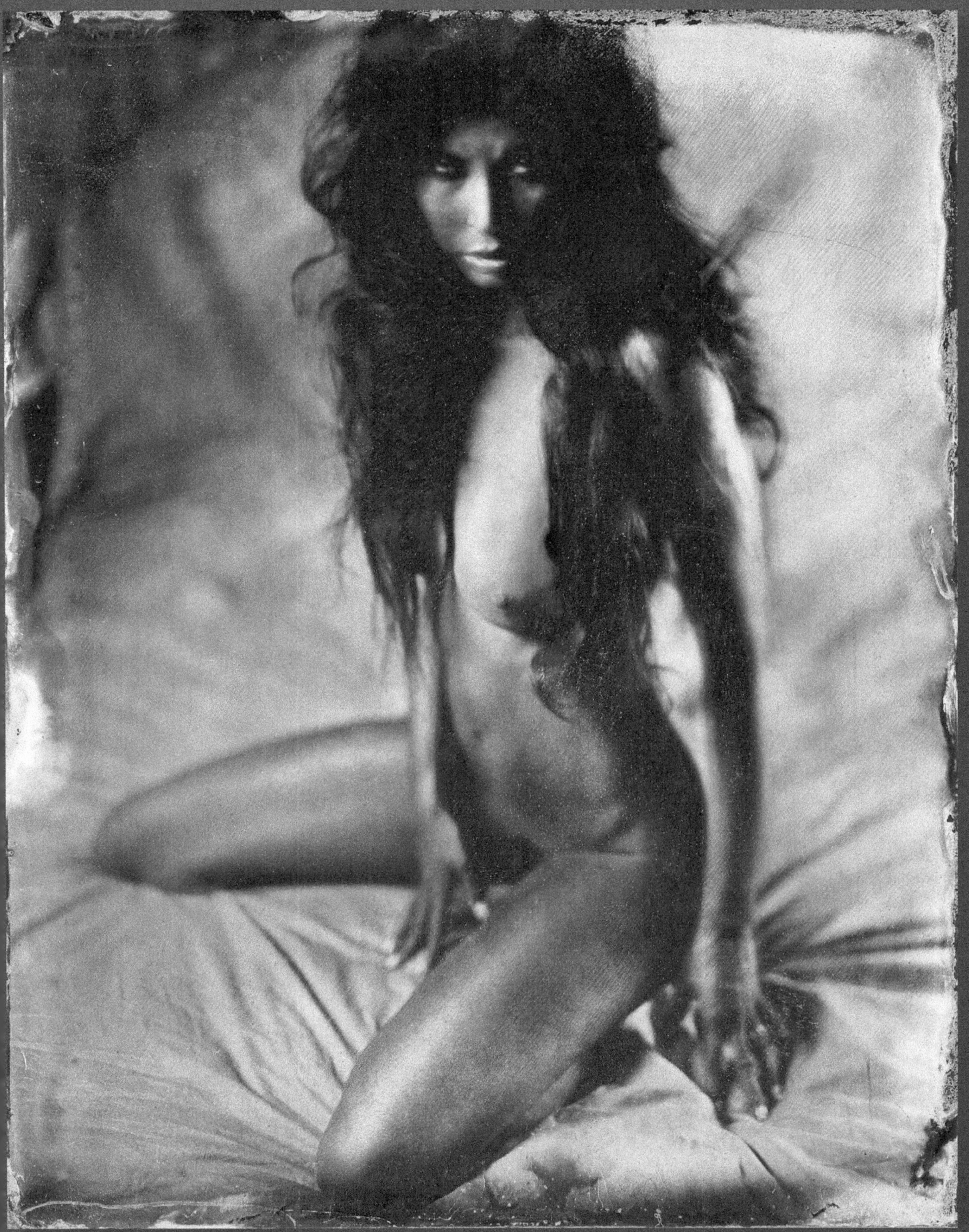

IGOR VASILIADIS

IGOR VASILIADIS

Excitement

Doubtfulness

100601-0001

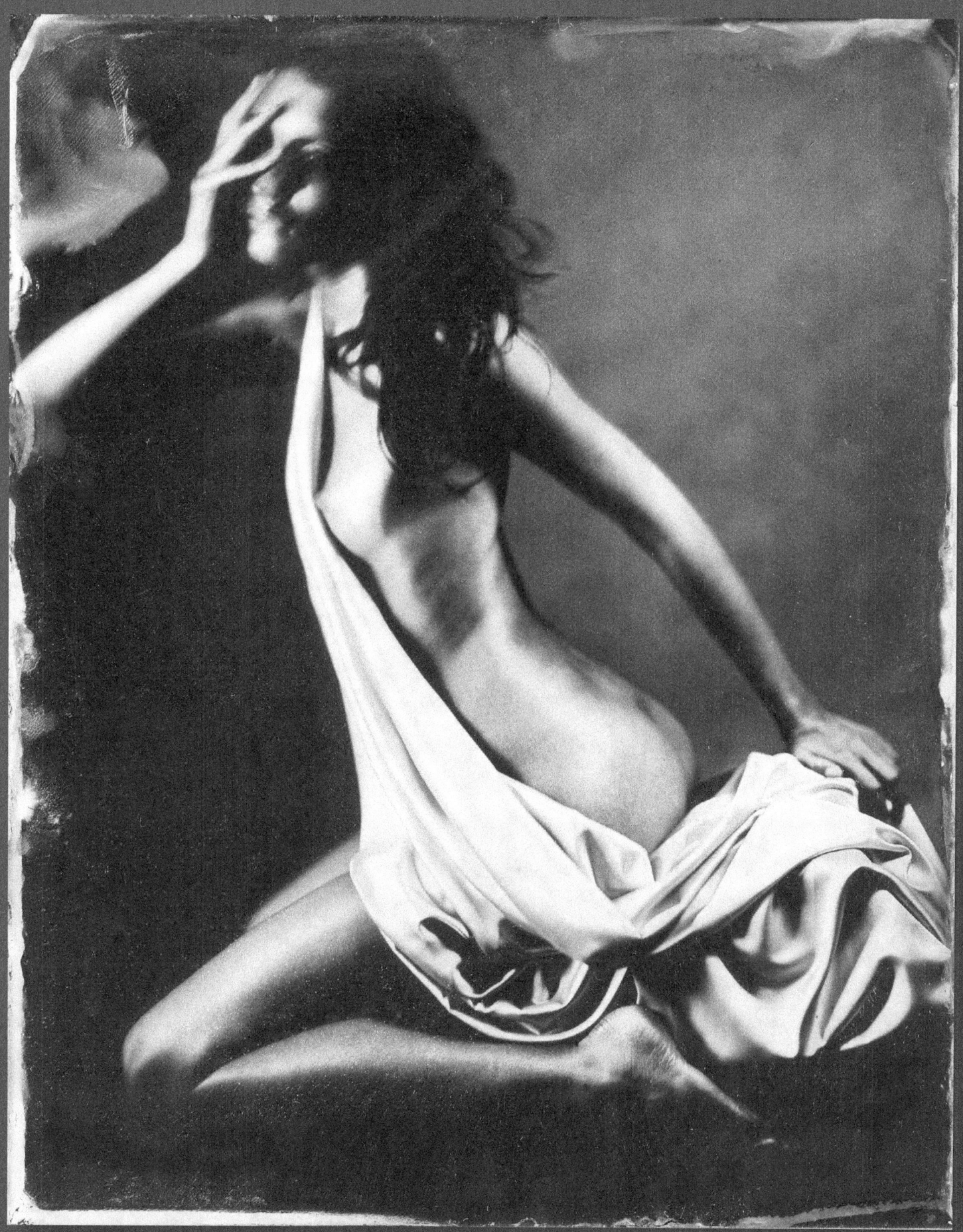

IGOR VASILIADIS

Pleasure

Calmness

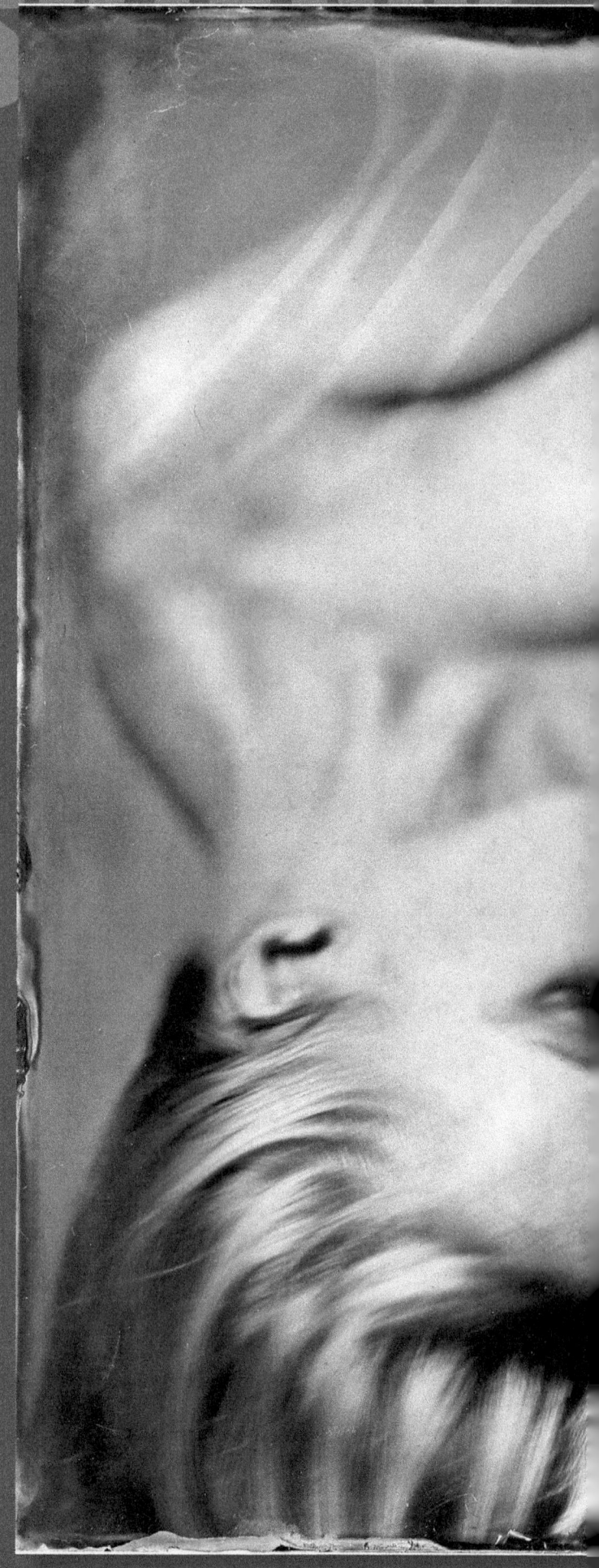

100625-0001

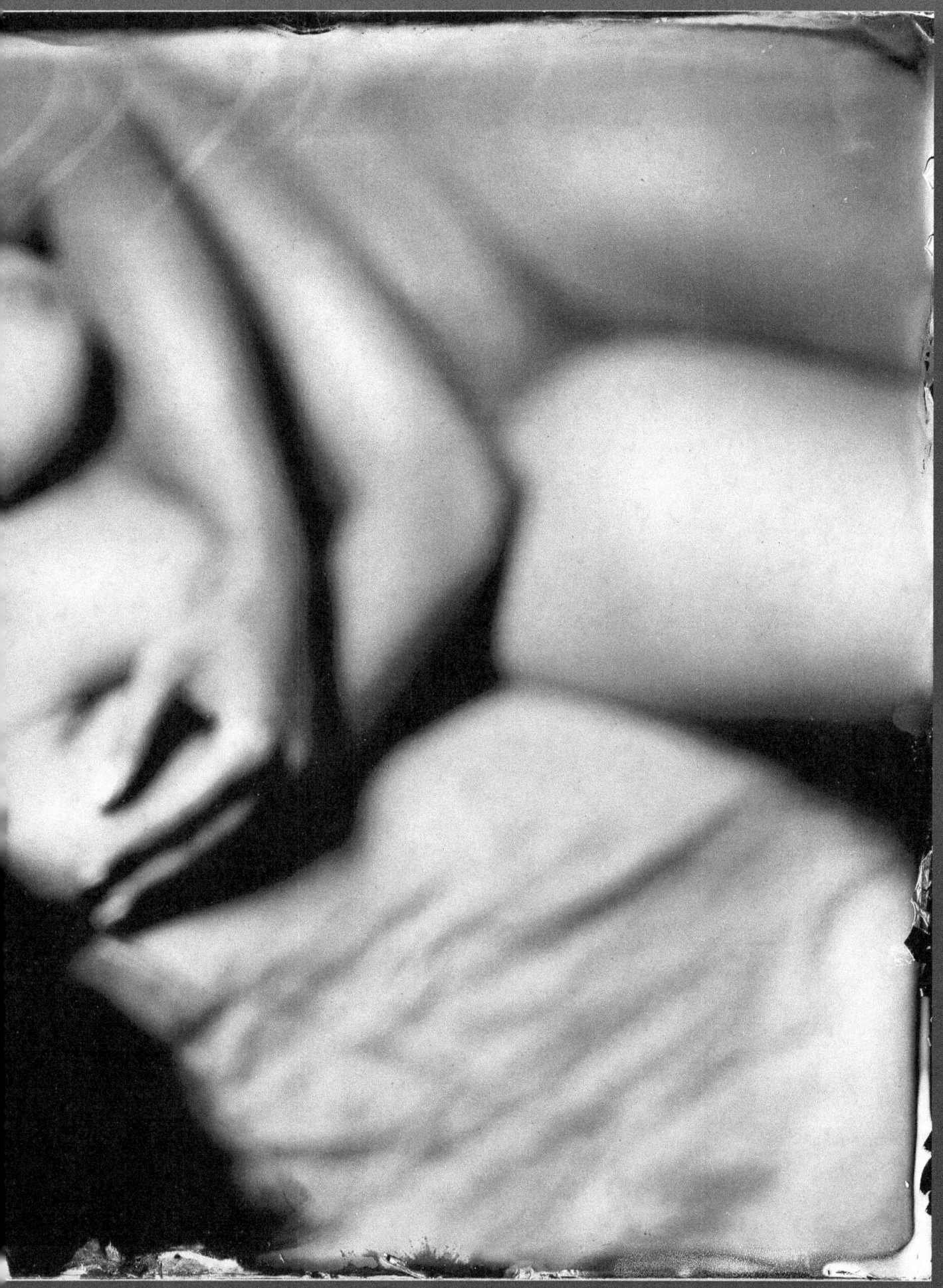

IGOR VASILIADIS

Contemplation
Obedience

100312-0001

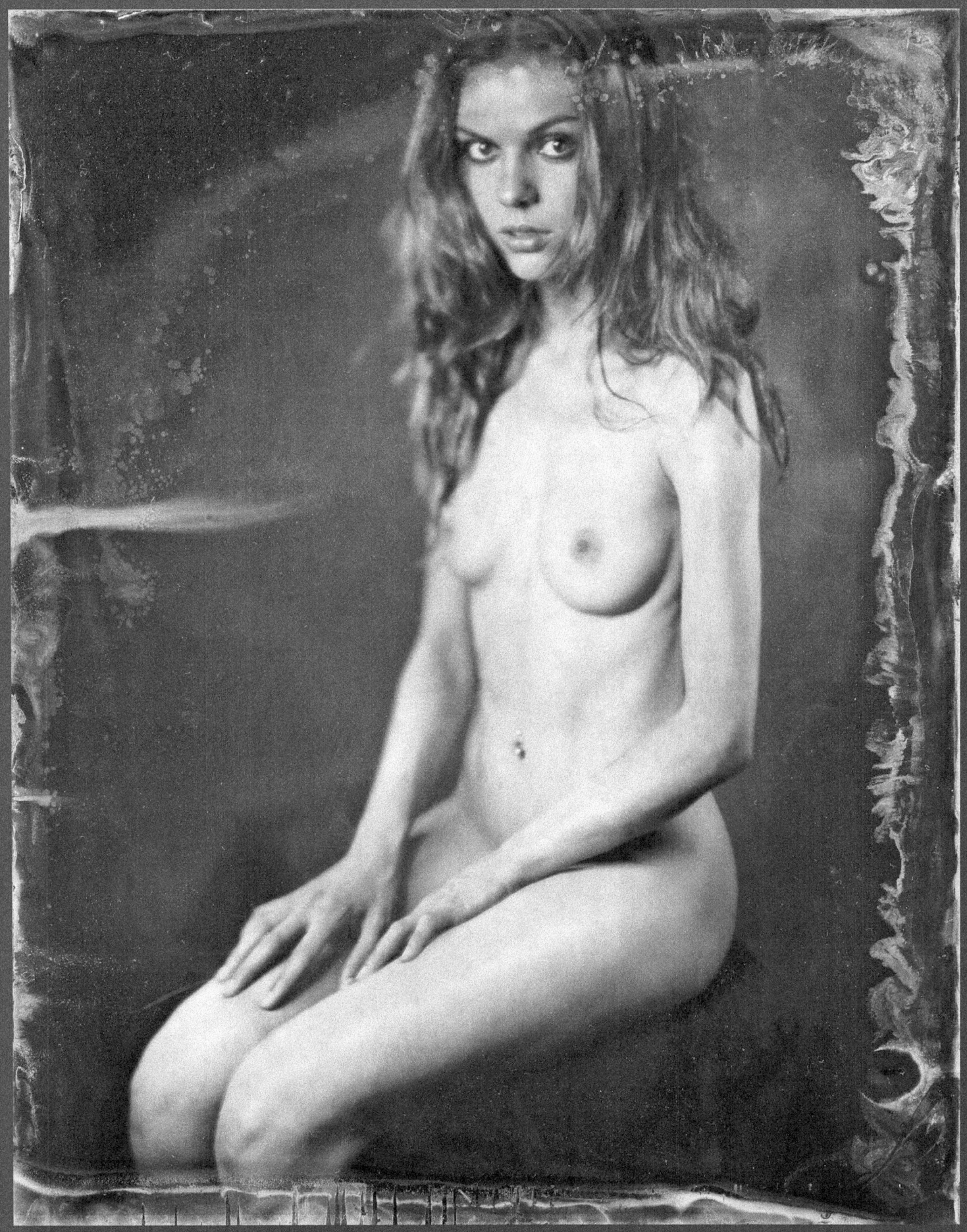

IGOR VASILIADIS

Pleasure

Forbiddance

100628-0005

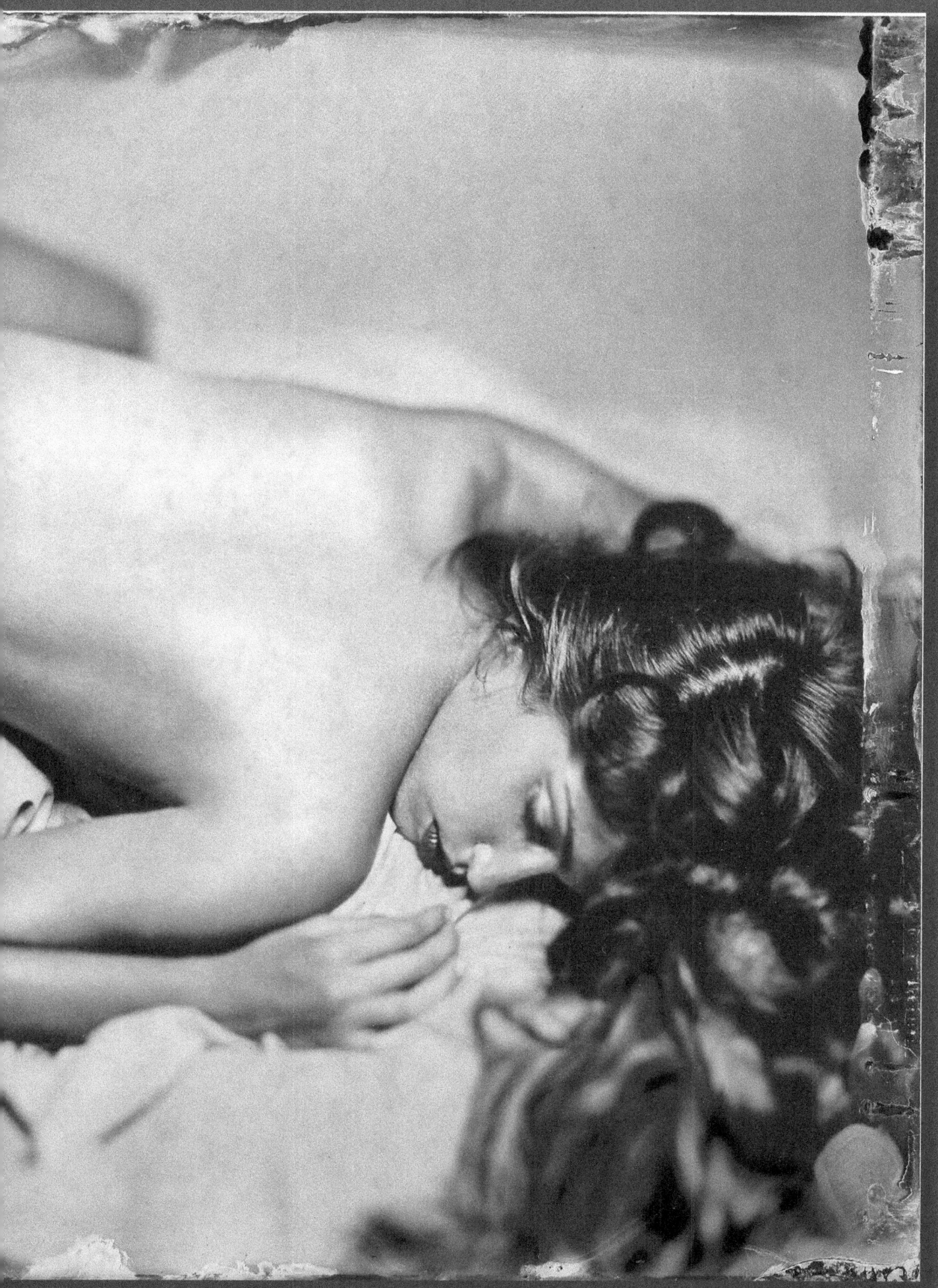

Loneliness

Mortification

100630-0002

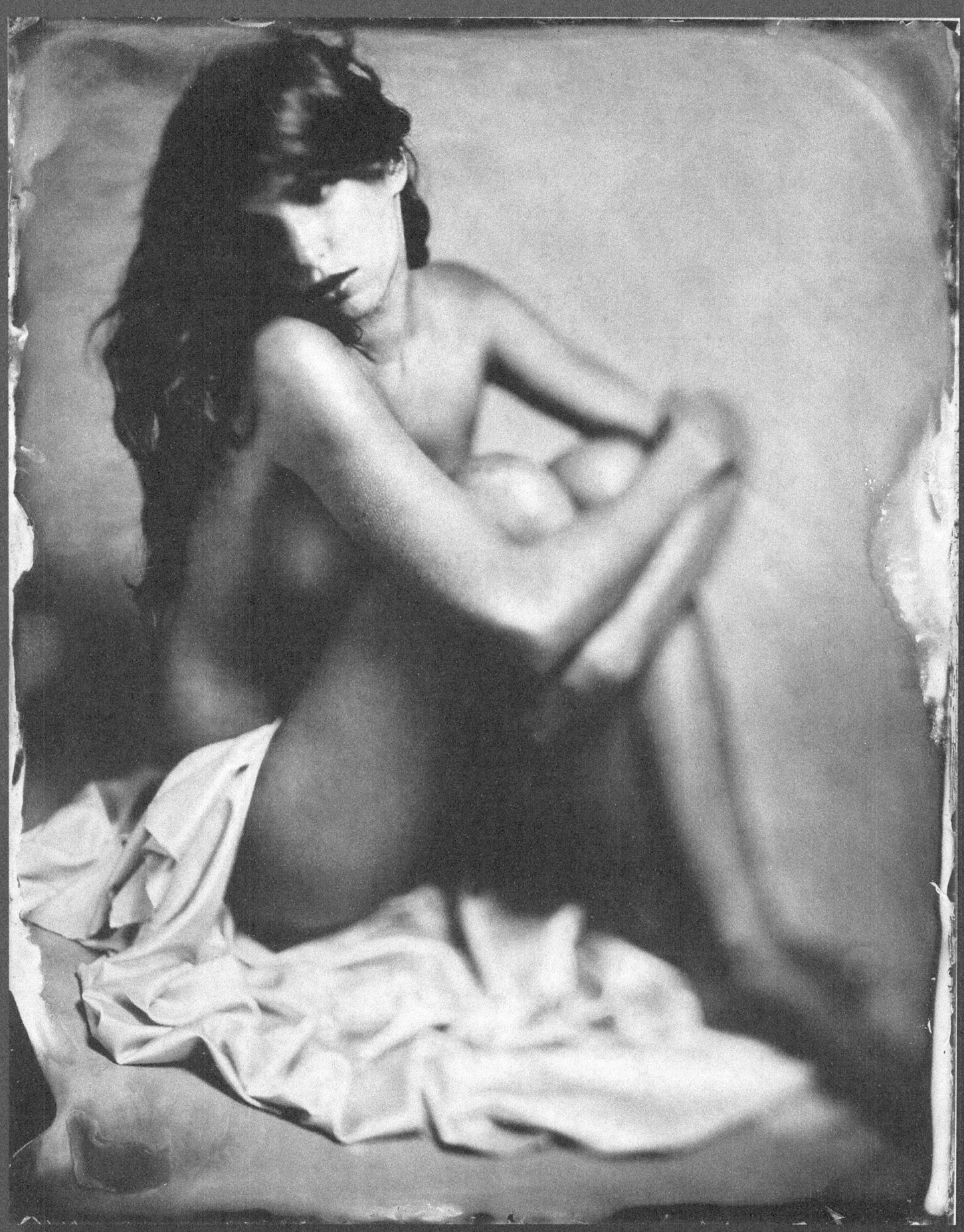

IGOR VASILIADIS

100712-0001

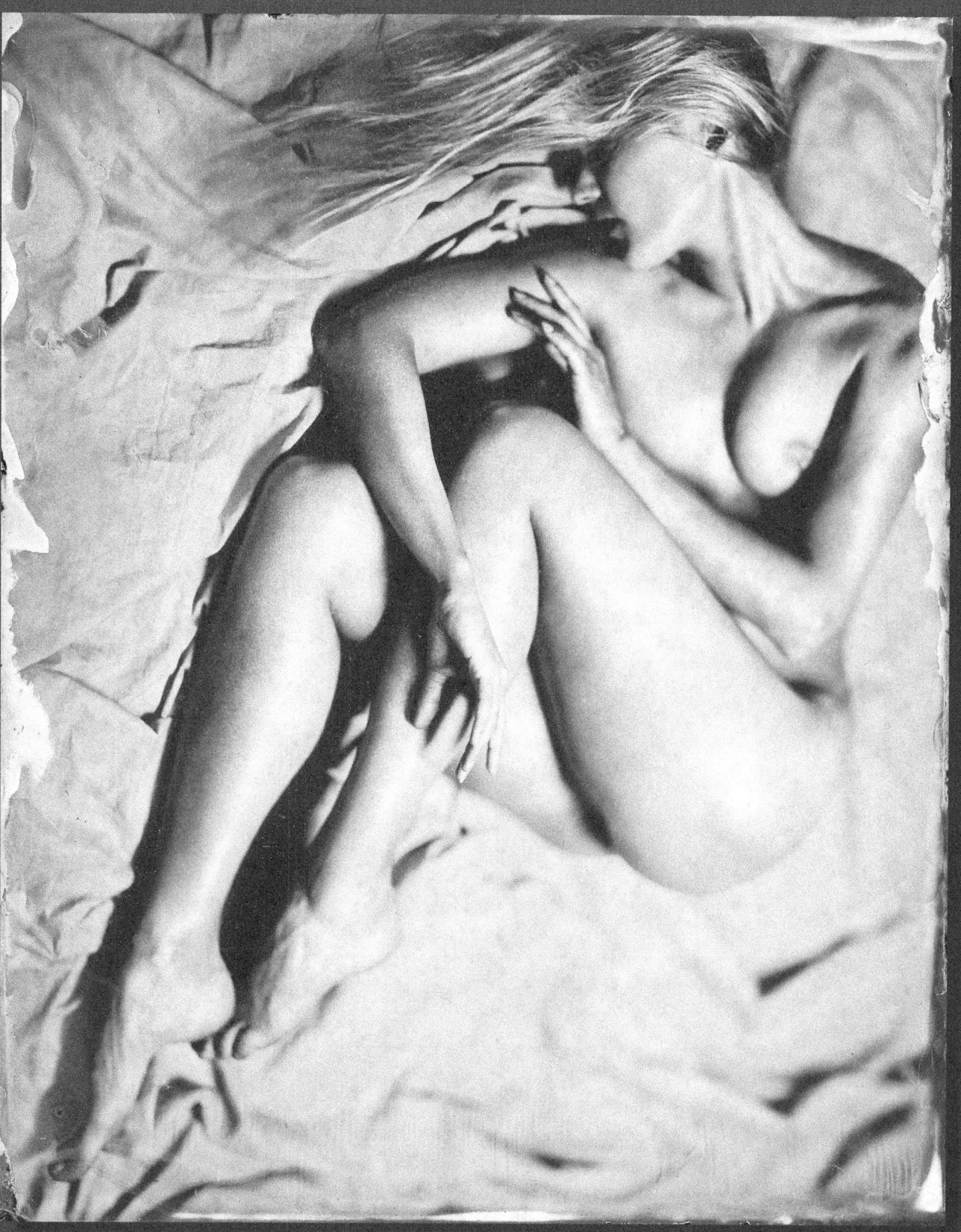

IGOR VASILIADIS

100712-0002

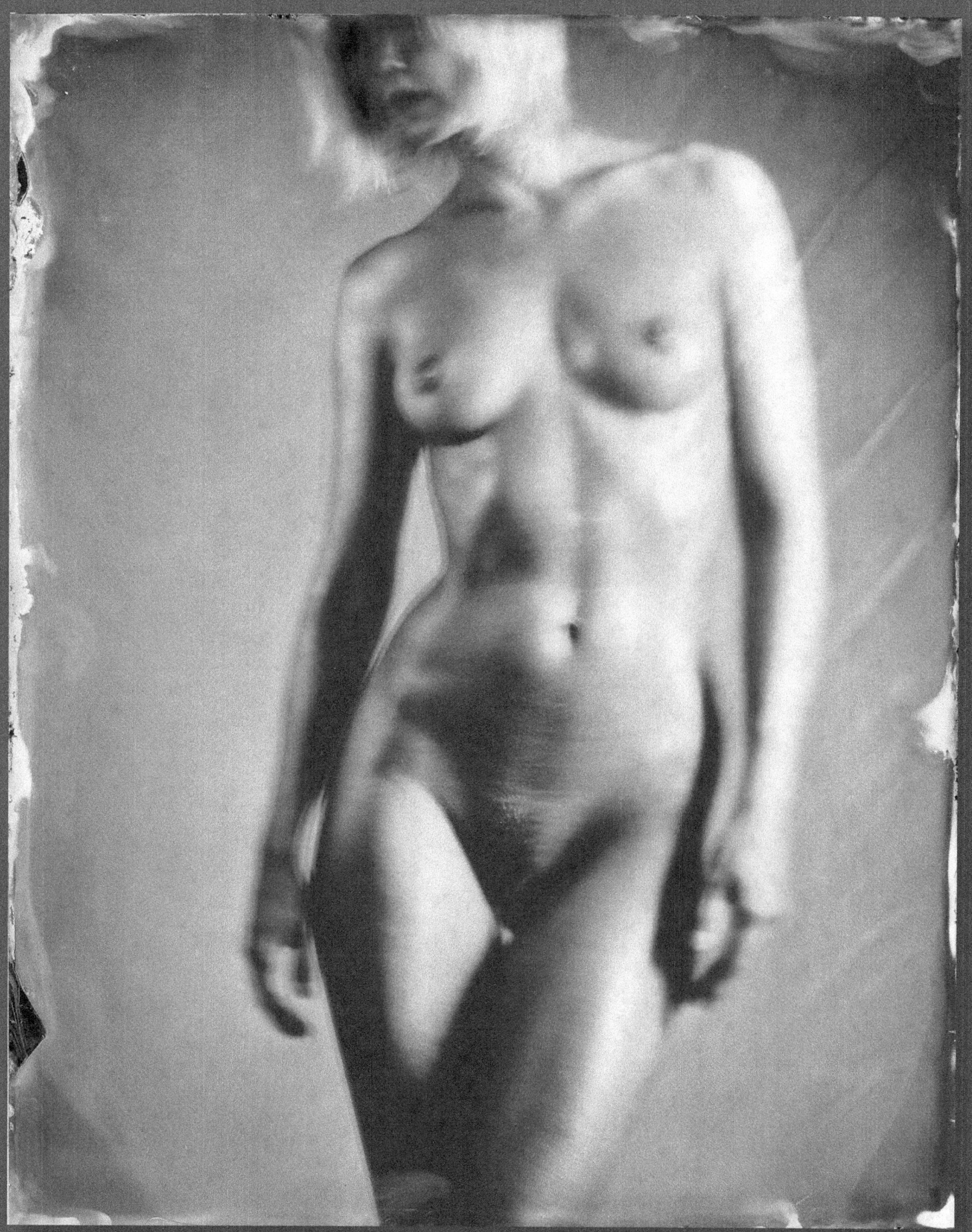

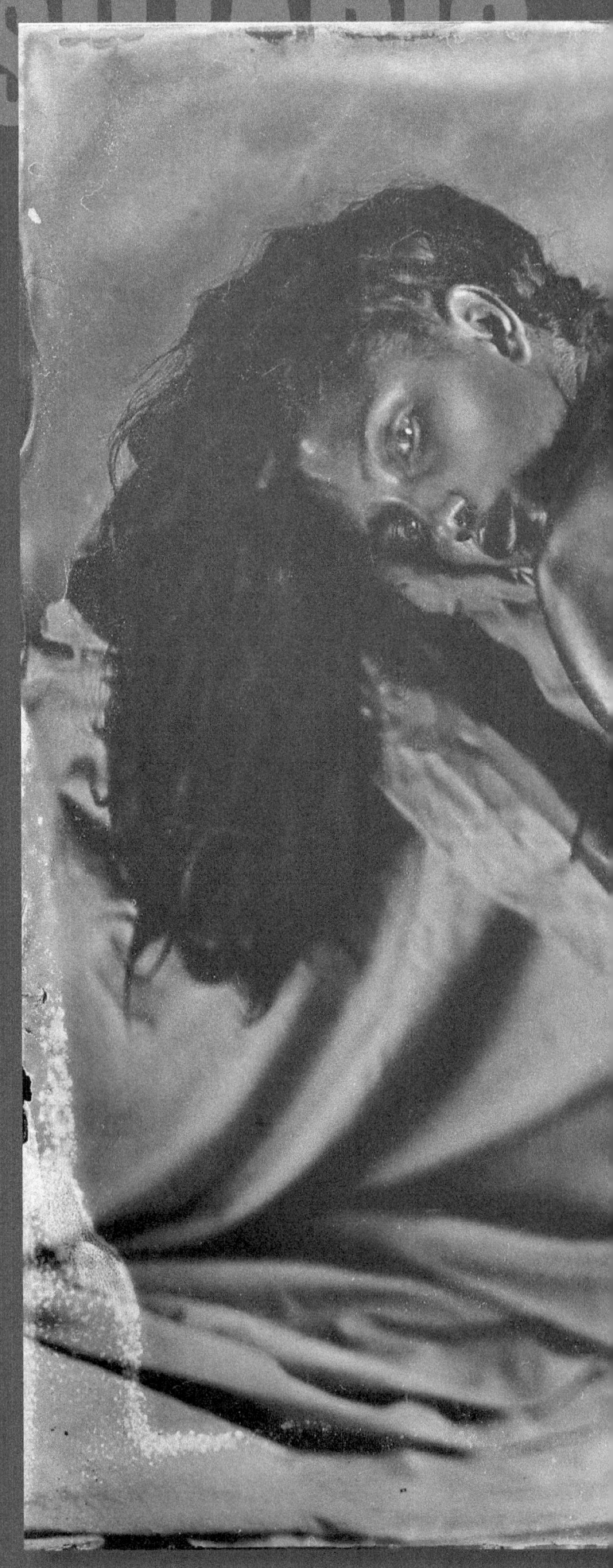

Trust

Contemplation

100730-0001

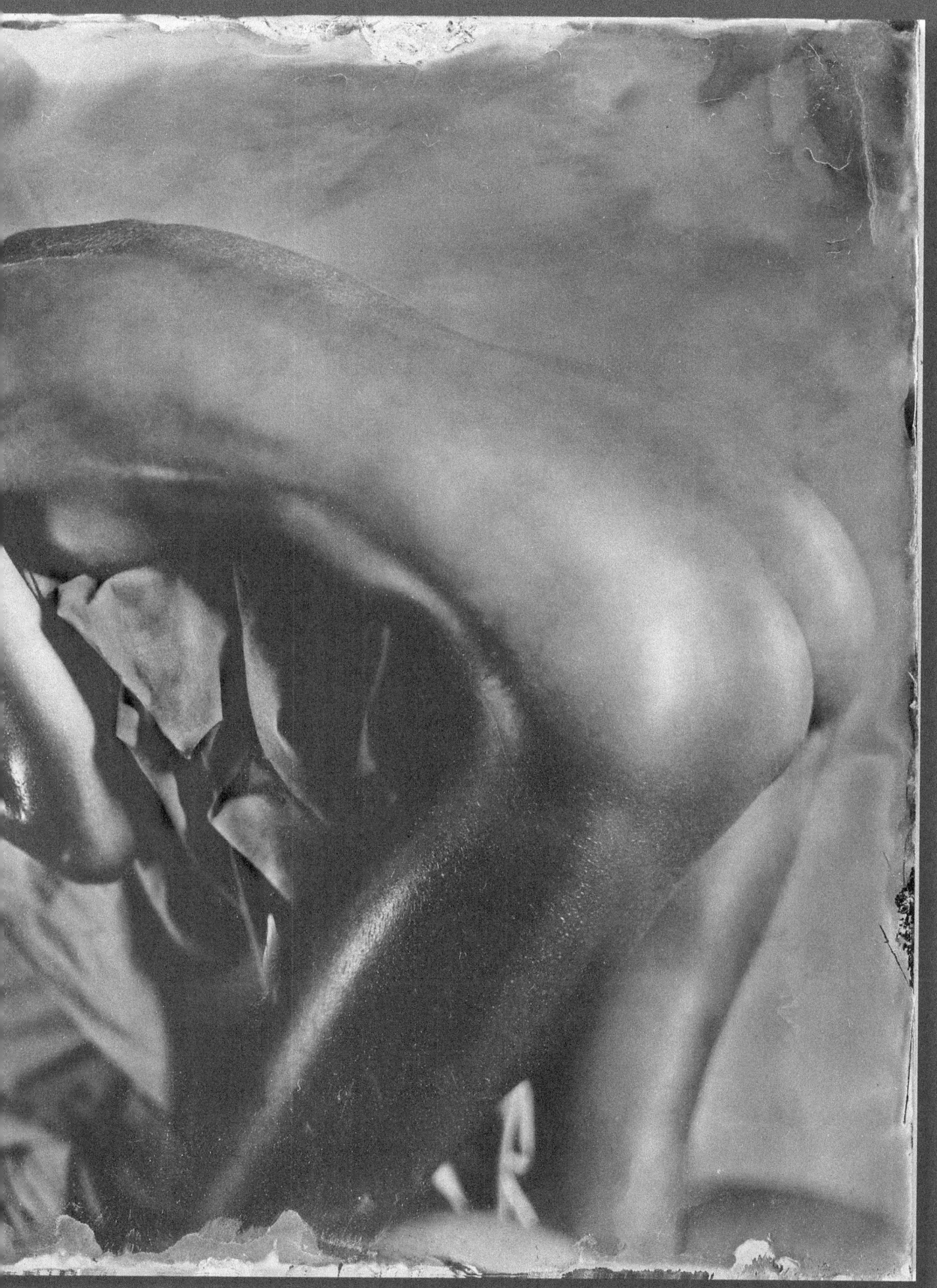

IGOR VASILIADIS

Disbelief

Anticipation

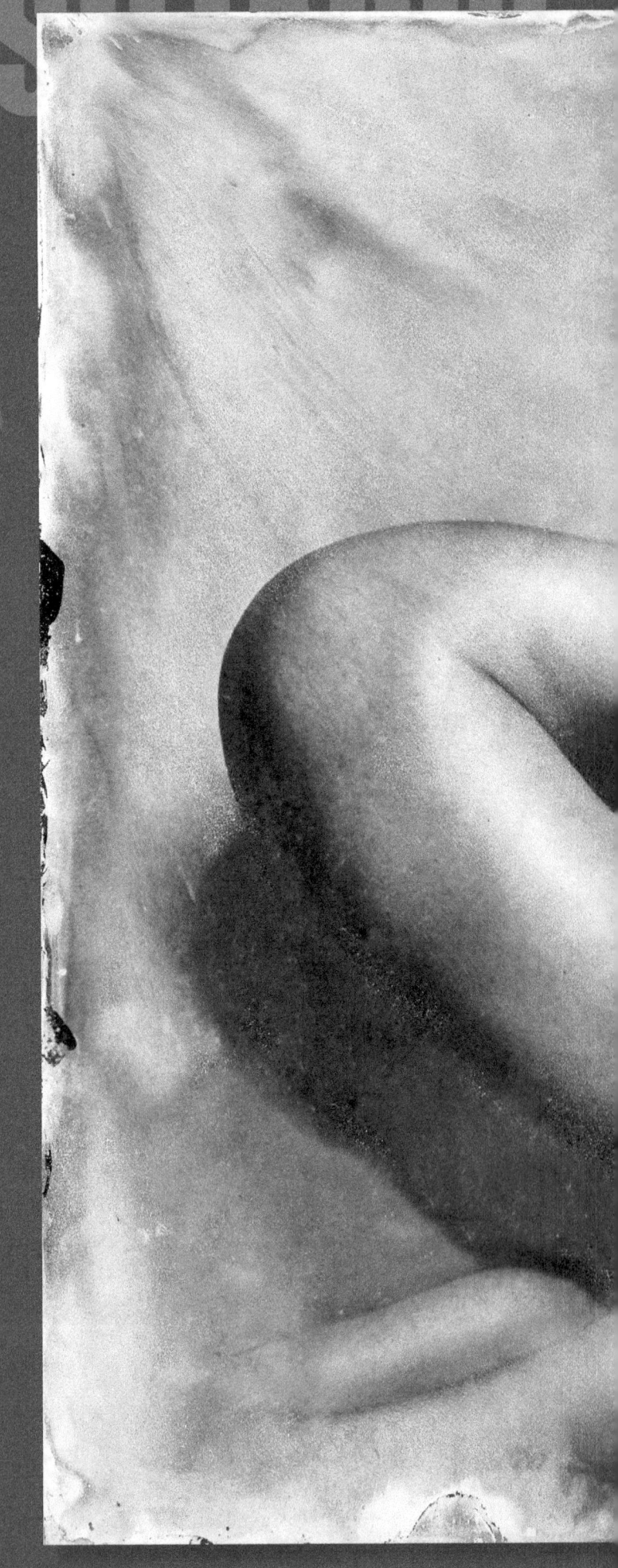

100824-0002

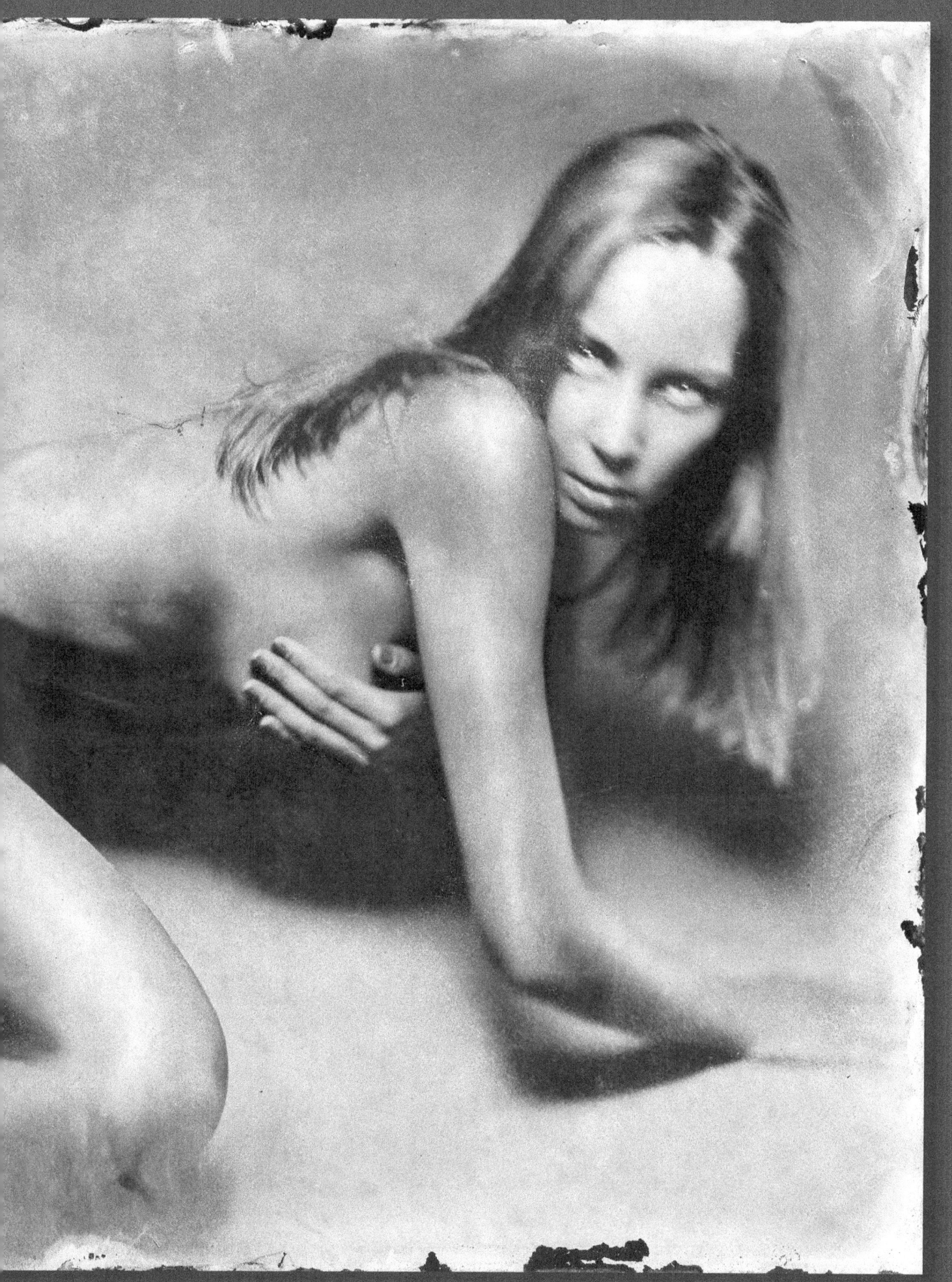

IGOR VASILIADIS

100826-0001

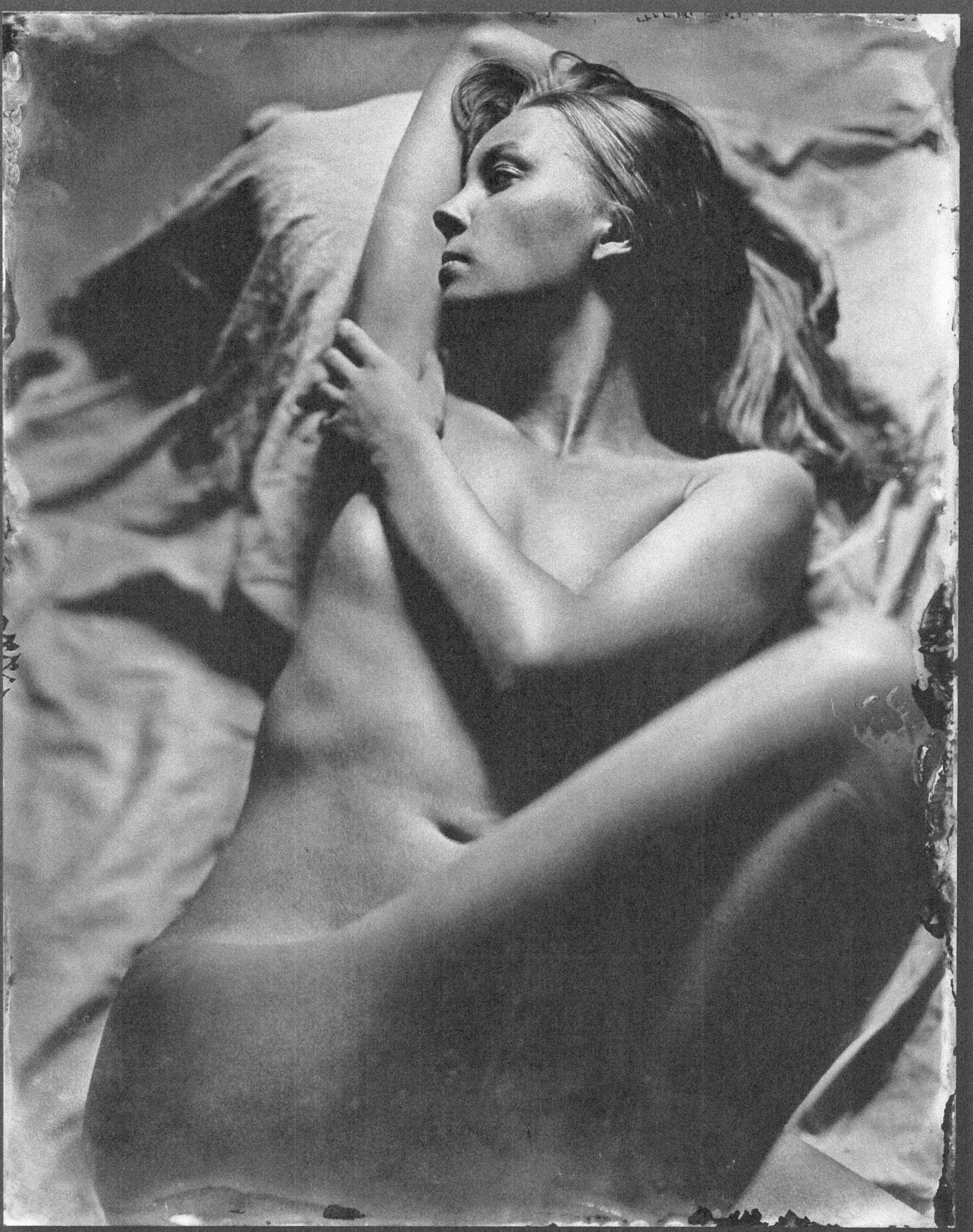

IGOR VASILIADIS

Perviousness Entrancement

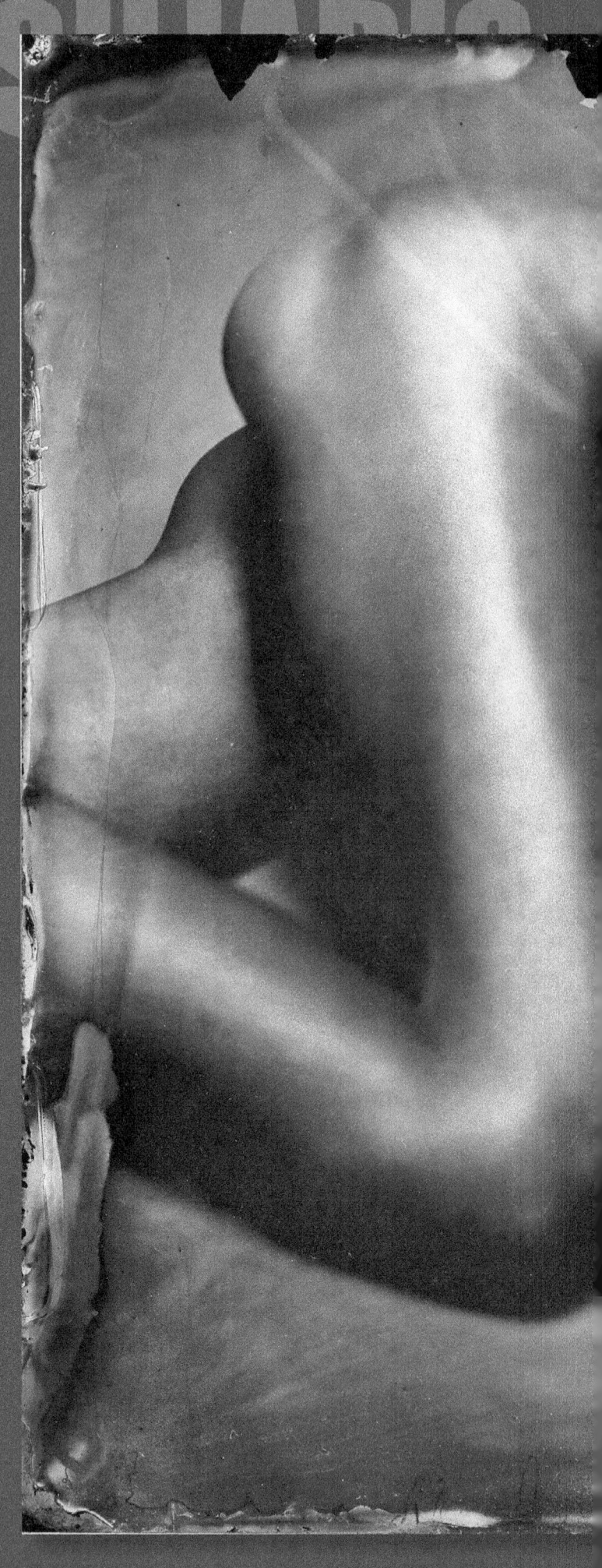

101130-0001

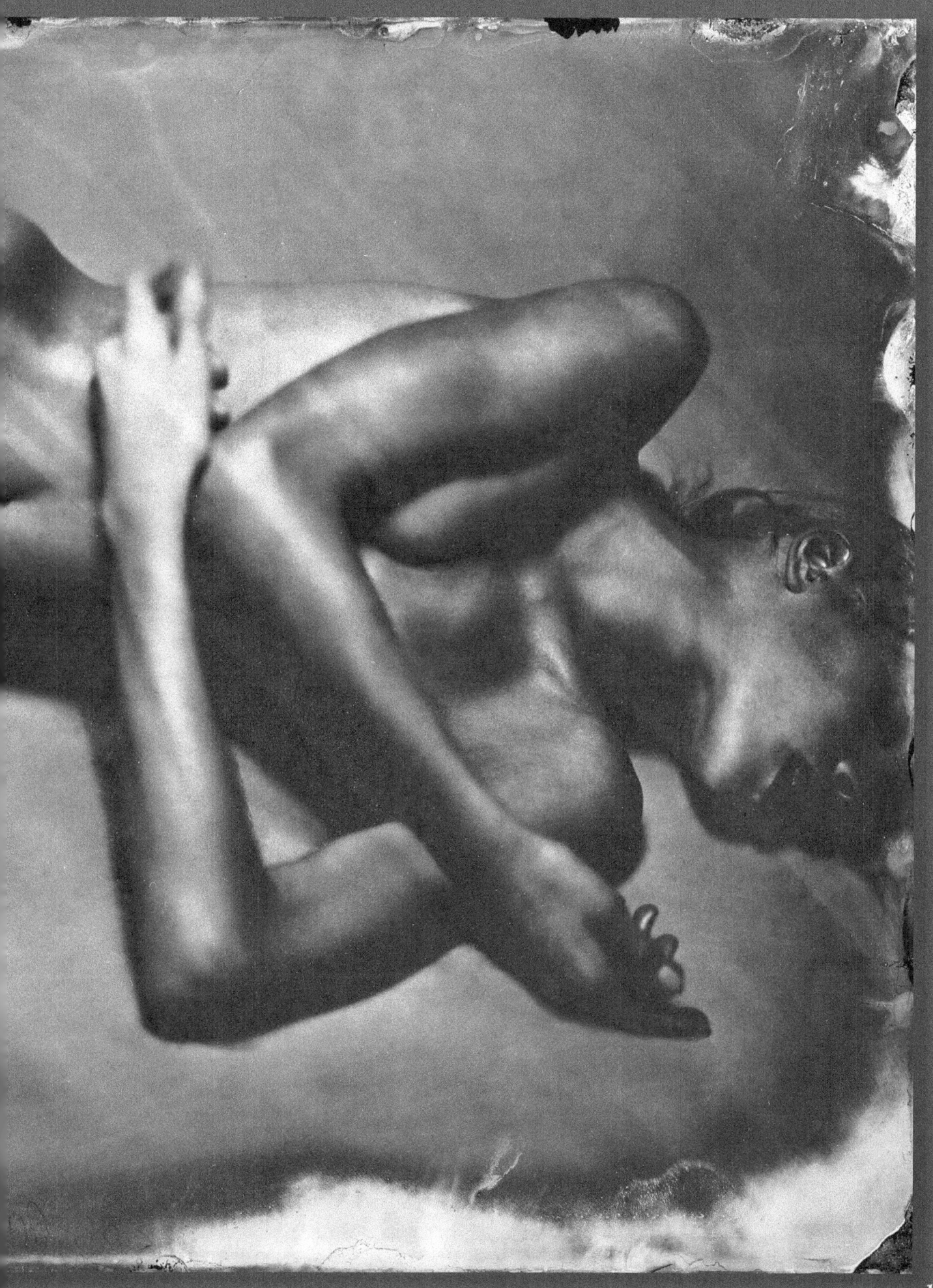

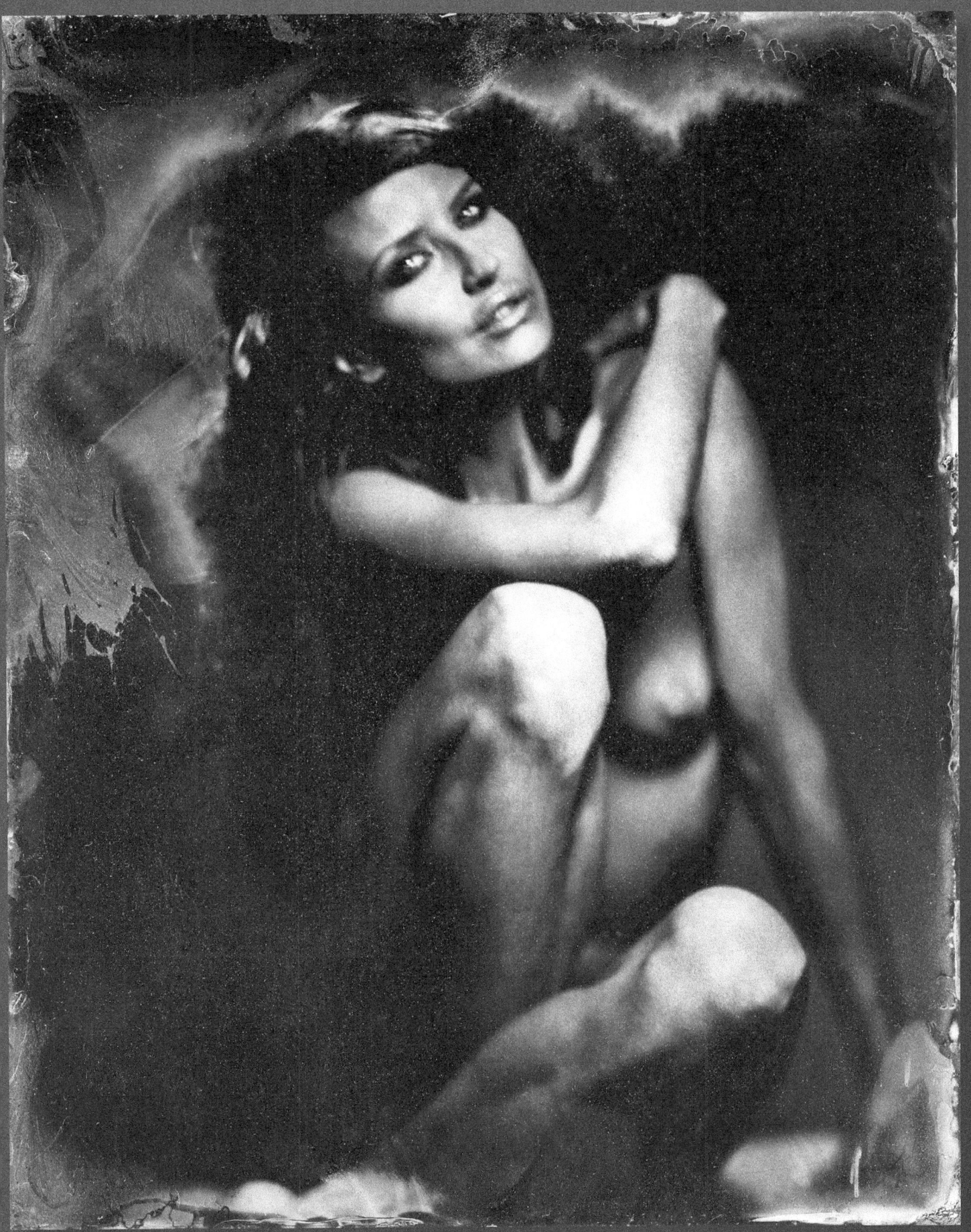

IGOR VASILIADIS

110221-0003

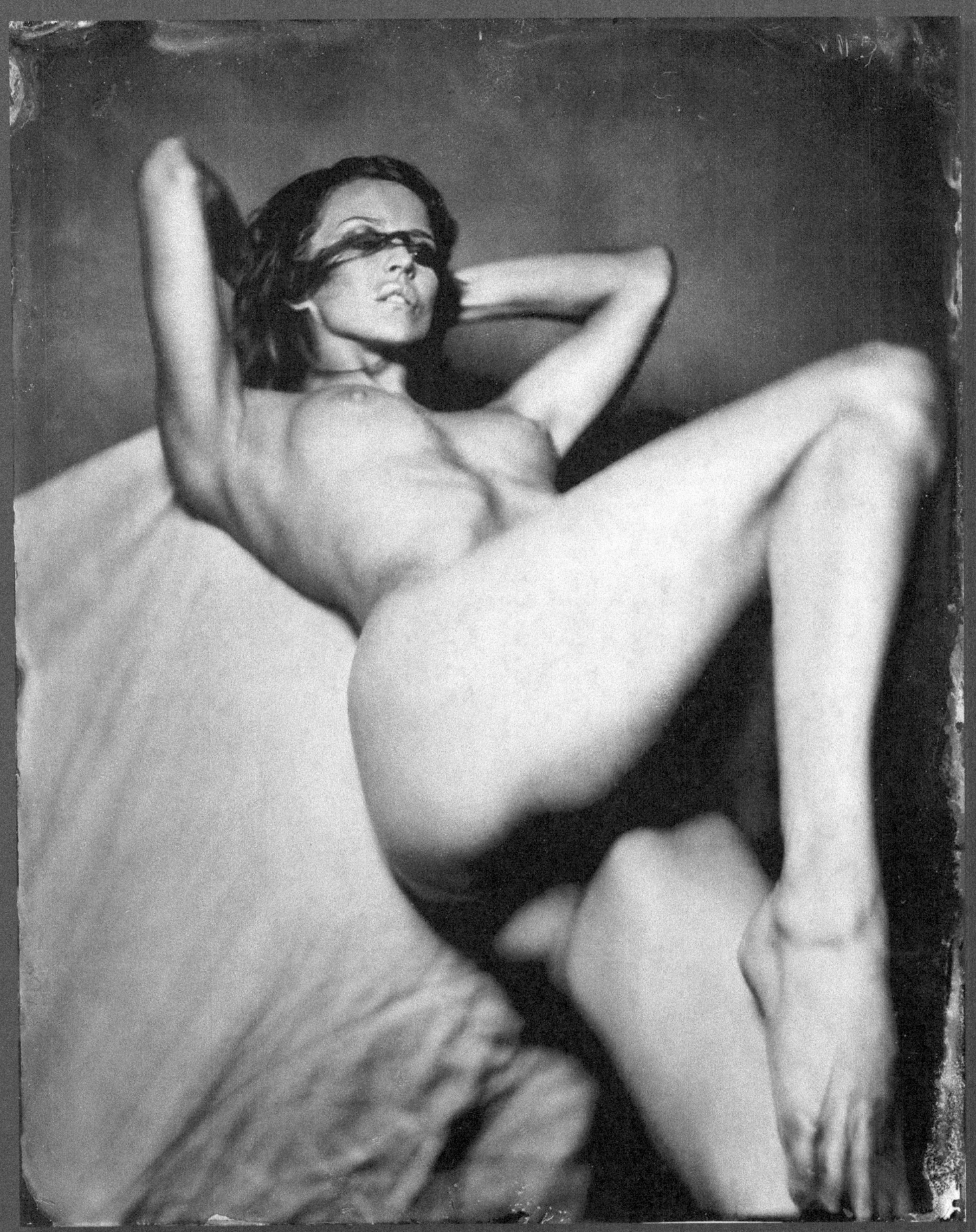

IGOR VASILIADIS

Extasy
Concentration

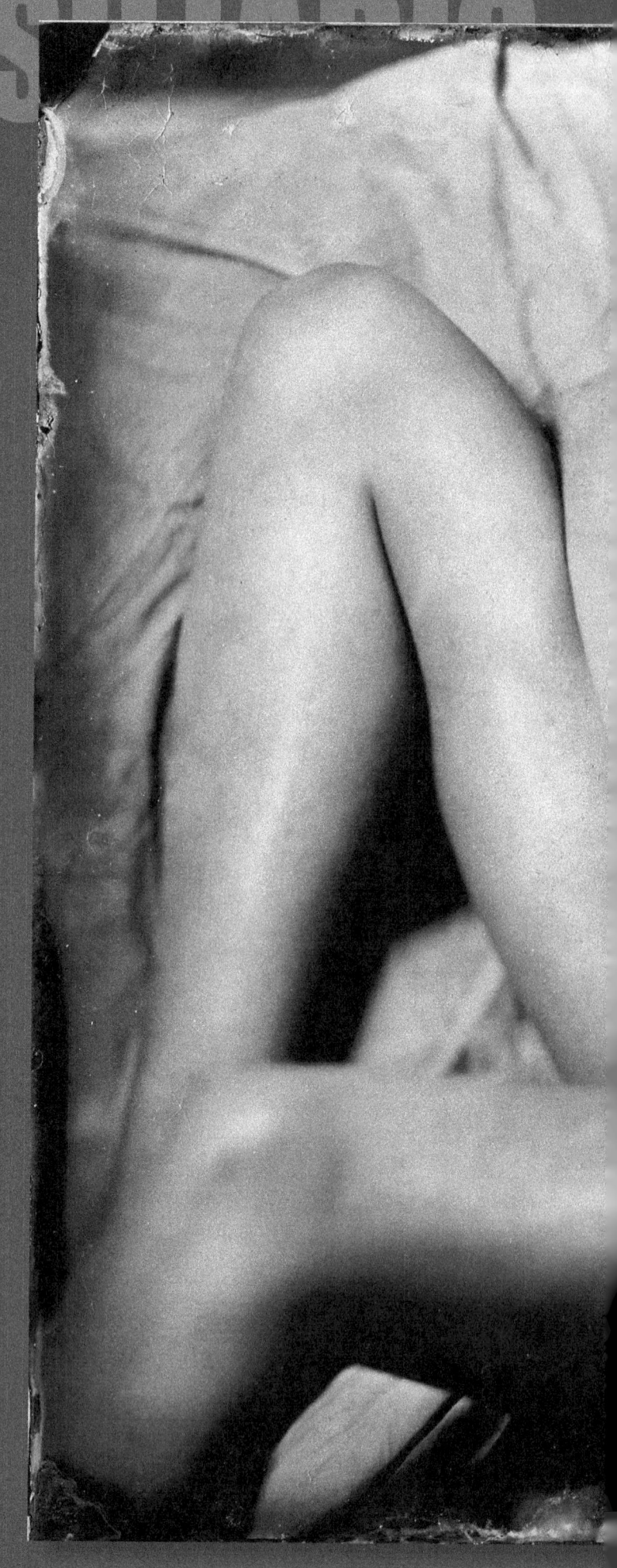

110513-0001

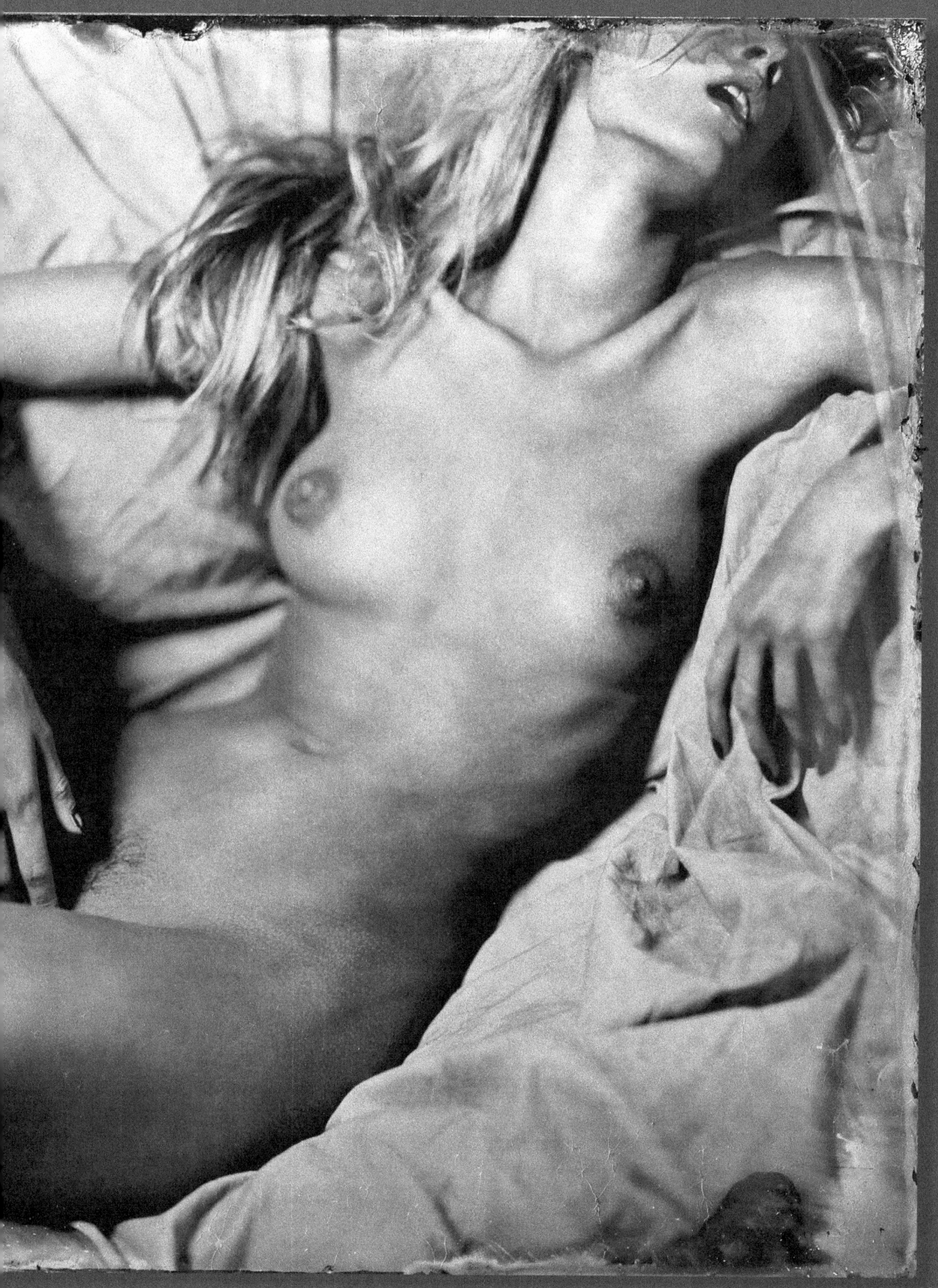

Sculptural Quiescence

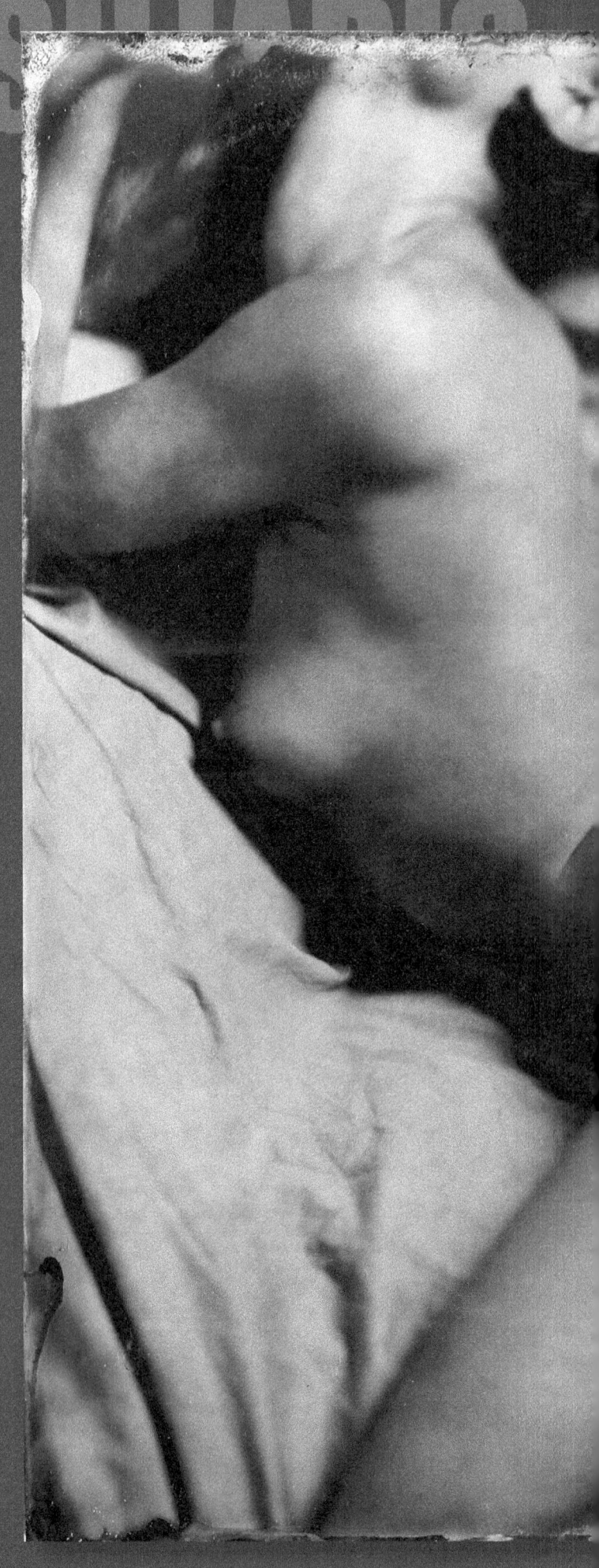

110513-0002

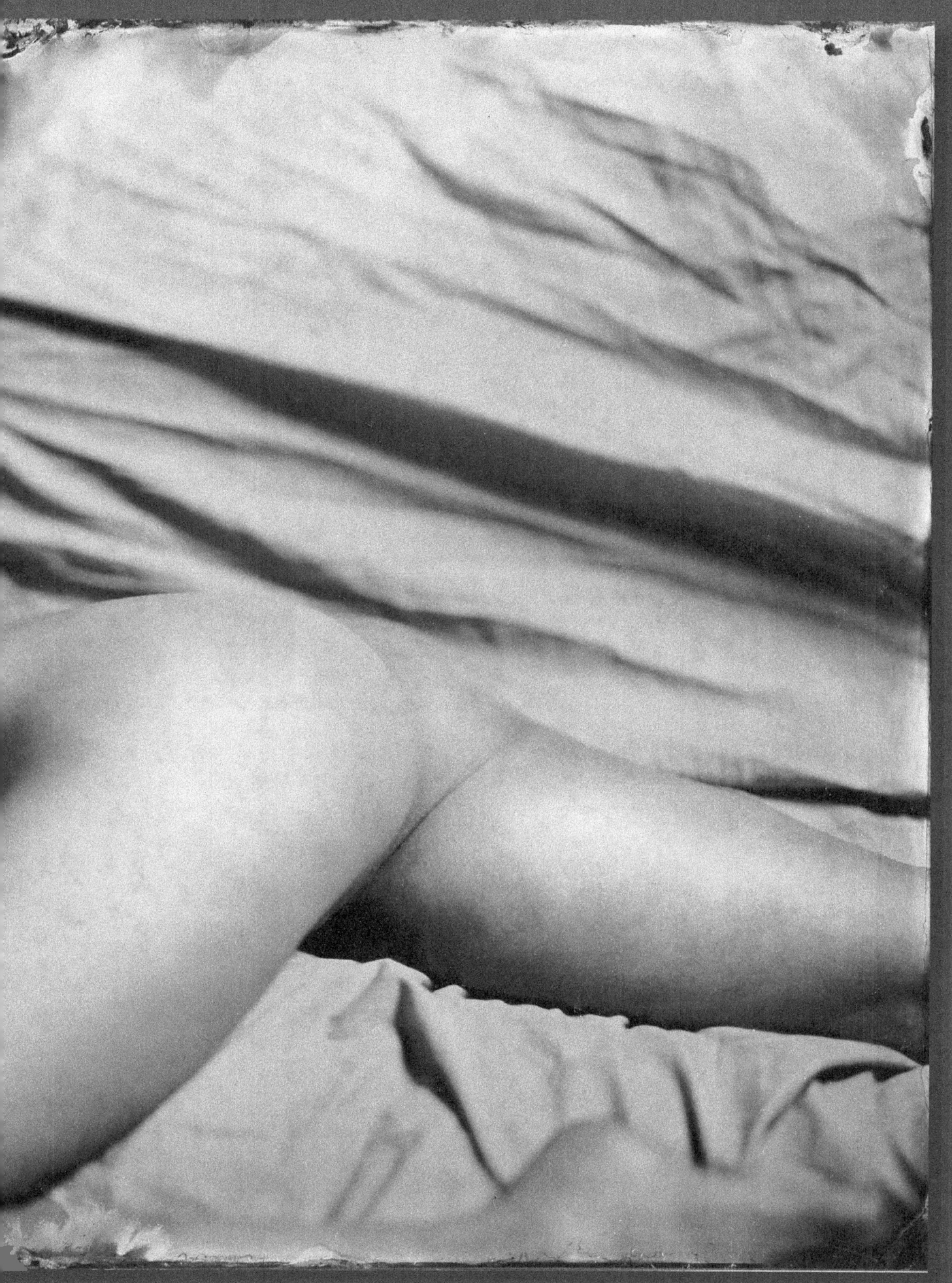

IGOR VASILIADIS

Eternity

Pleasure

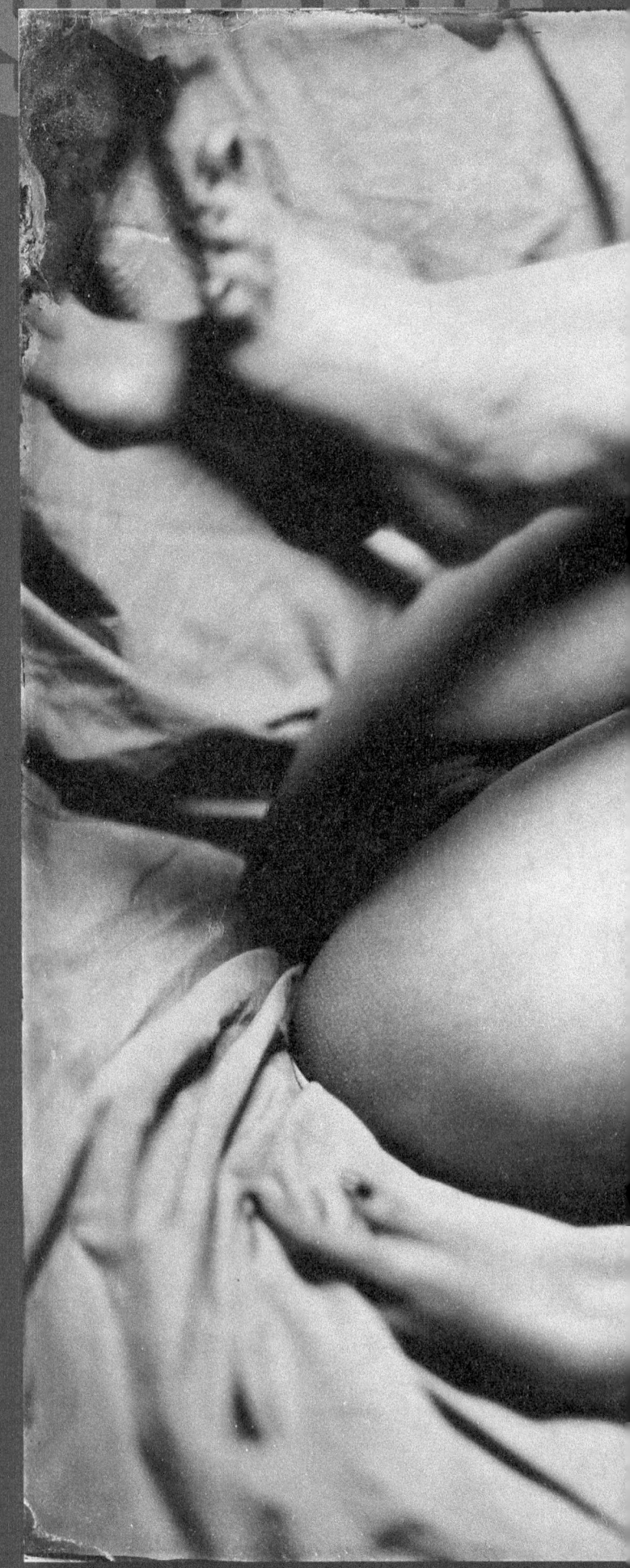

110513-0003

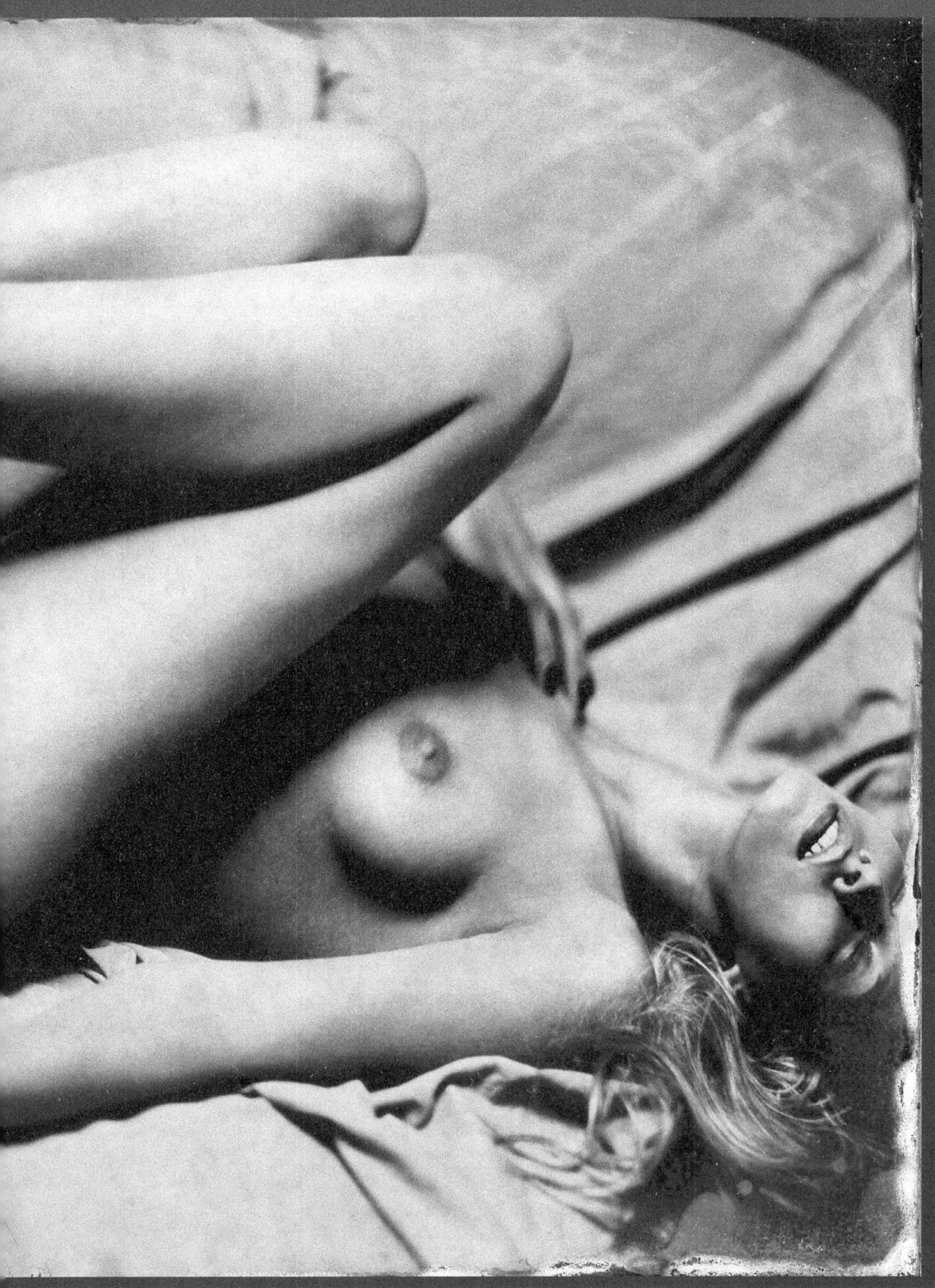

IGOR VASILIADIS

110726-0001

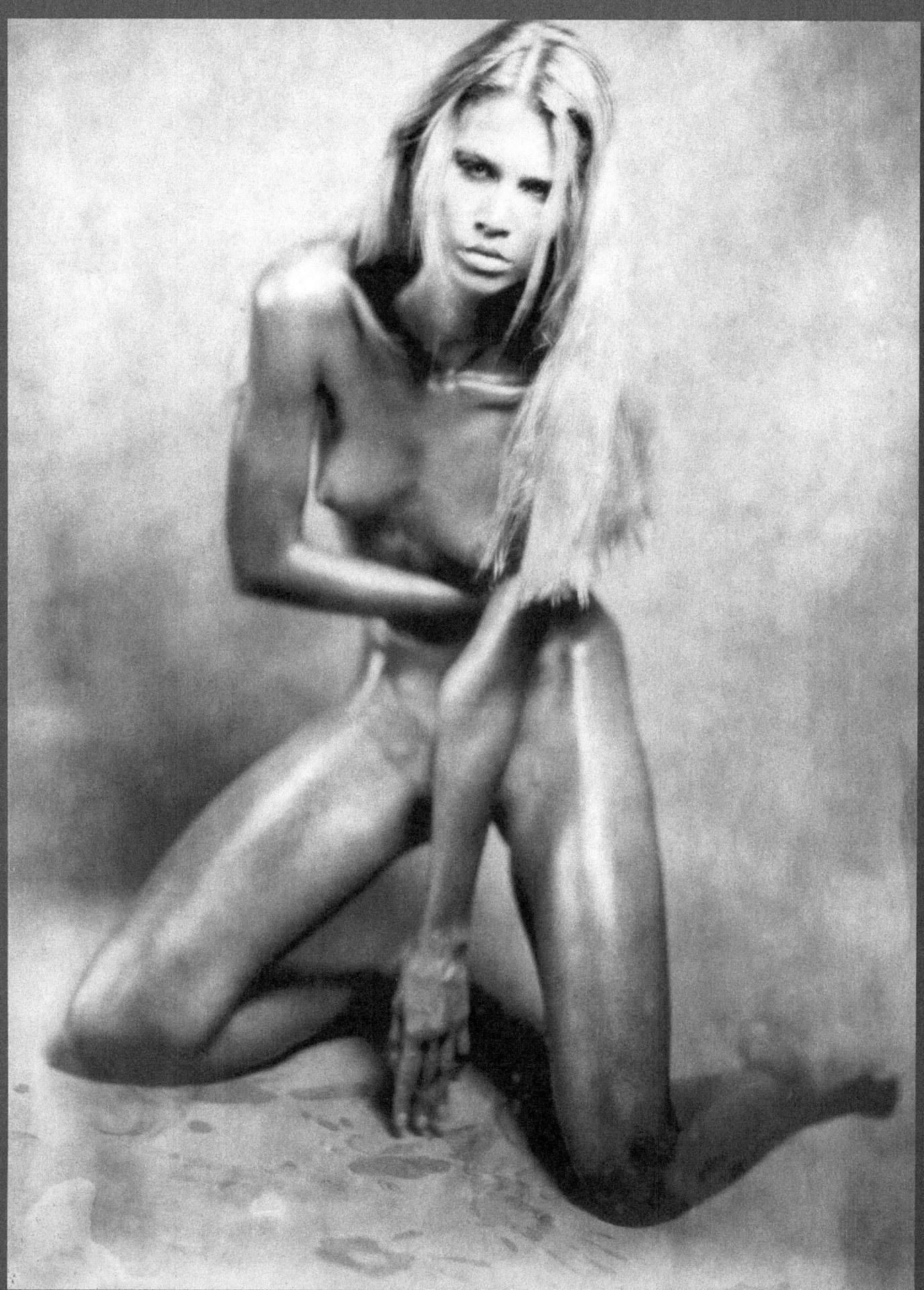

IGOR VASILIADIS

110726-0004

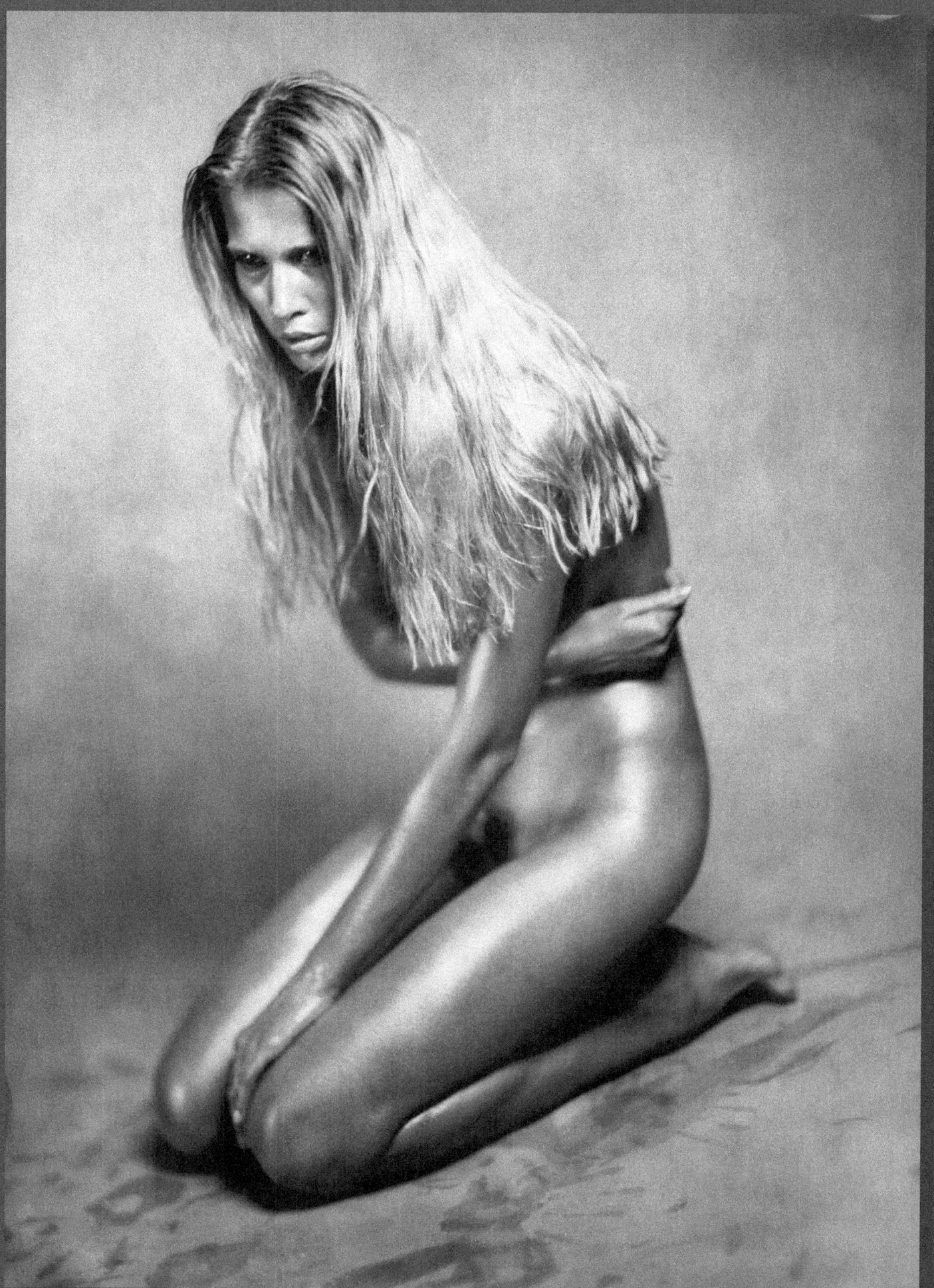

IGOR VASILIADIS

Aspiration
High hopes

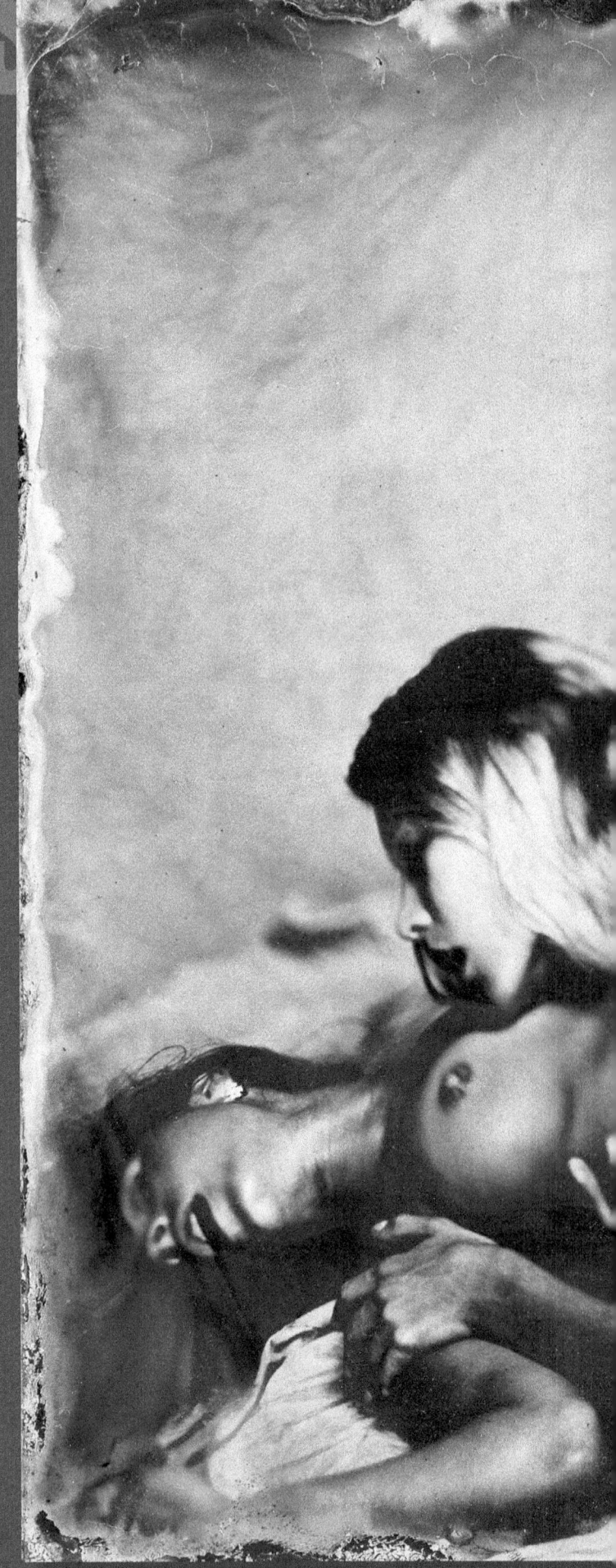

110909-0001

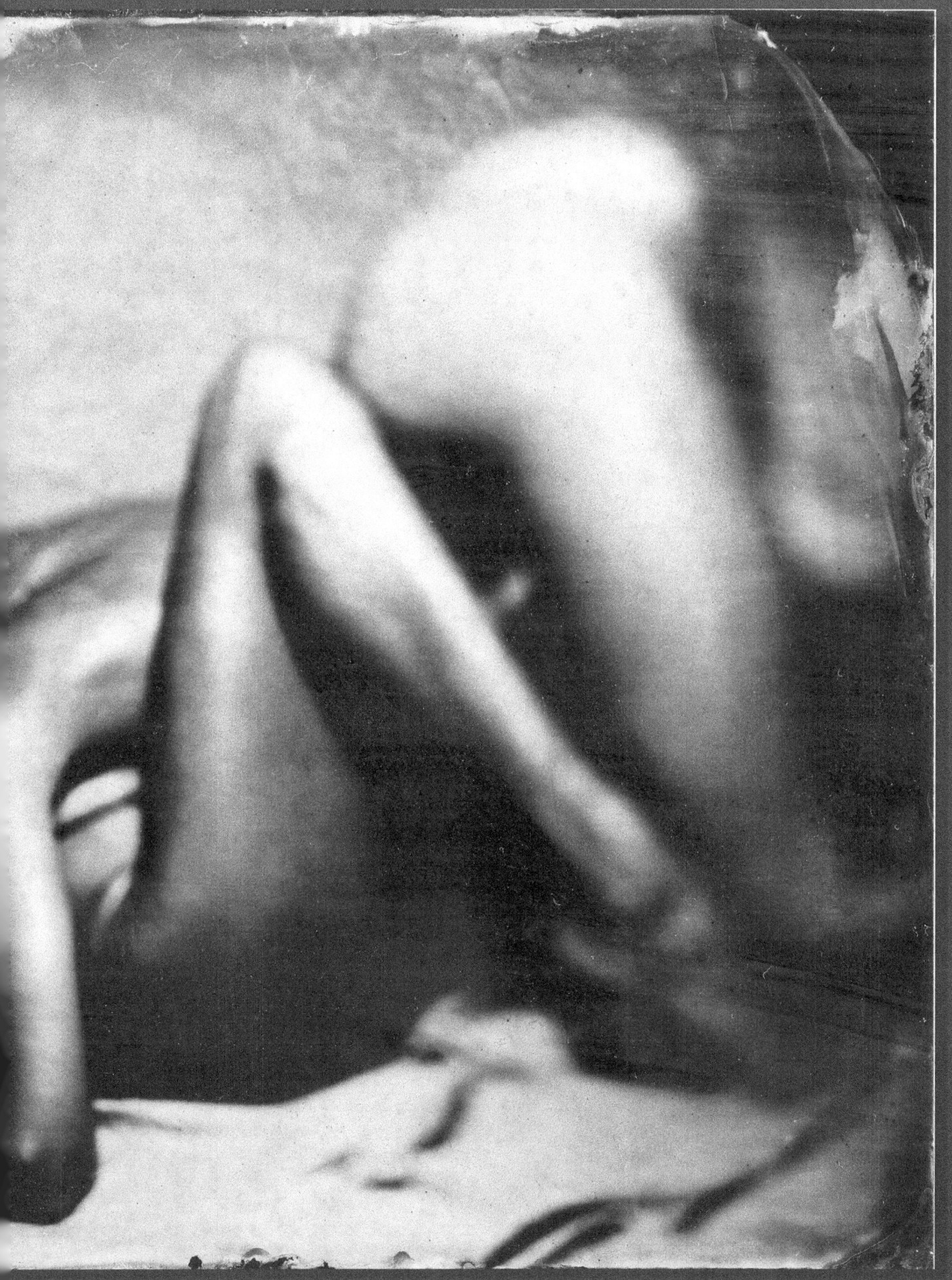

110804-0001

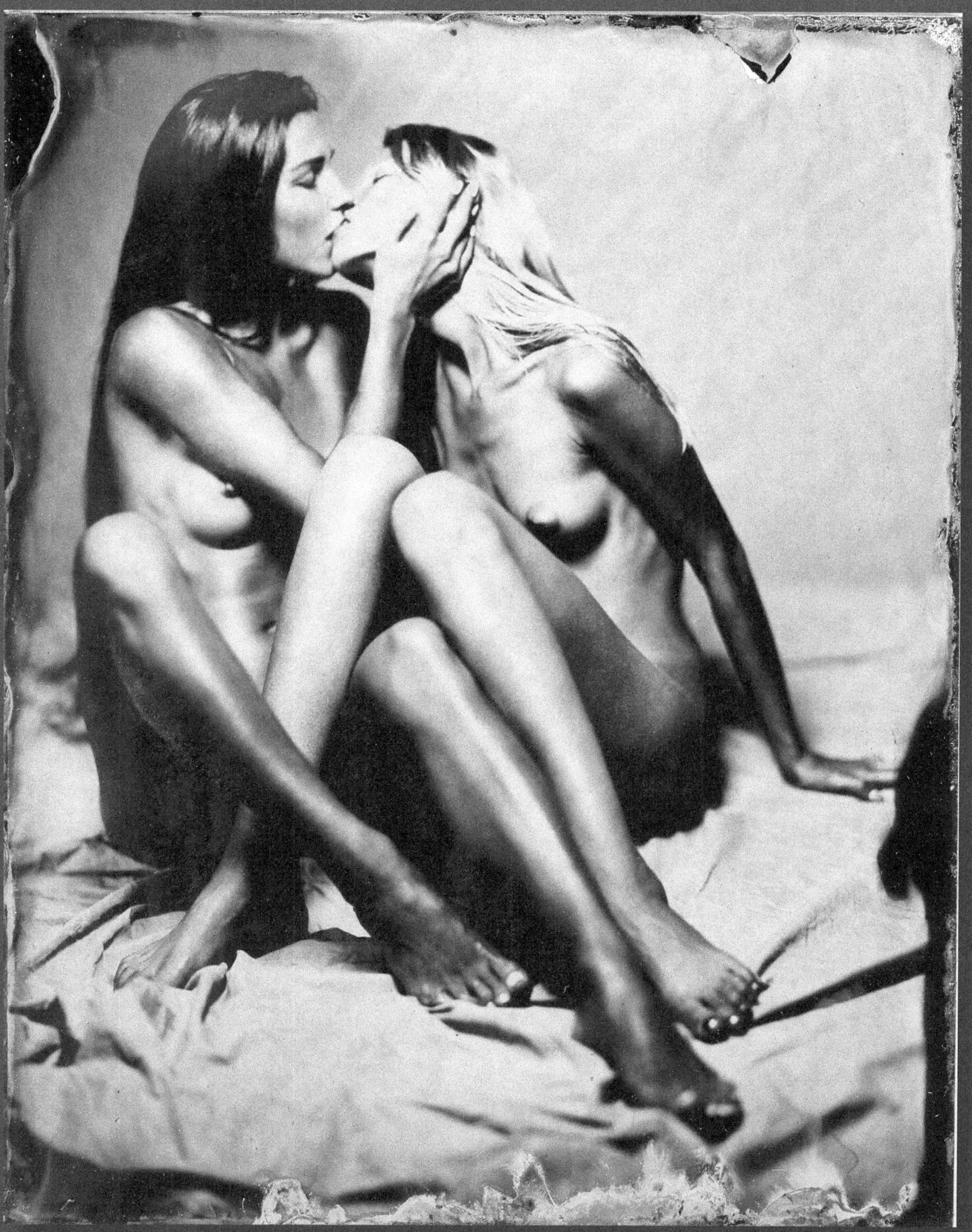

Consonance

Balance

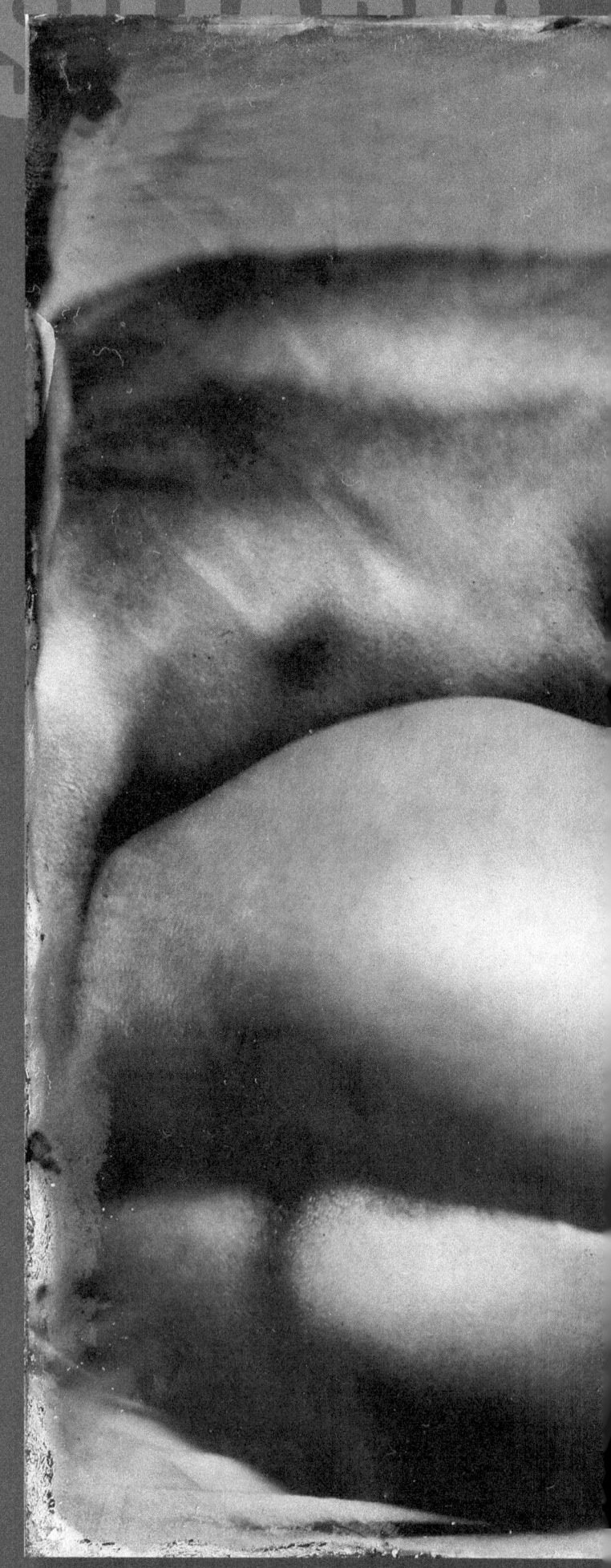

110909-0002

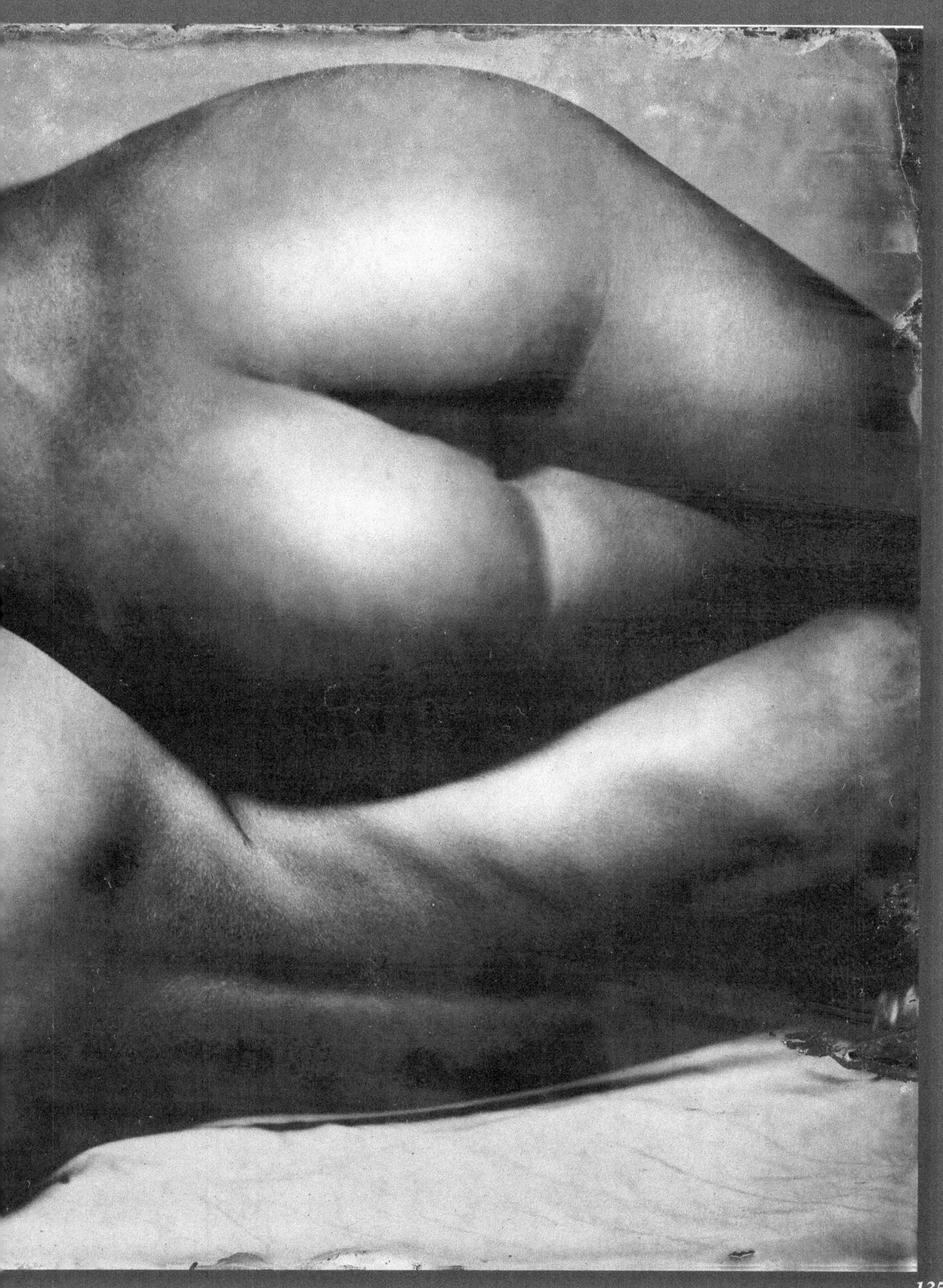

IGOR VASILIADIS

Eyes don't lie

081008-002

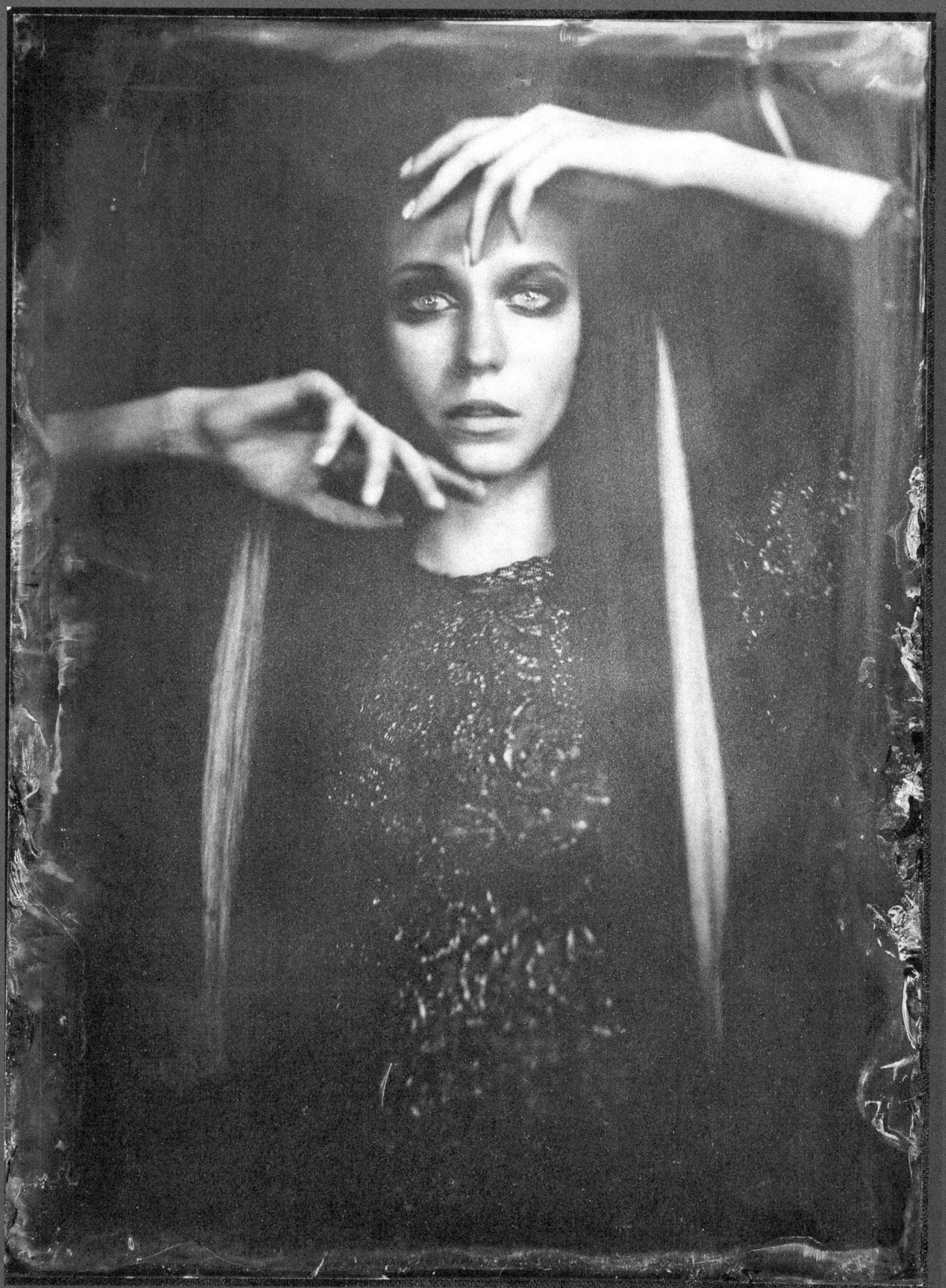

IGOR VASILIADIS

IGOR VASILIADIS

Concentration

Comtemplation

091219-0002

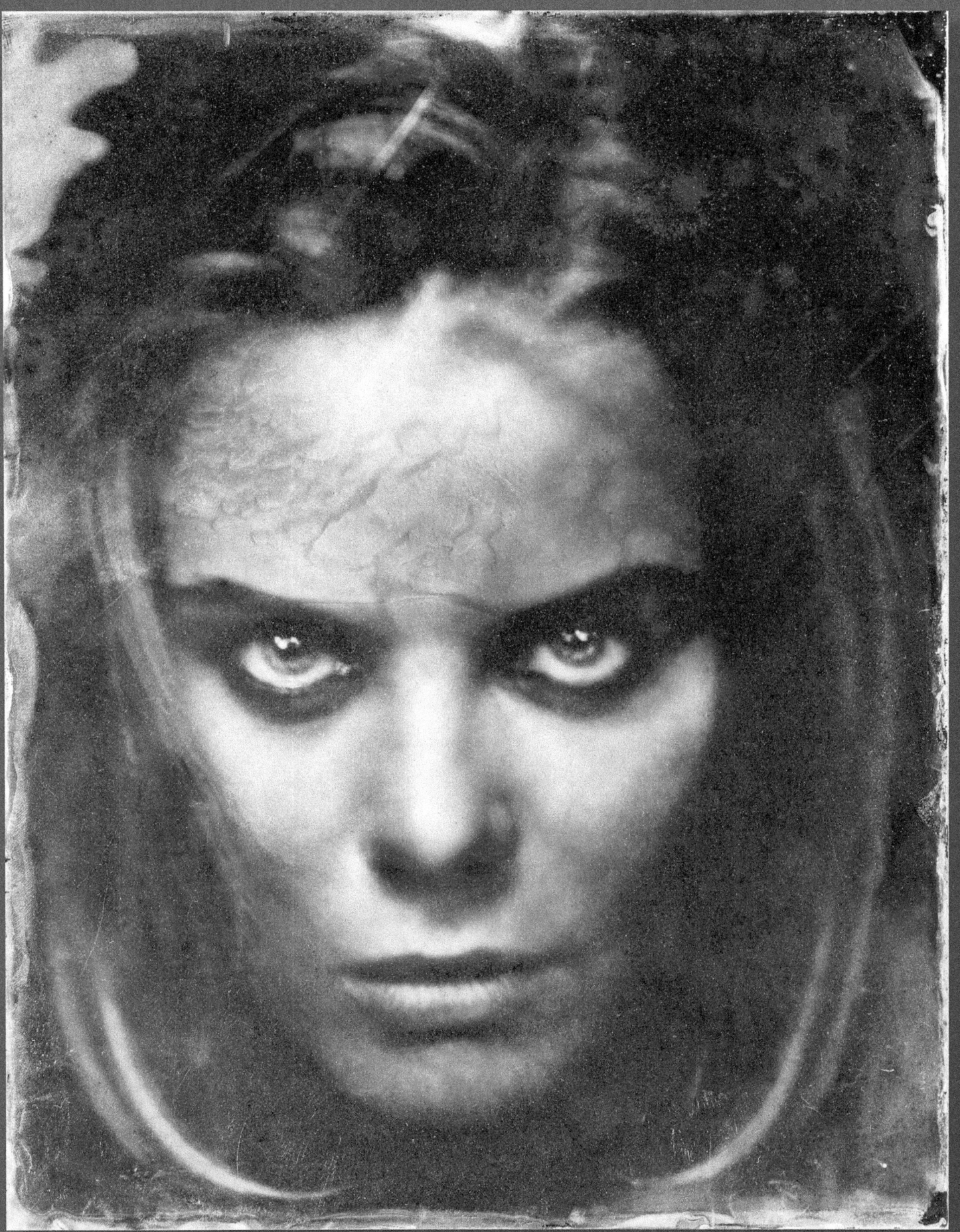

IGOR VASILIADIS

Irreality

Ethnicity

100628-0002

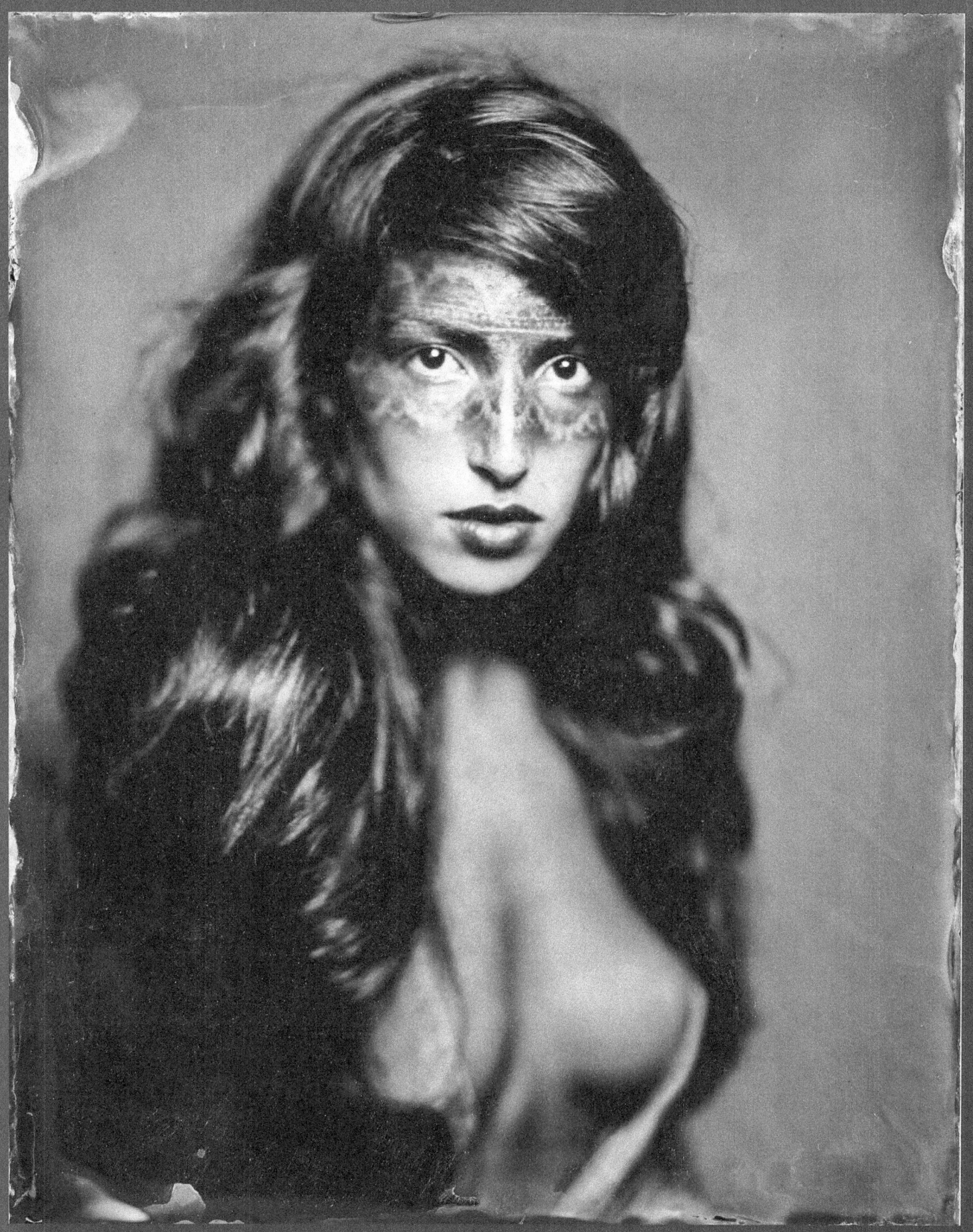

Fantasies
Affectation

090704-0005

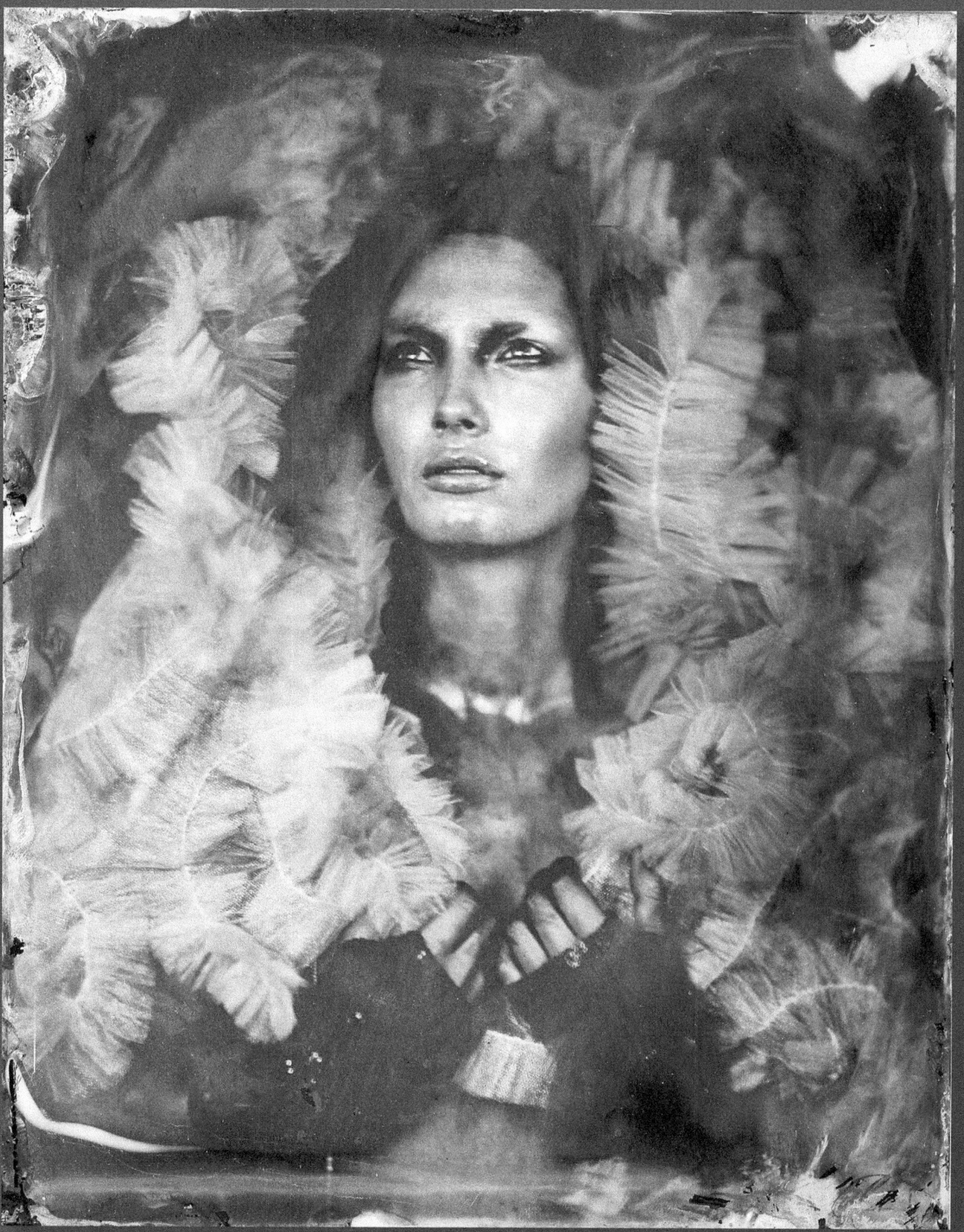

IGOR VASILIADIS

090523-0001

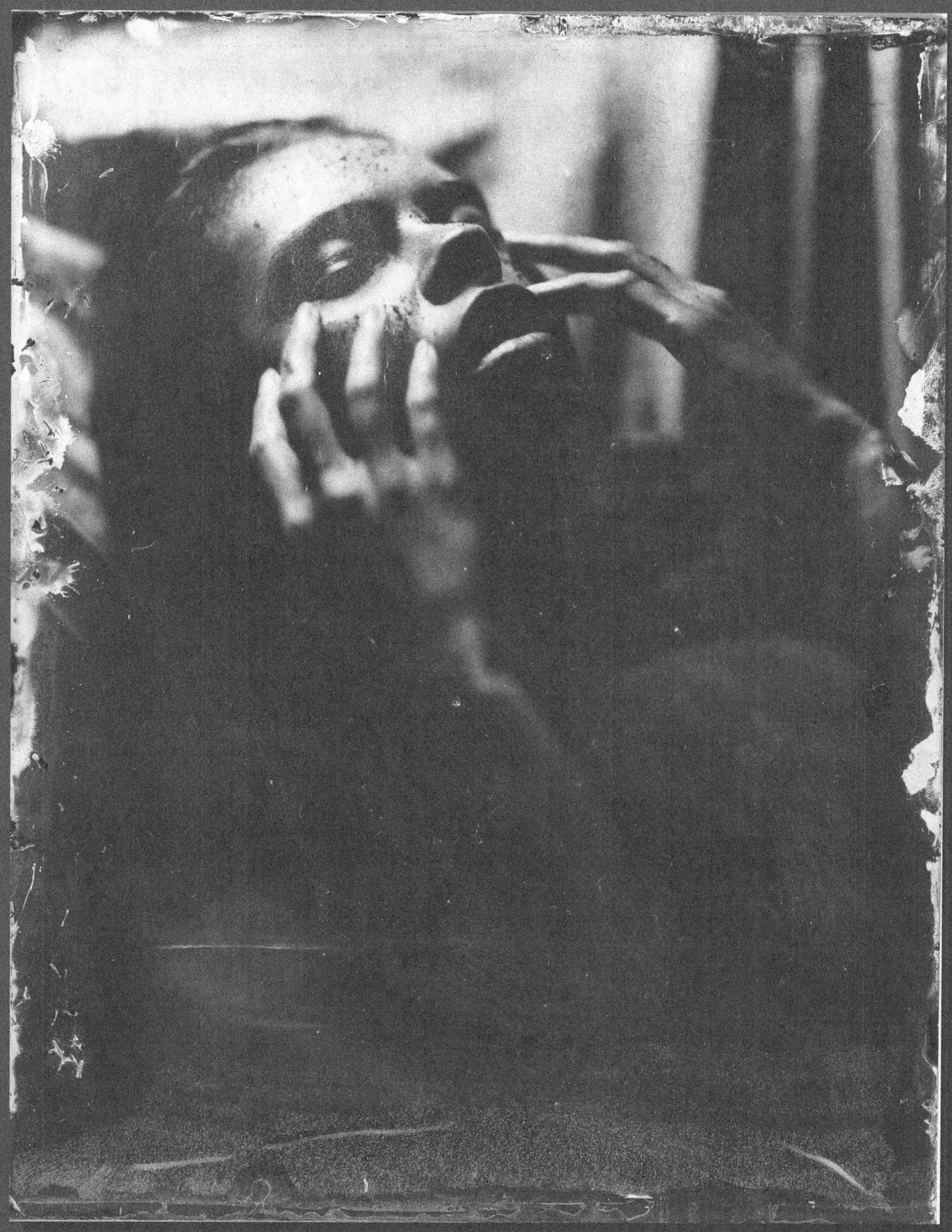

IGOR VASILIADIS

090926-0001

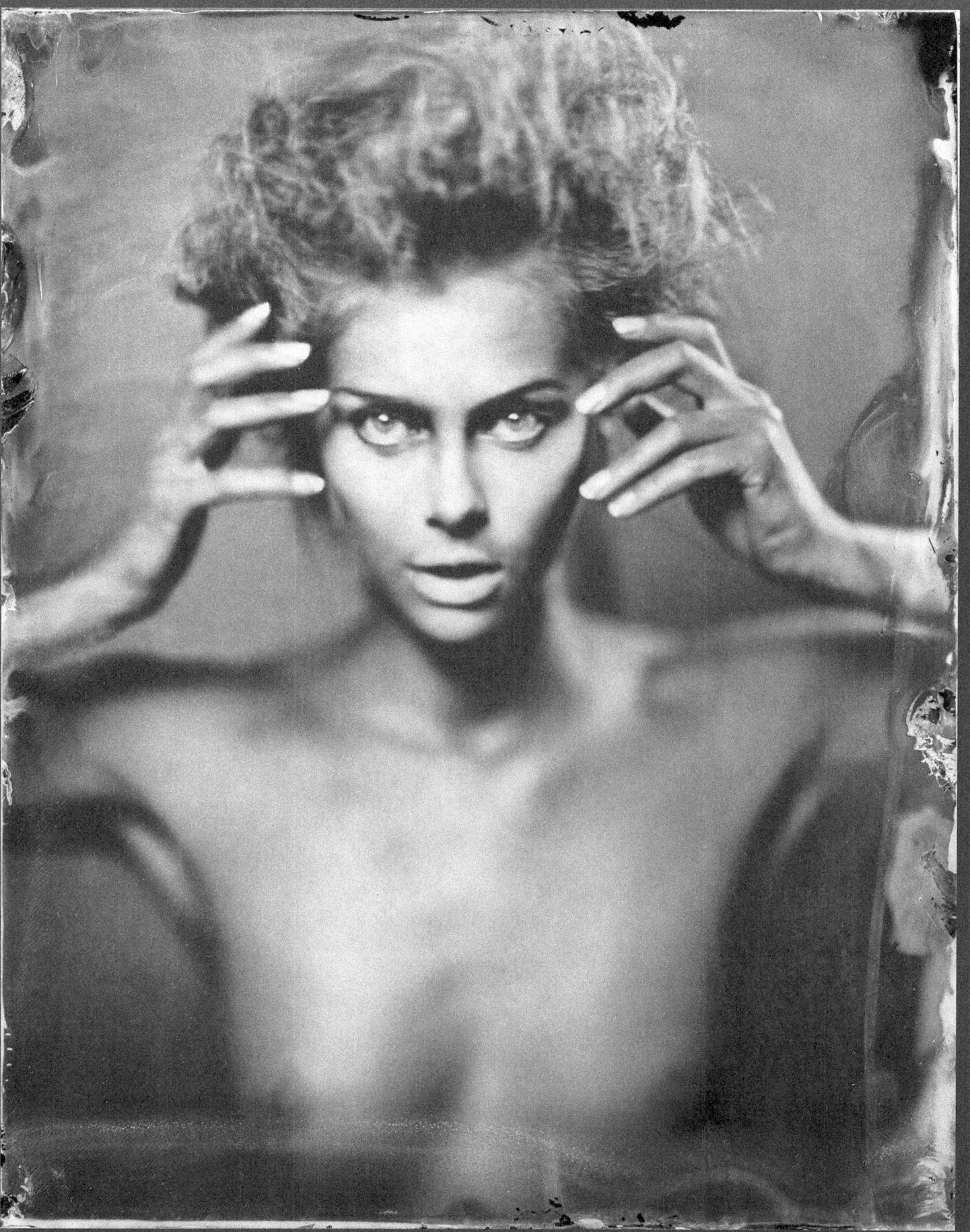

090926-0003

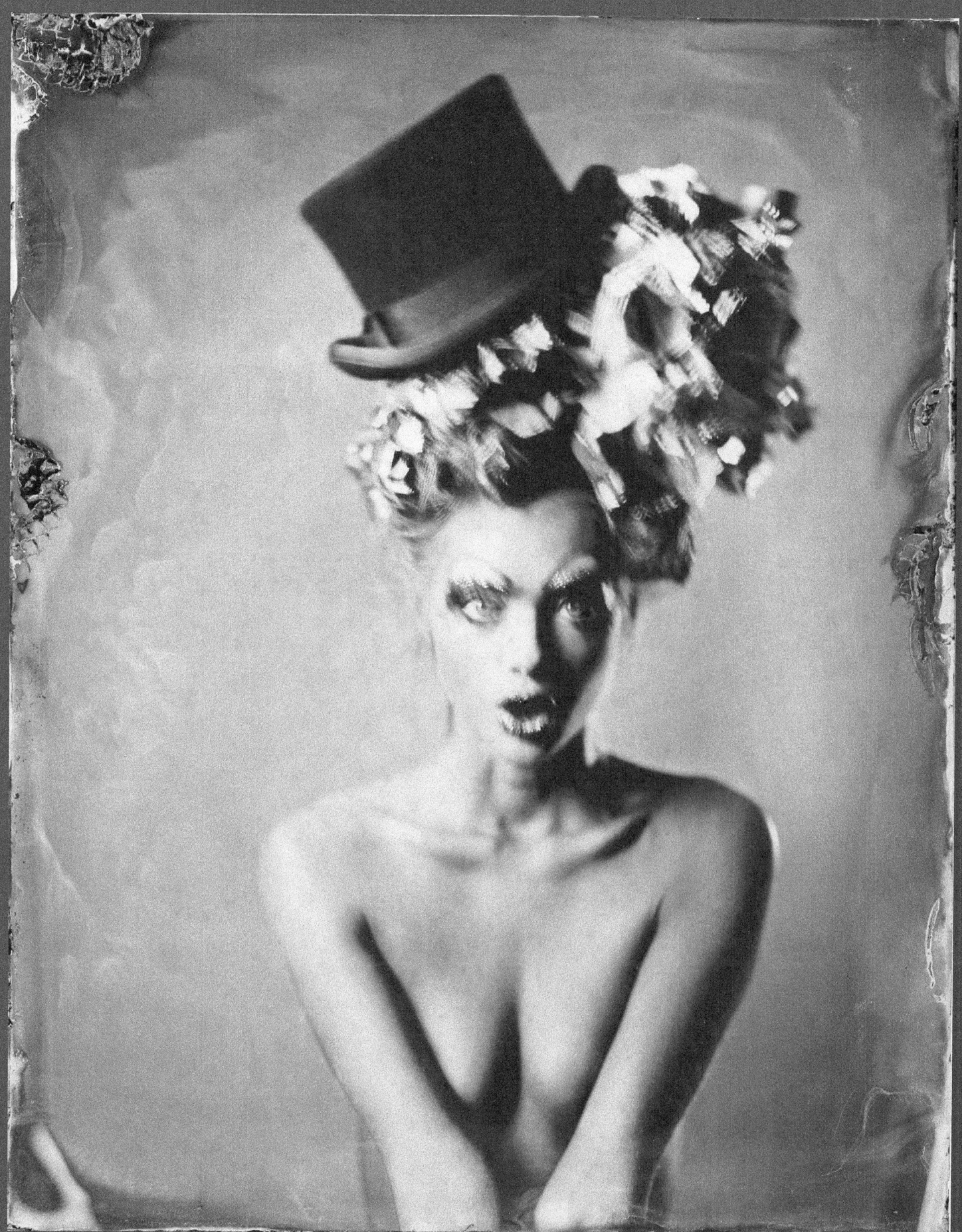

Timeless Detachment

090726-0004

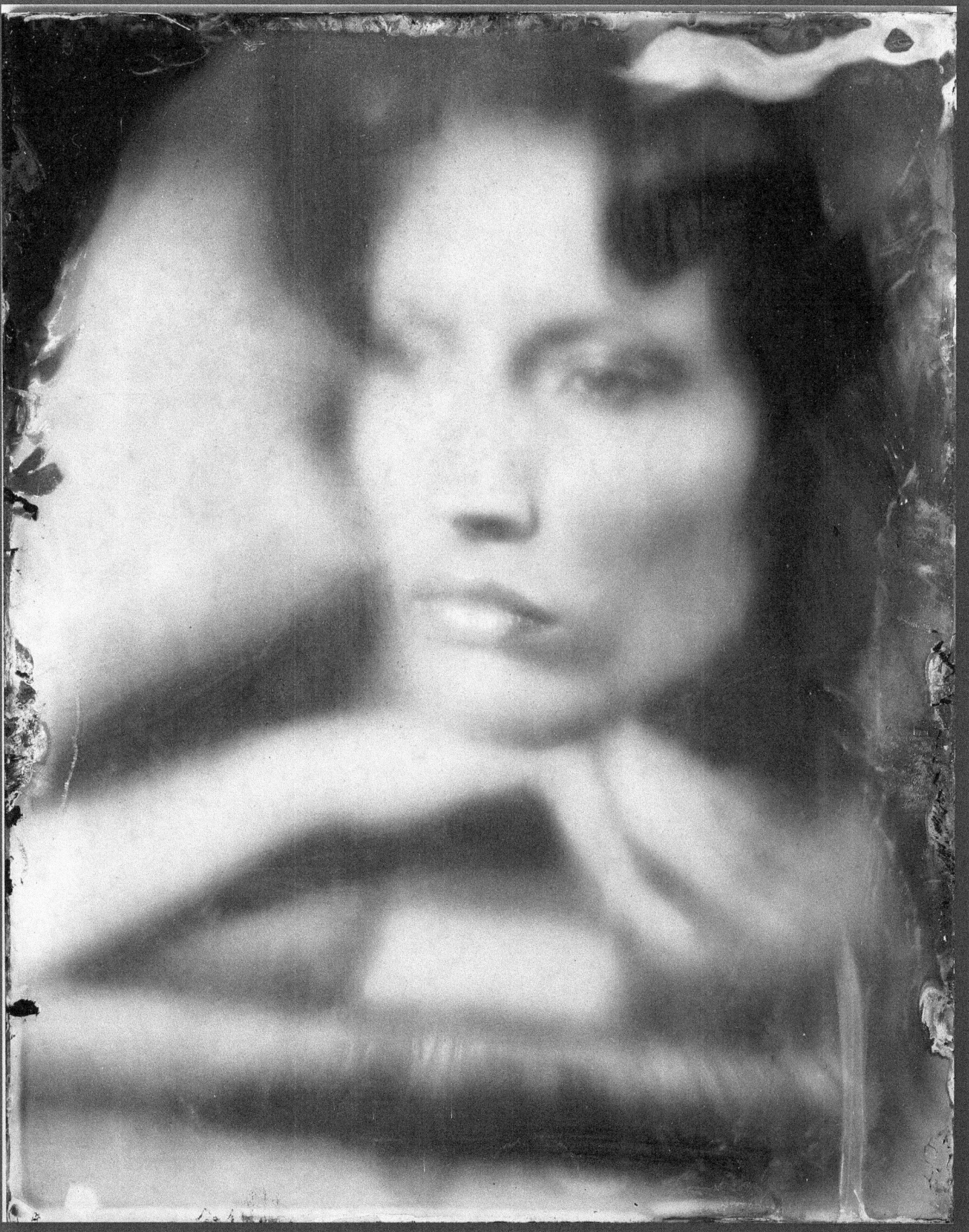

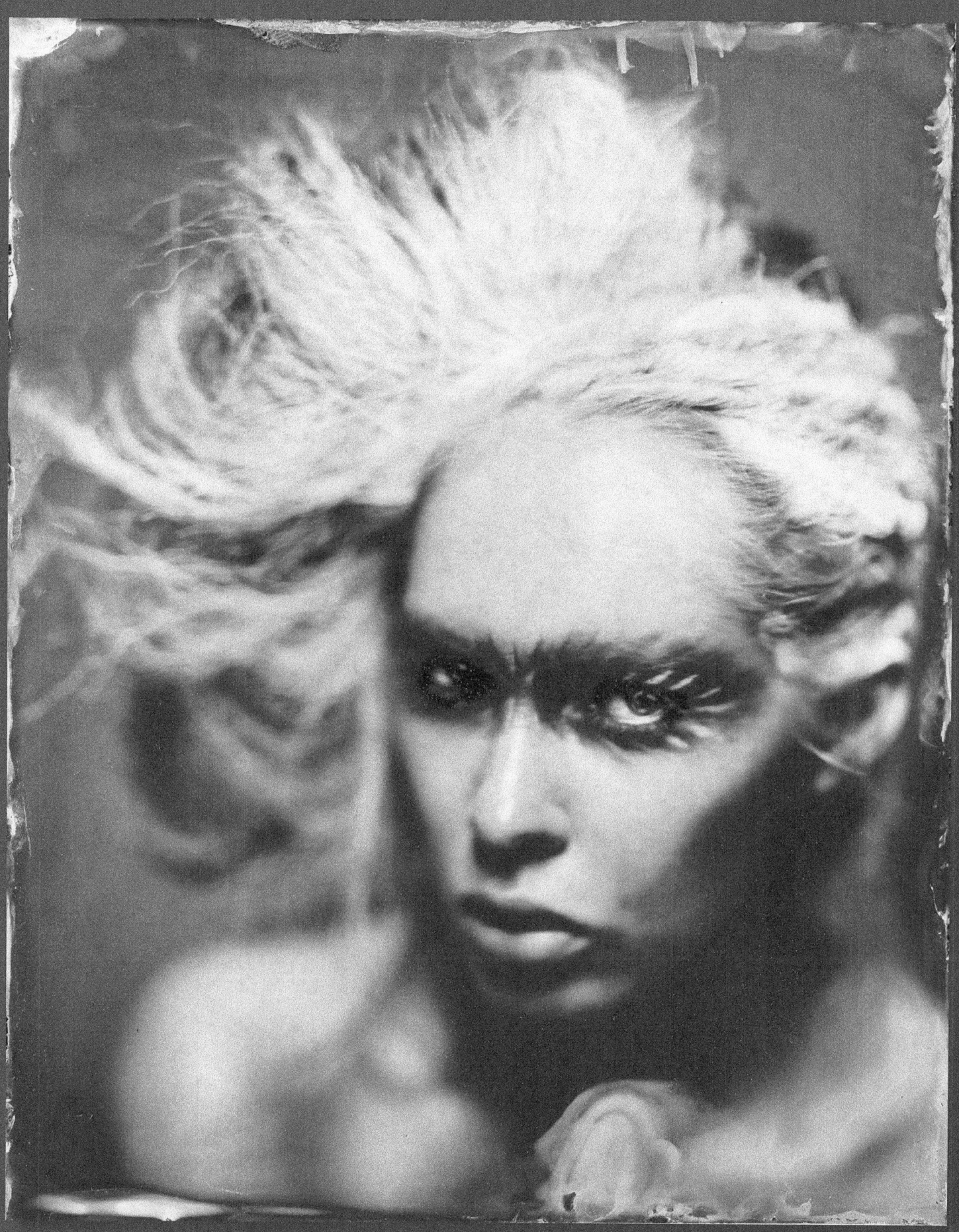

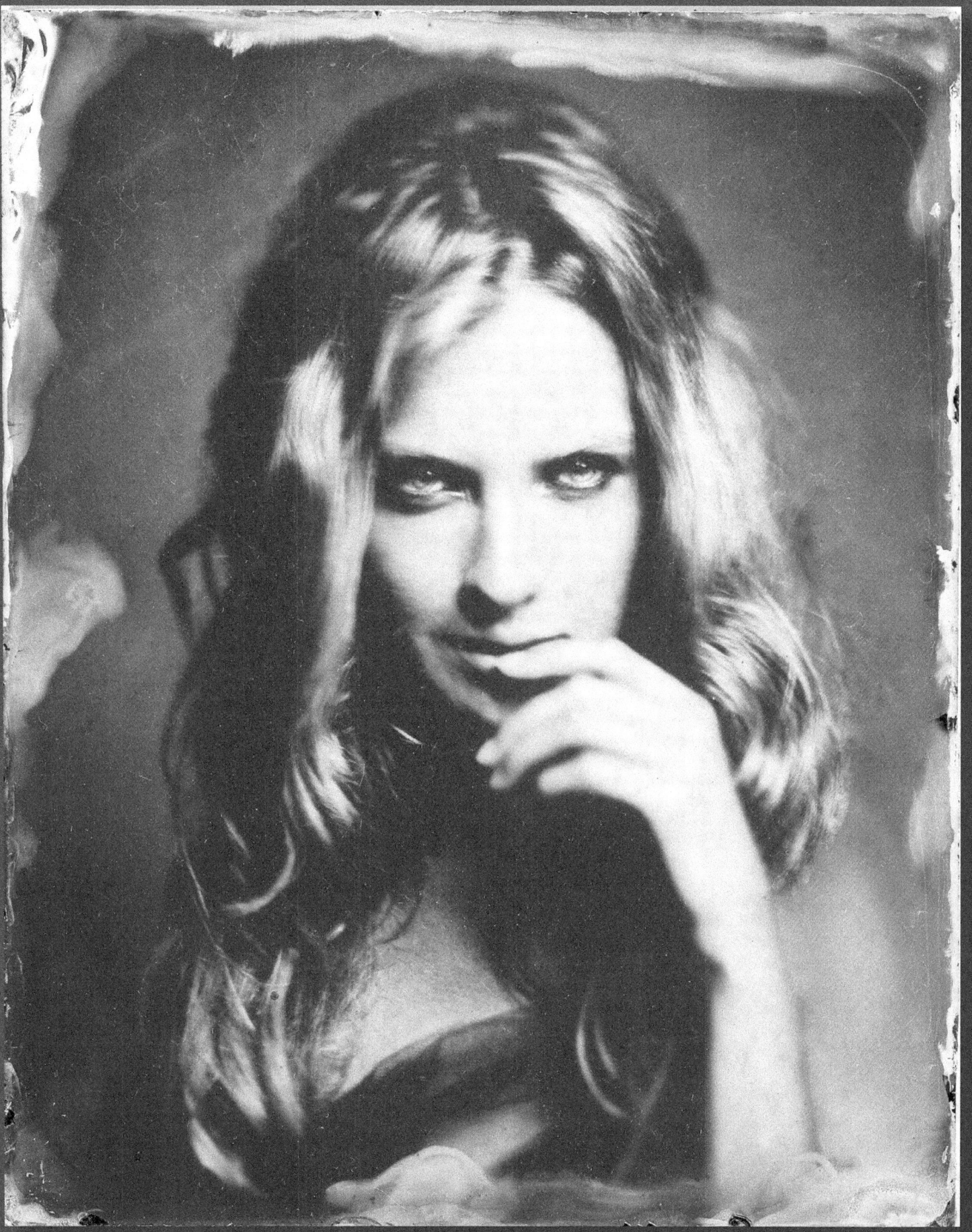

IGOR VASILIADIS

080816-0001

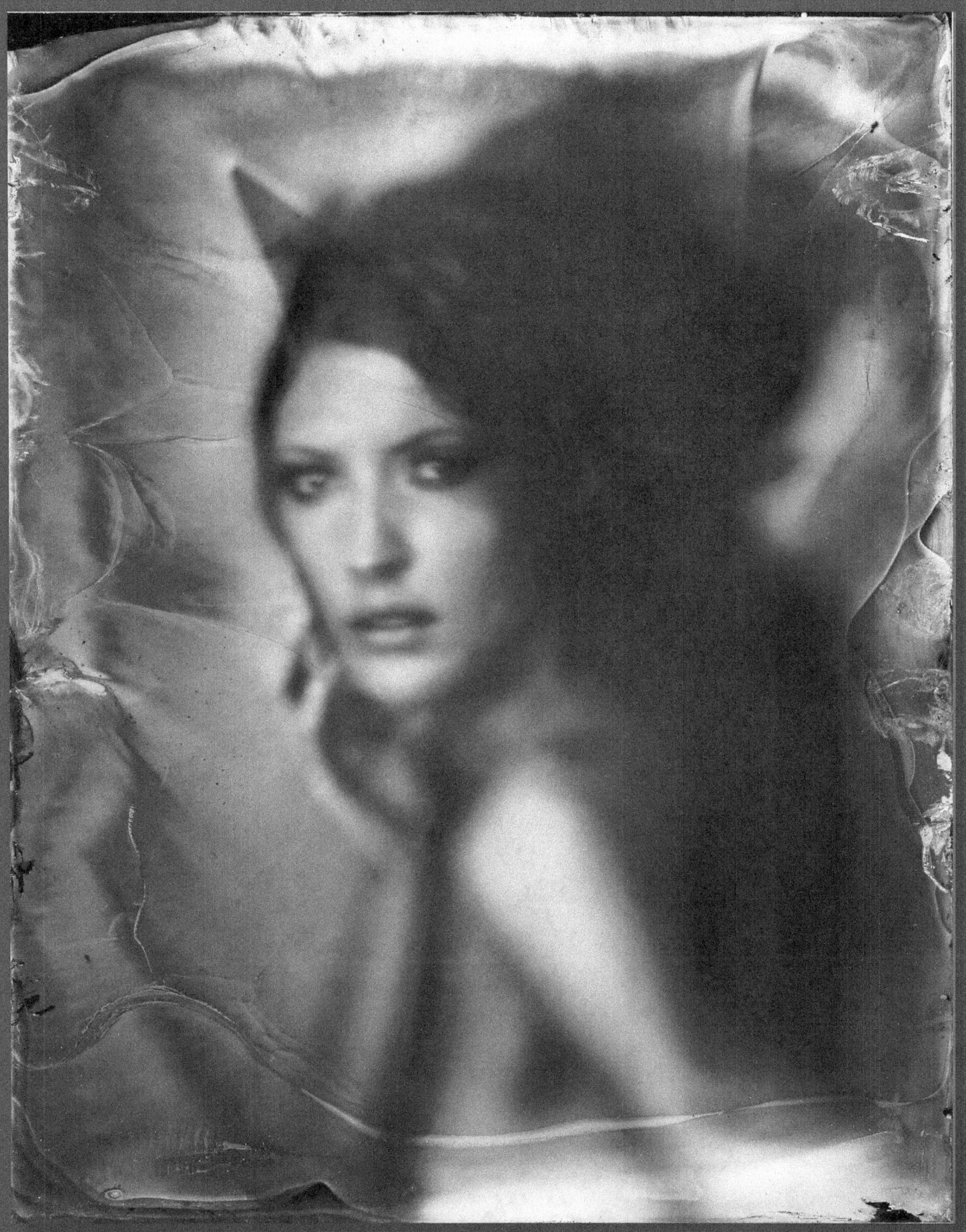

IGOR VASILIADIS

Eternal fashion

IGOR VASILIADIS

IGOR VASILIADIS

090704-0003

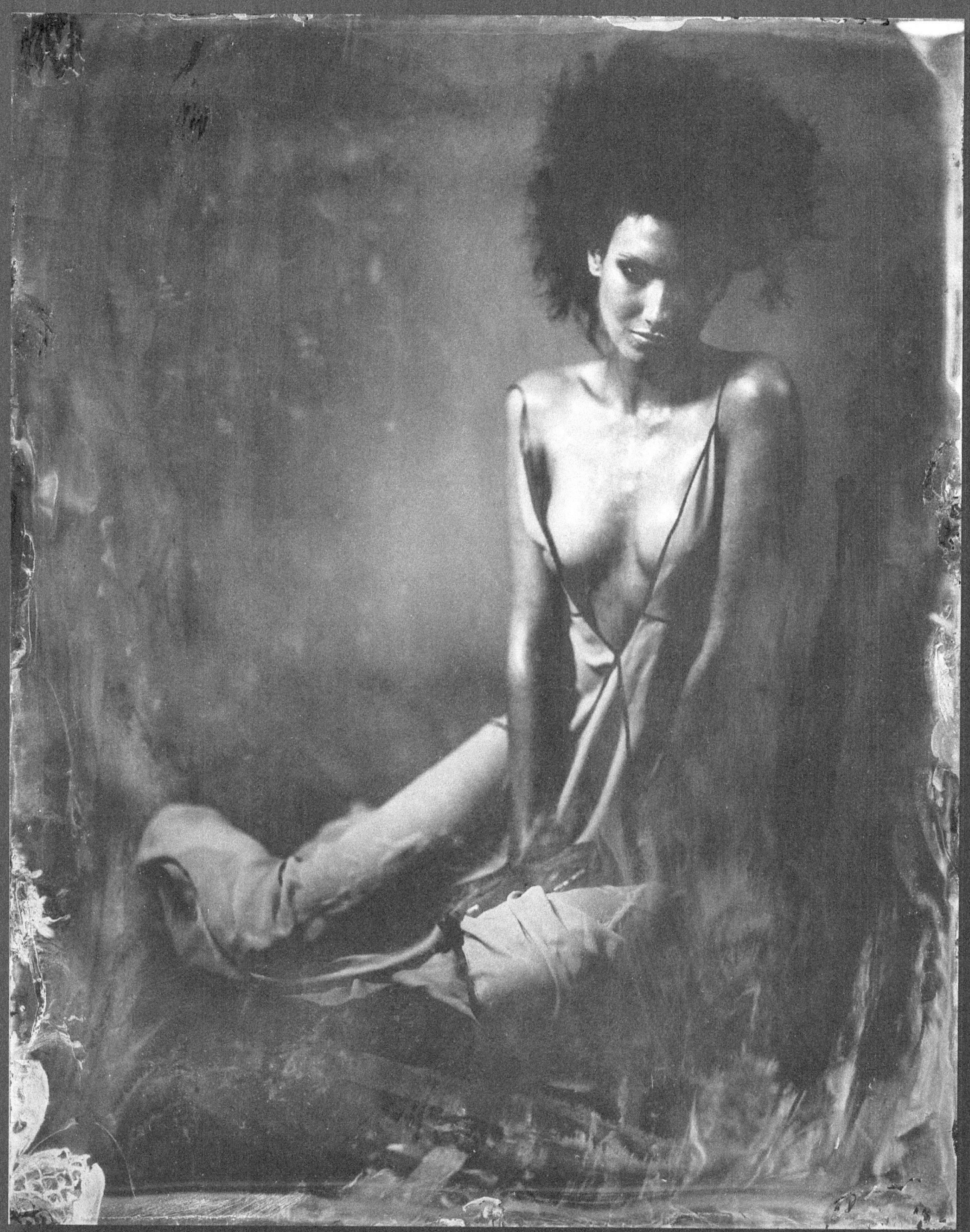

Reminiscence
Grief

081010-0001

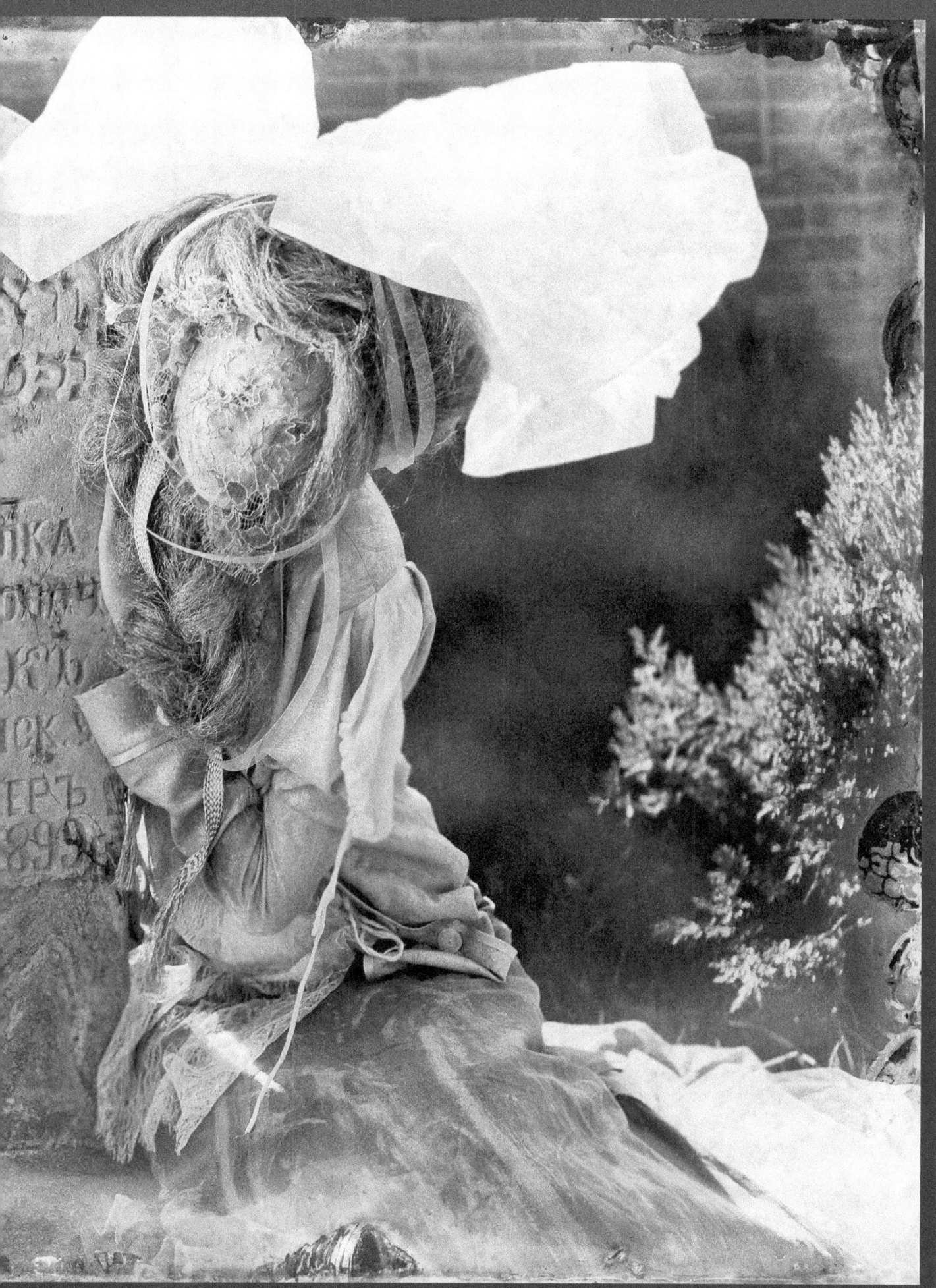

IGOR VASILIADIS

IGOR VASILIADIS

IGOR VASILIADIS

100628-0004

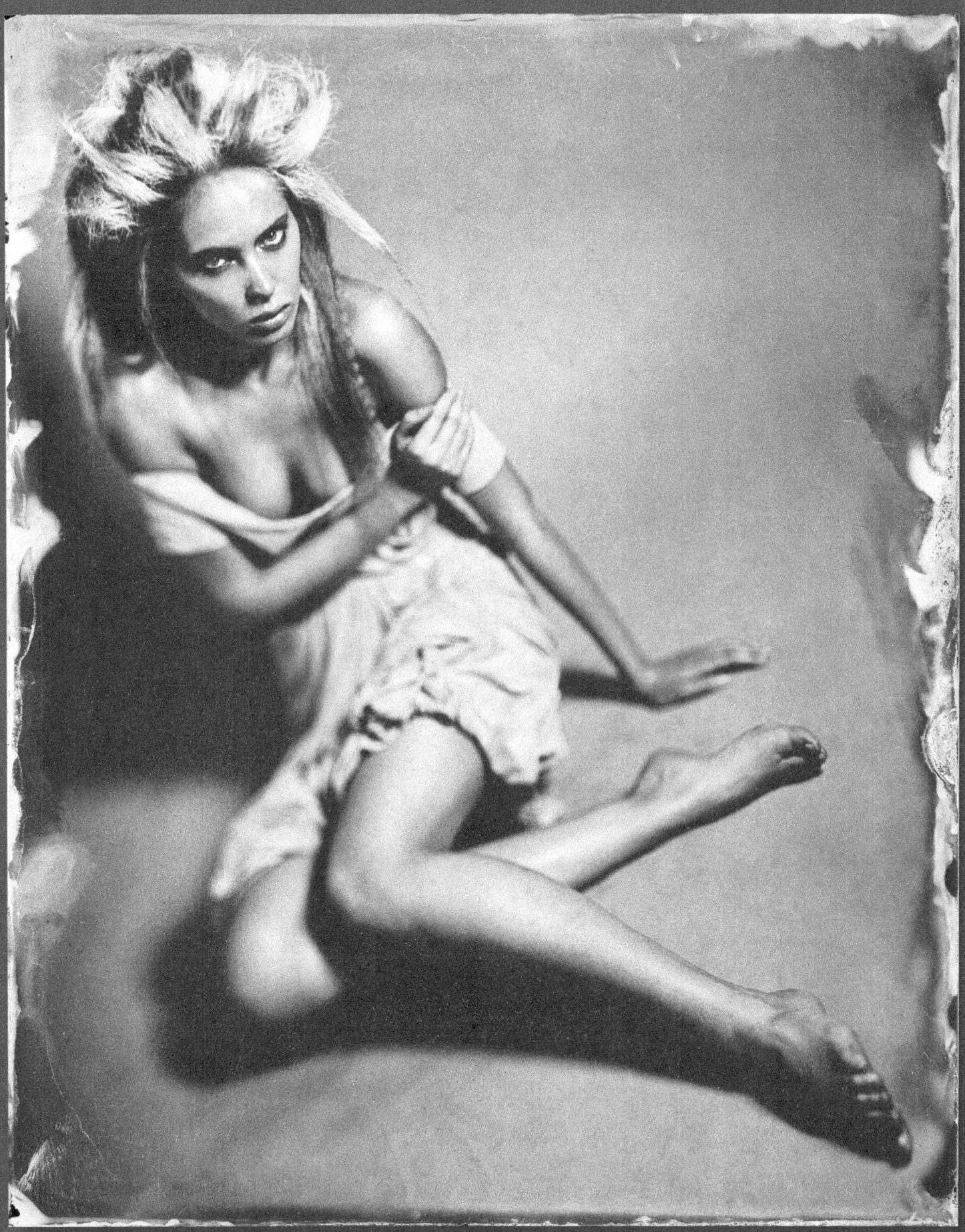

IGOR VA...

Reliance Inaccessibility

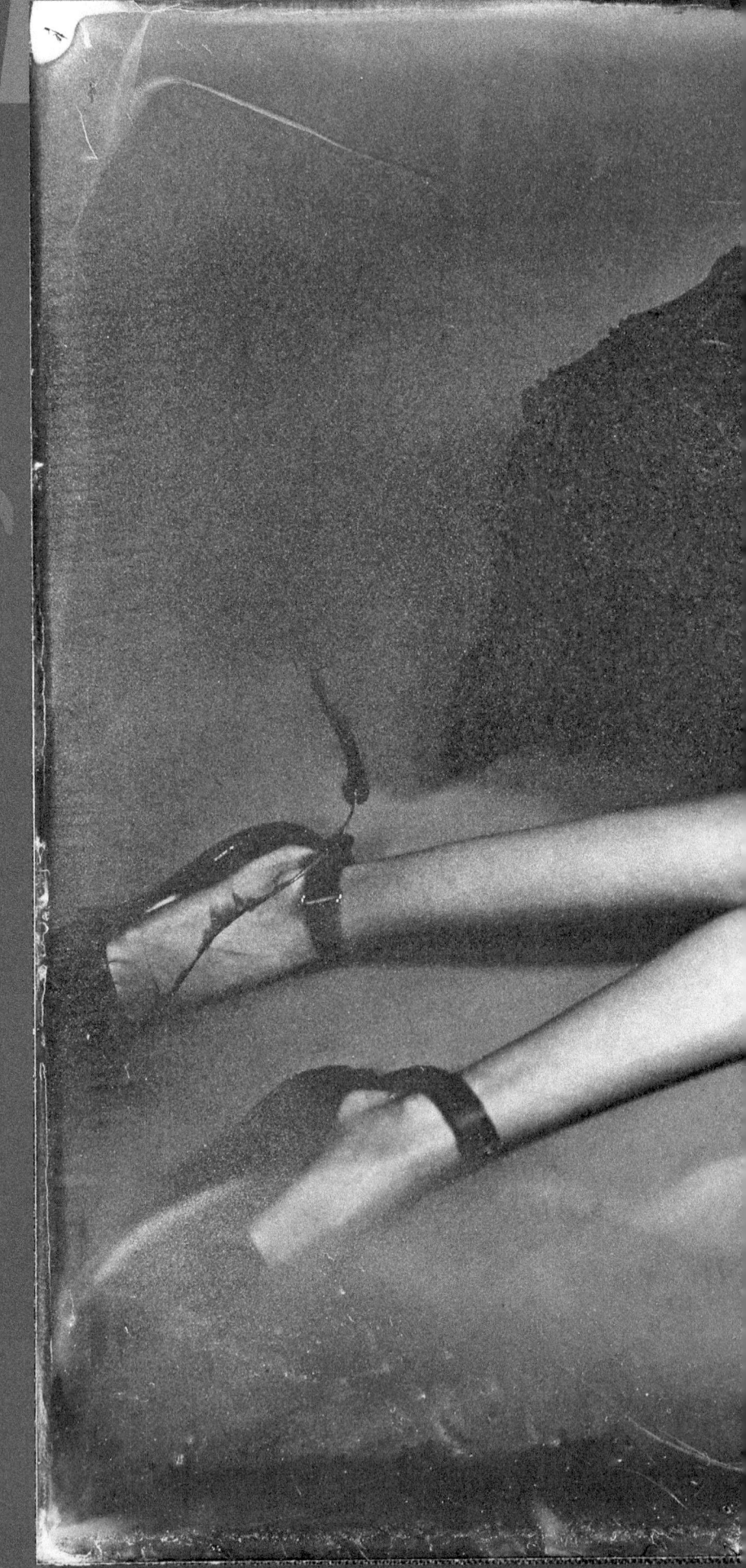

081008-004

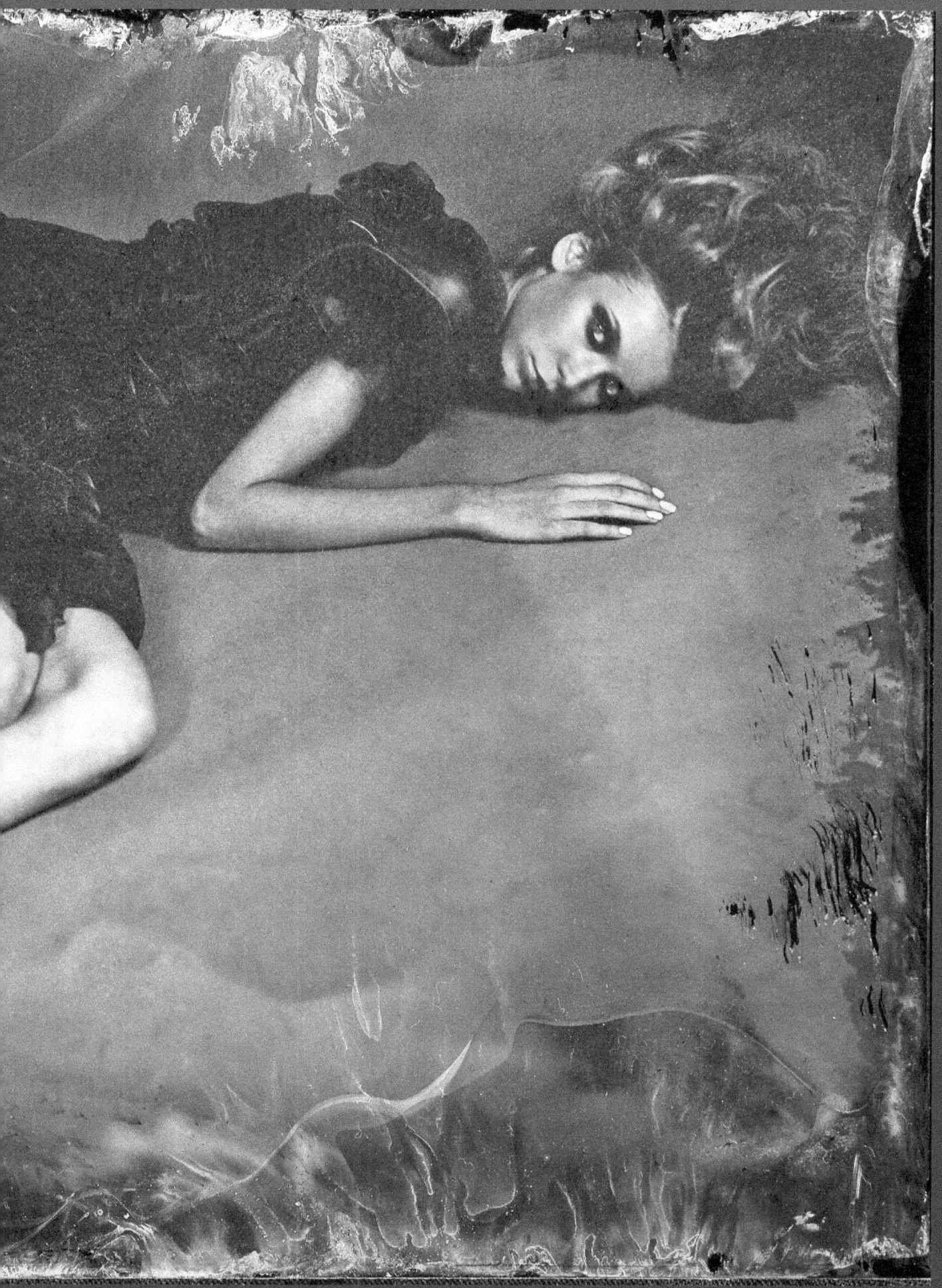

081008-001

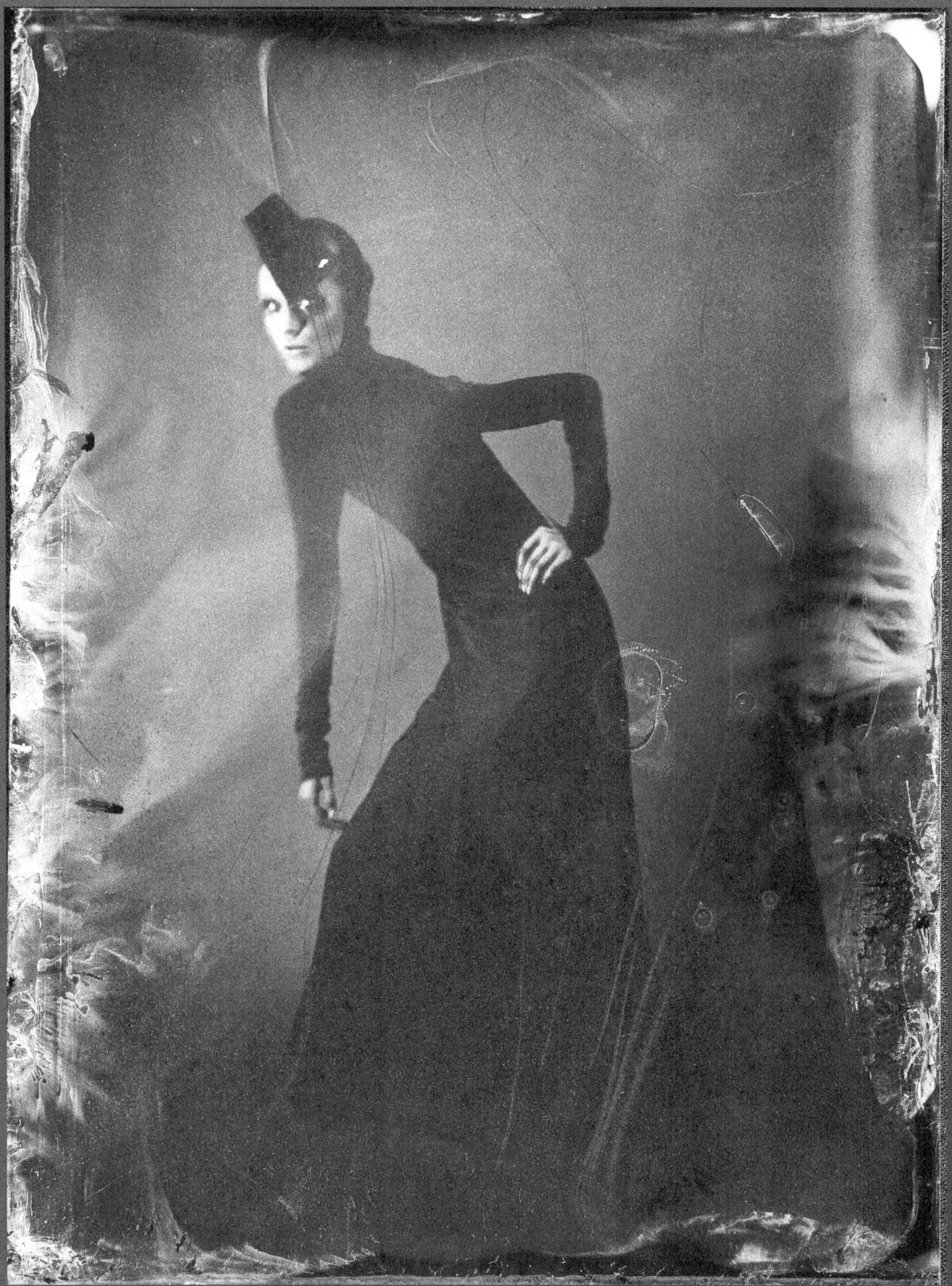

IGOR VASILIADIS

081008-003

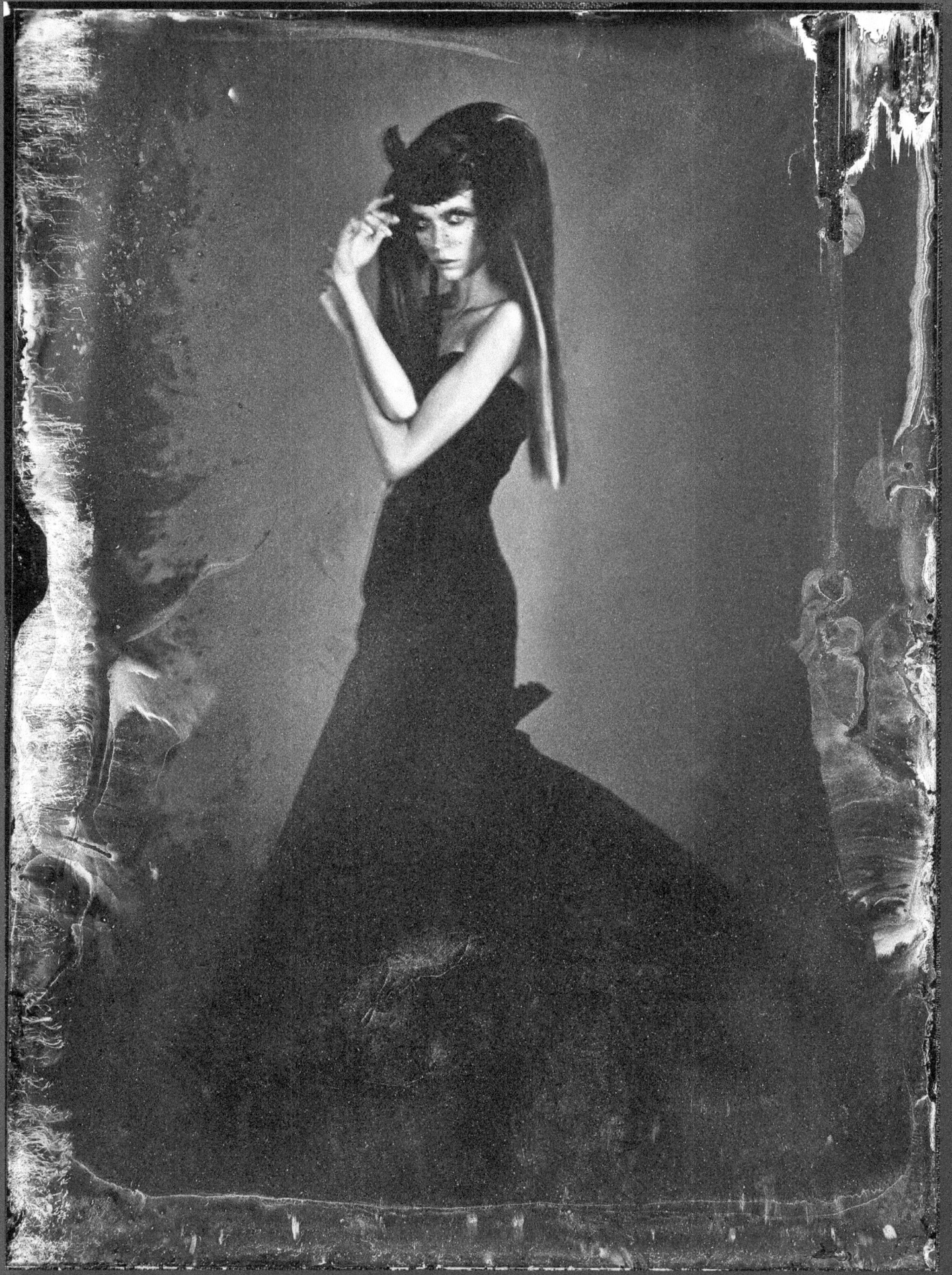

IGOR VASILIADIS

Quaintmess

Aftermativeness

090704-0004

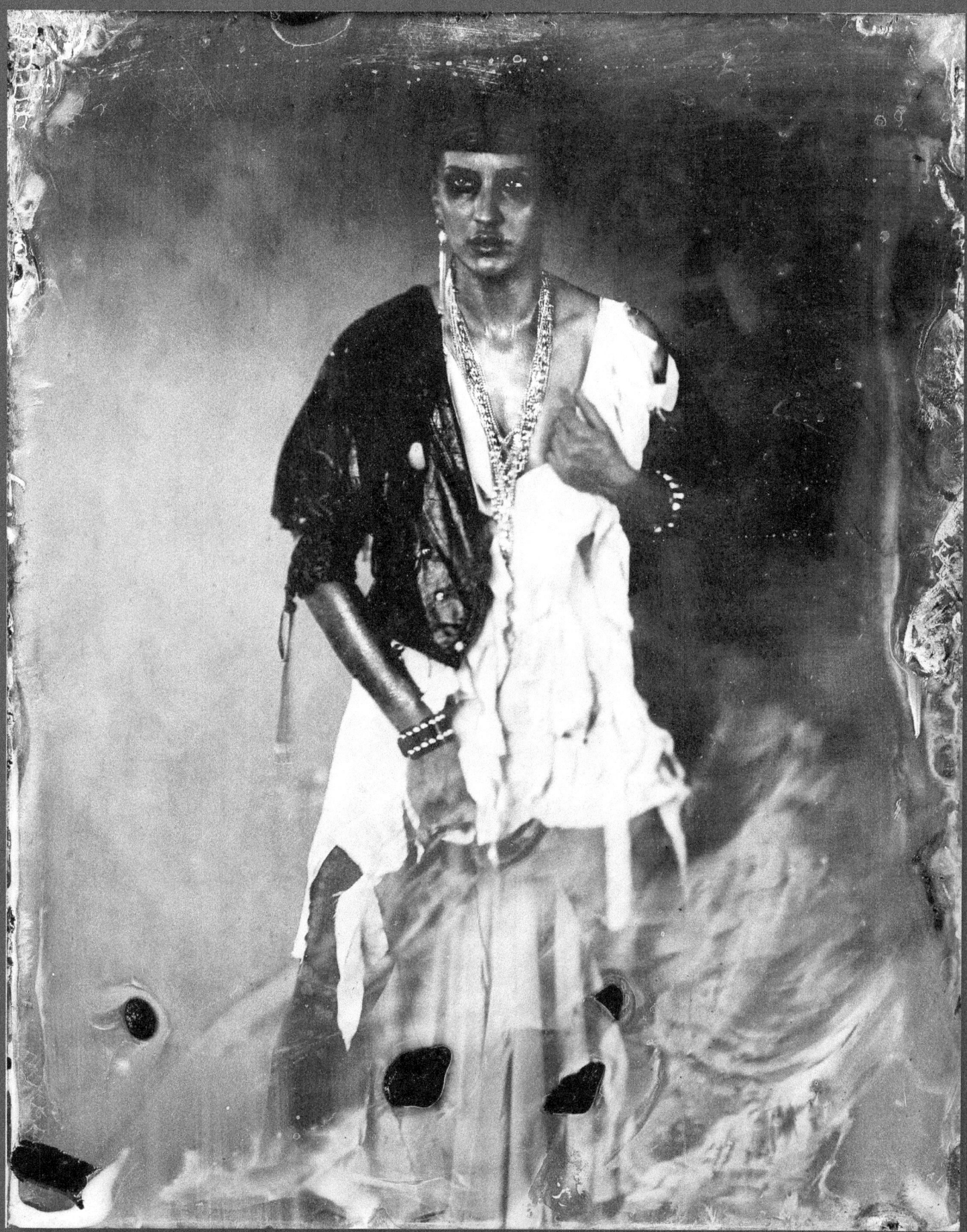

Immaculacy

Innocence

100614-0001

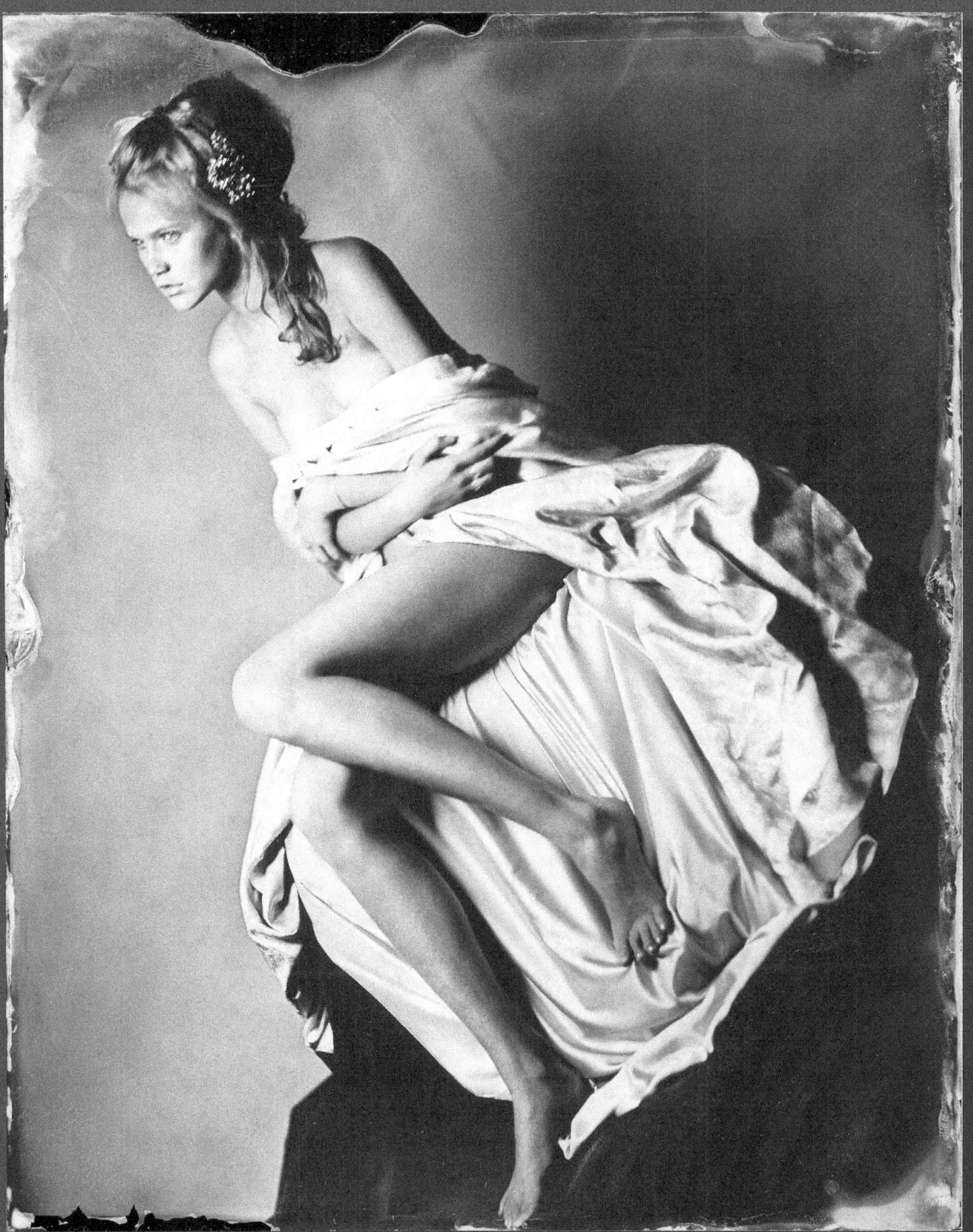

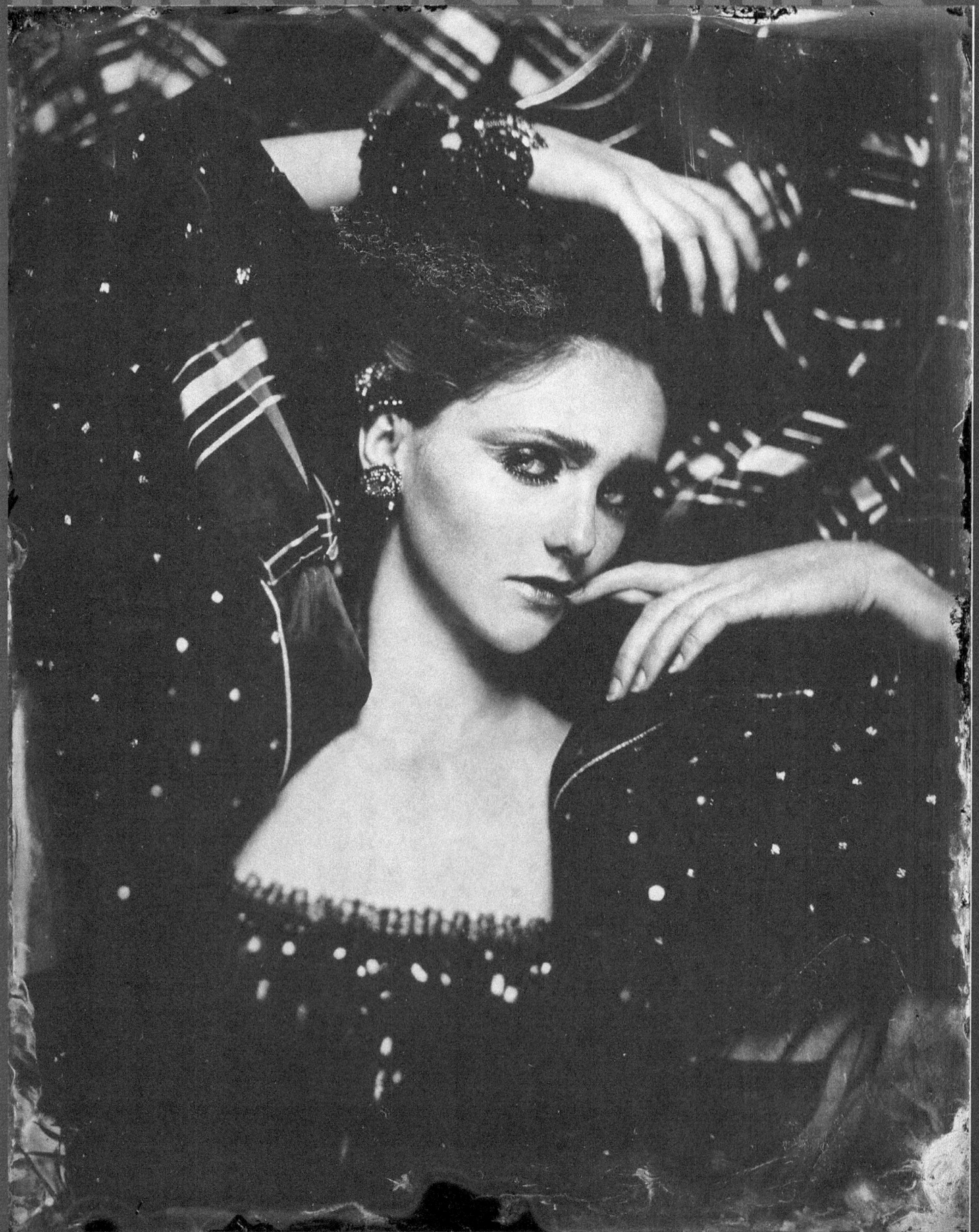

110317-0007

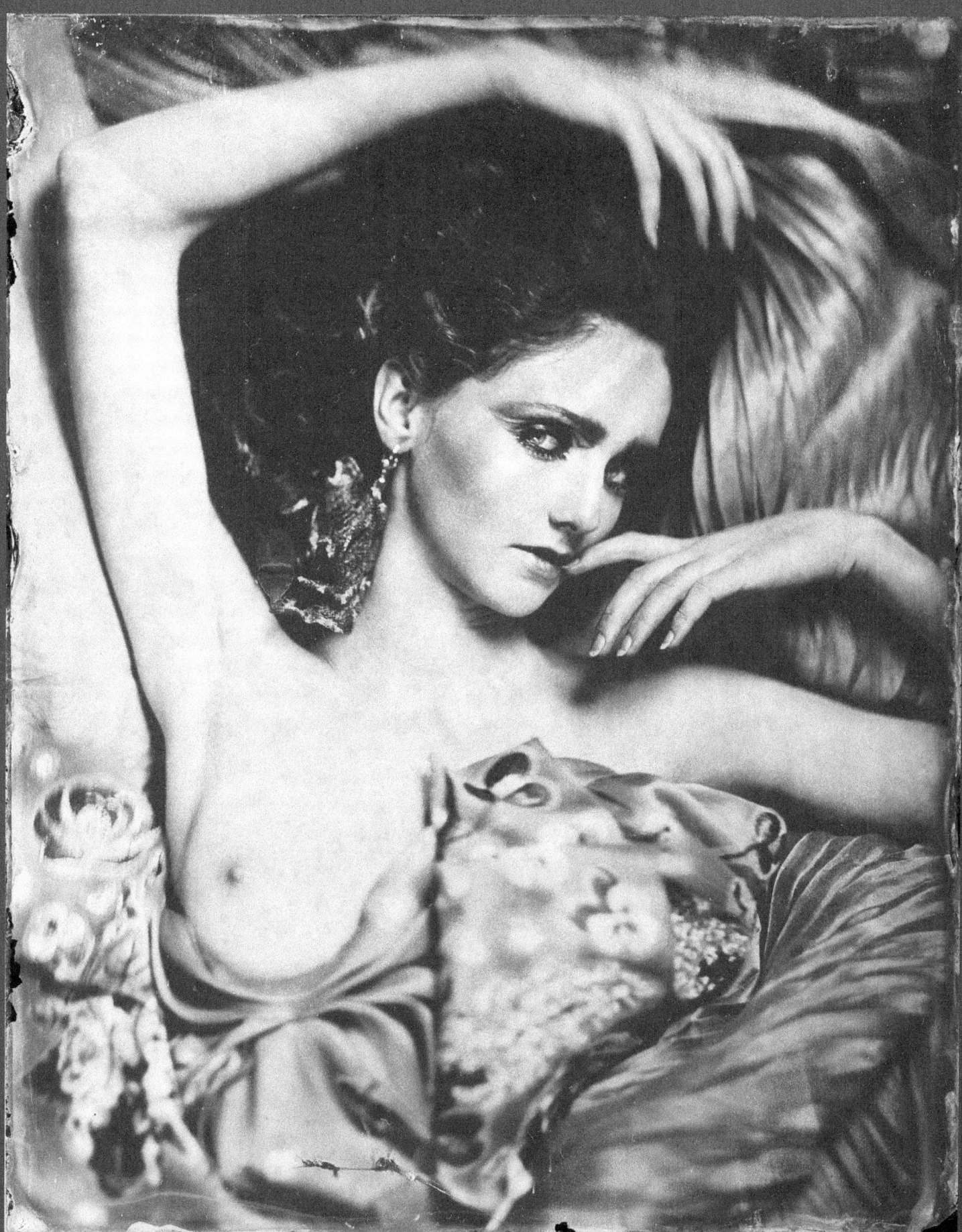

110317-0006

110324-0003

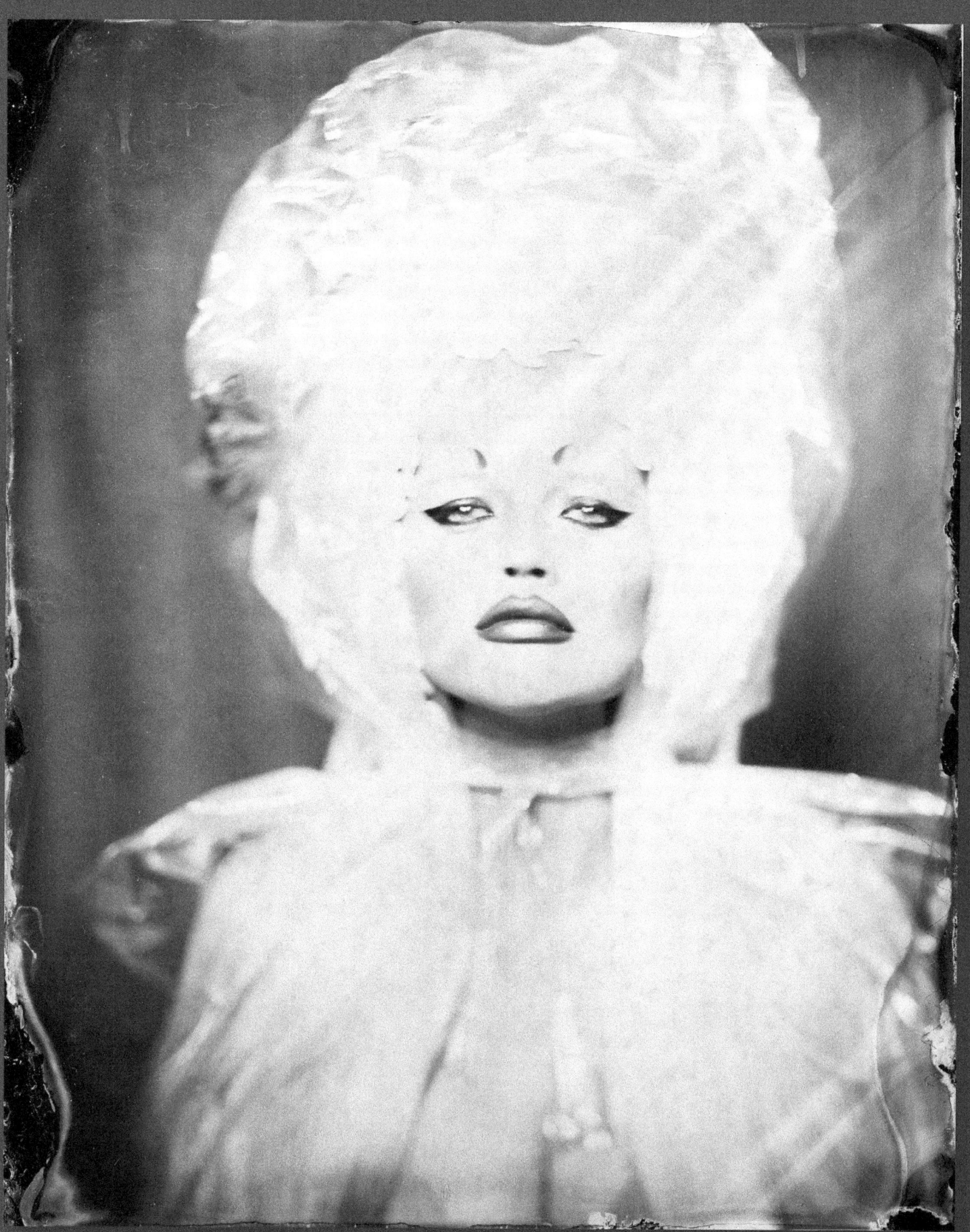

IGOR VASILIADIS

Flirting

Success

110324-0002

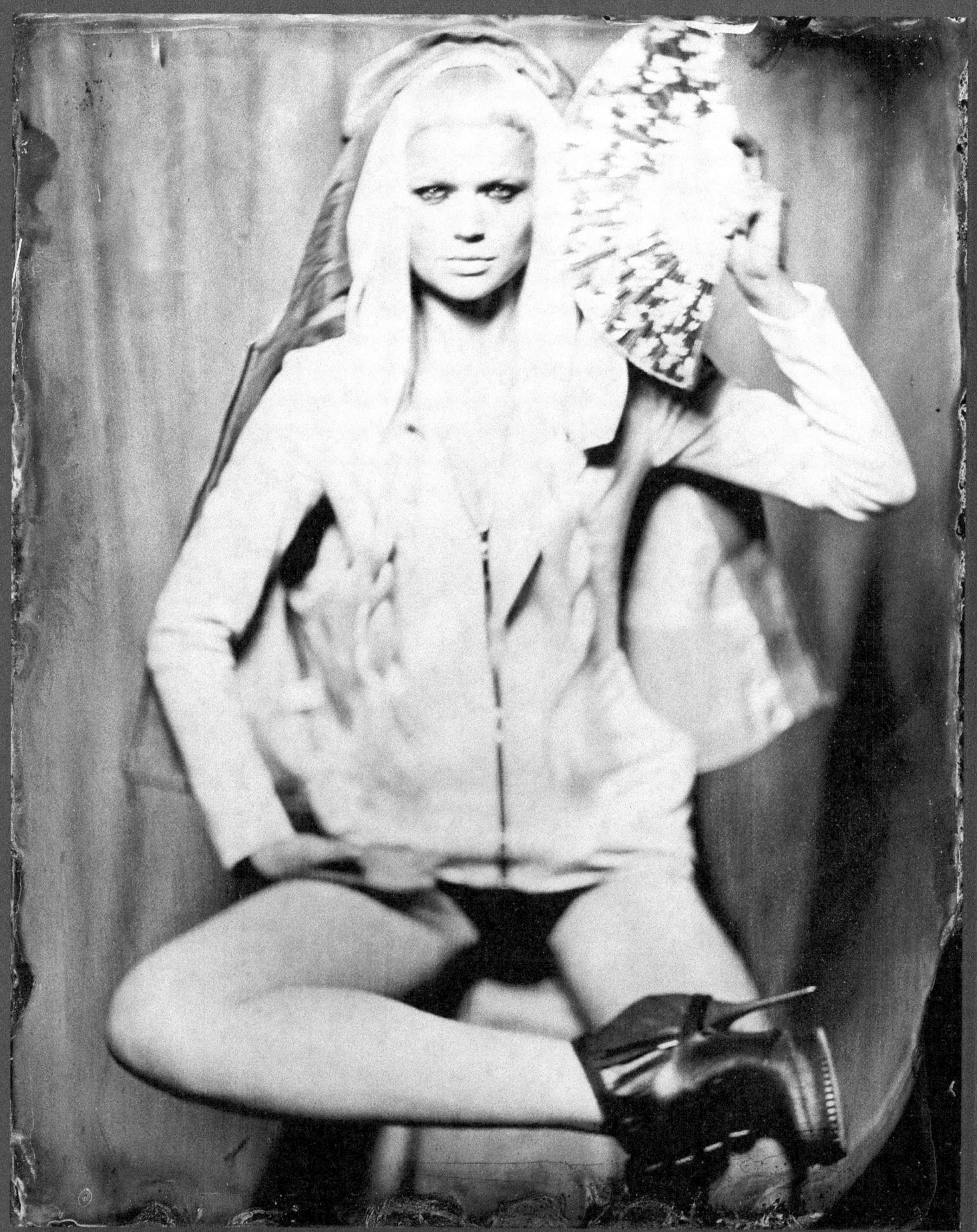

IGOR VASILIADIS

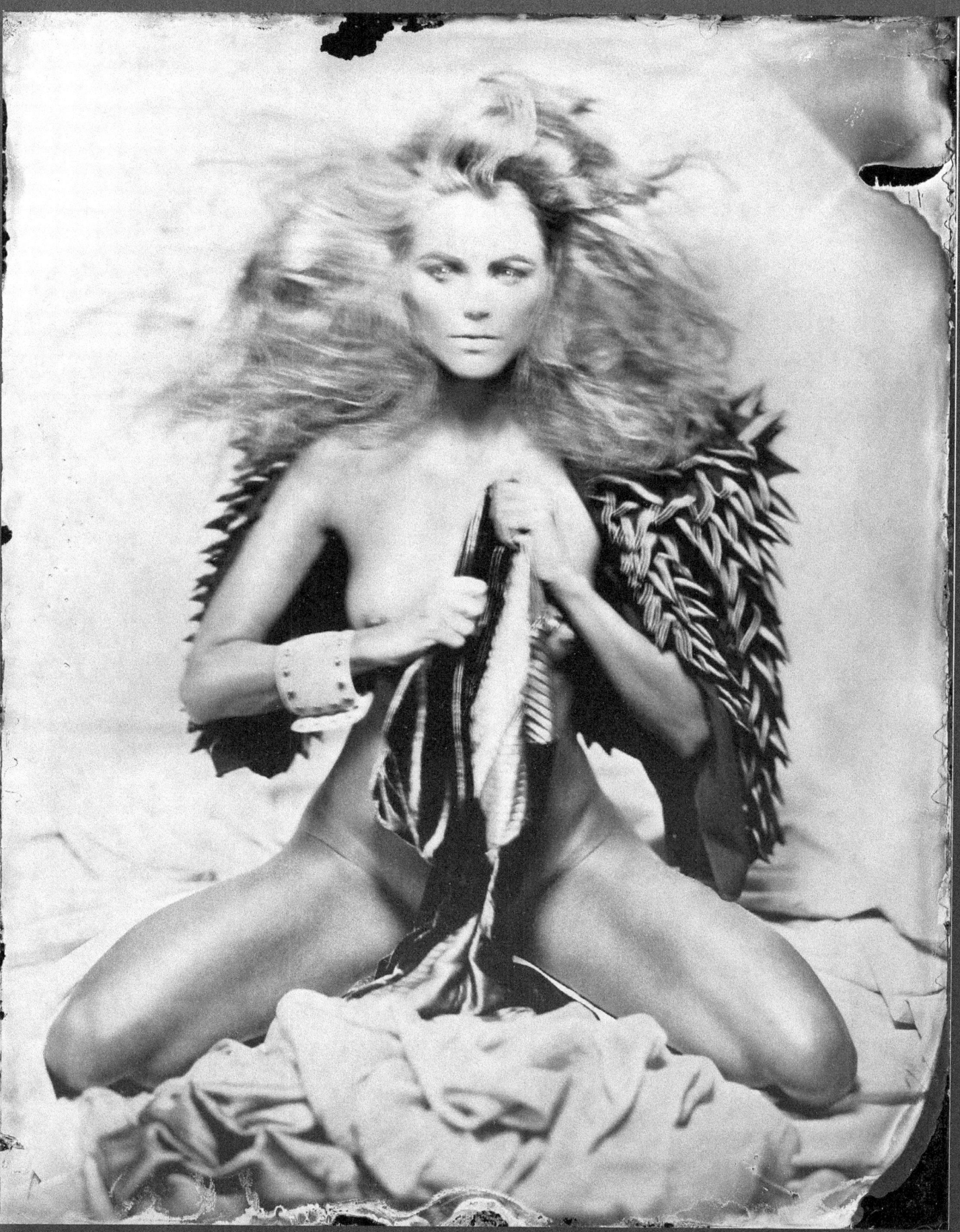

IGOR VASILIADIS

110317-0001

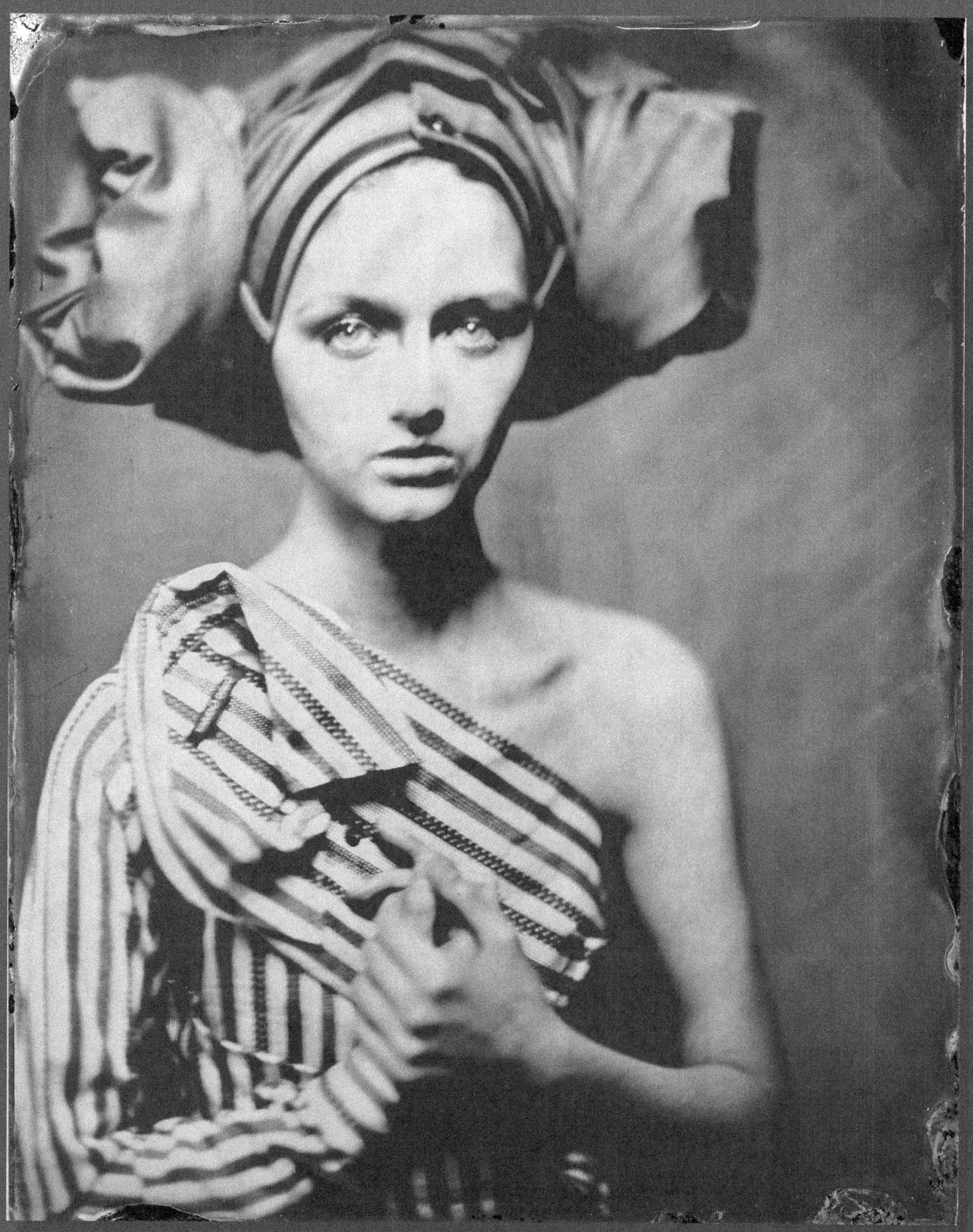

IGOR VASILIADIS

Calmness
Harmony

110317-0008

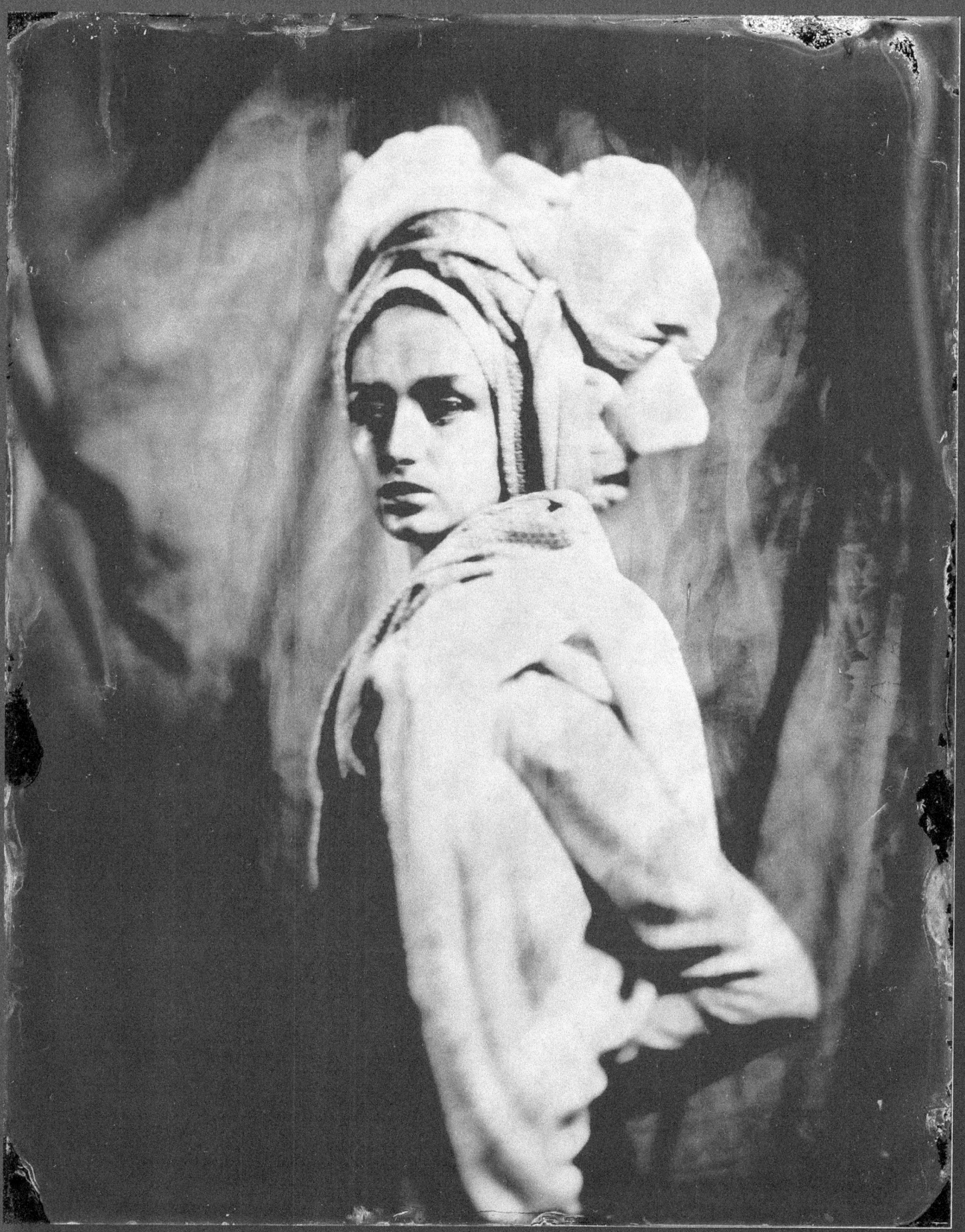

IGOR VASILIADIS

Elegancy

Daintiness

110324-0001

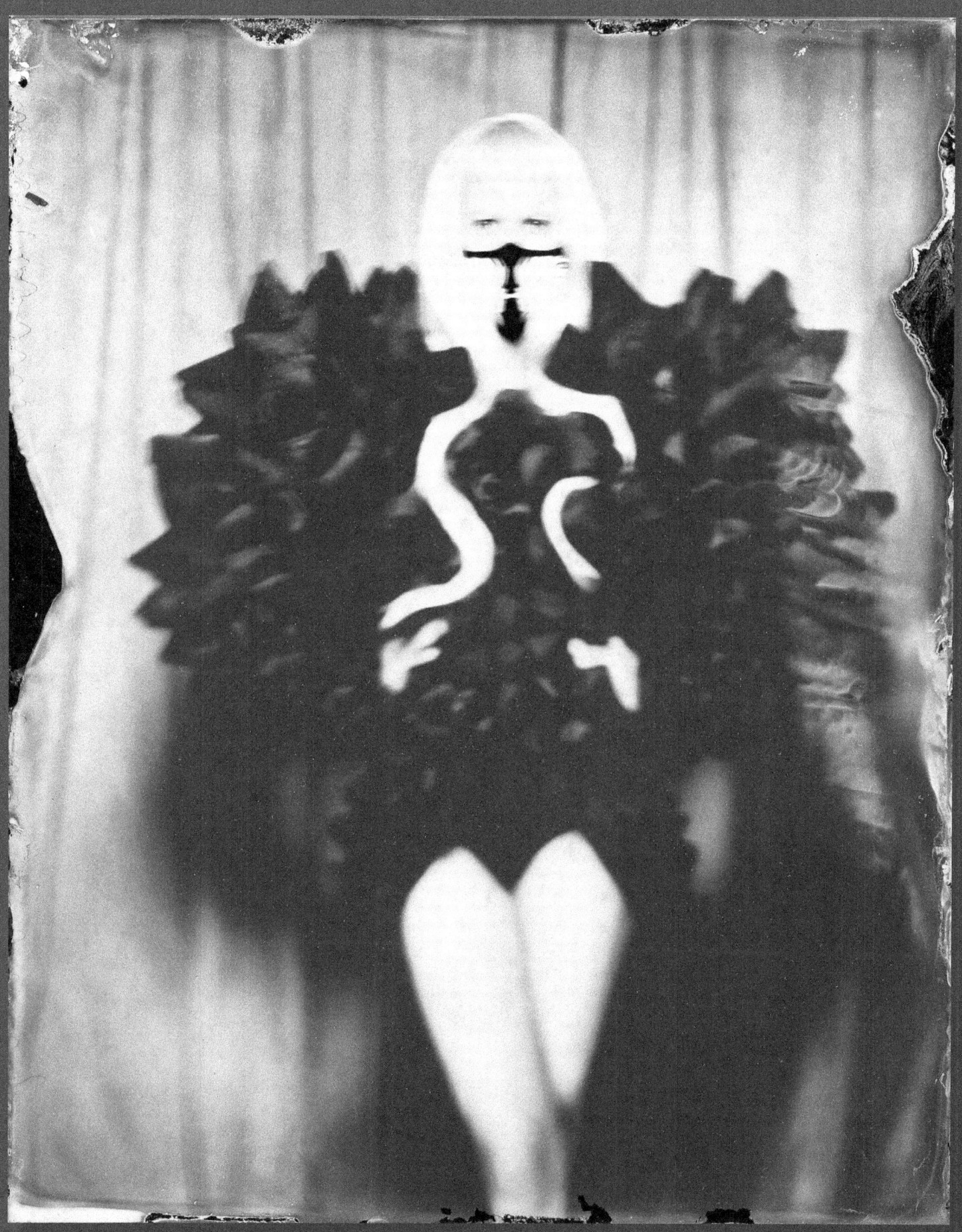

Purity
Subtlety

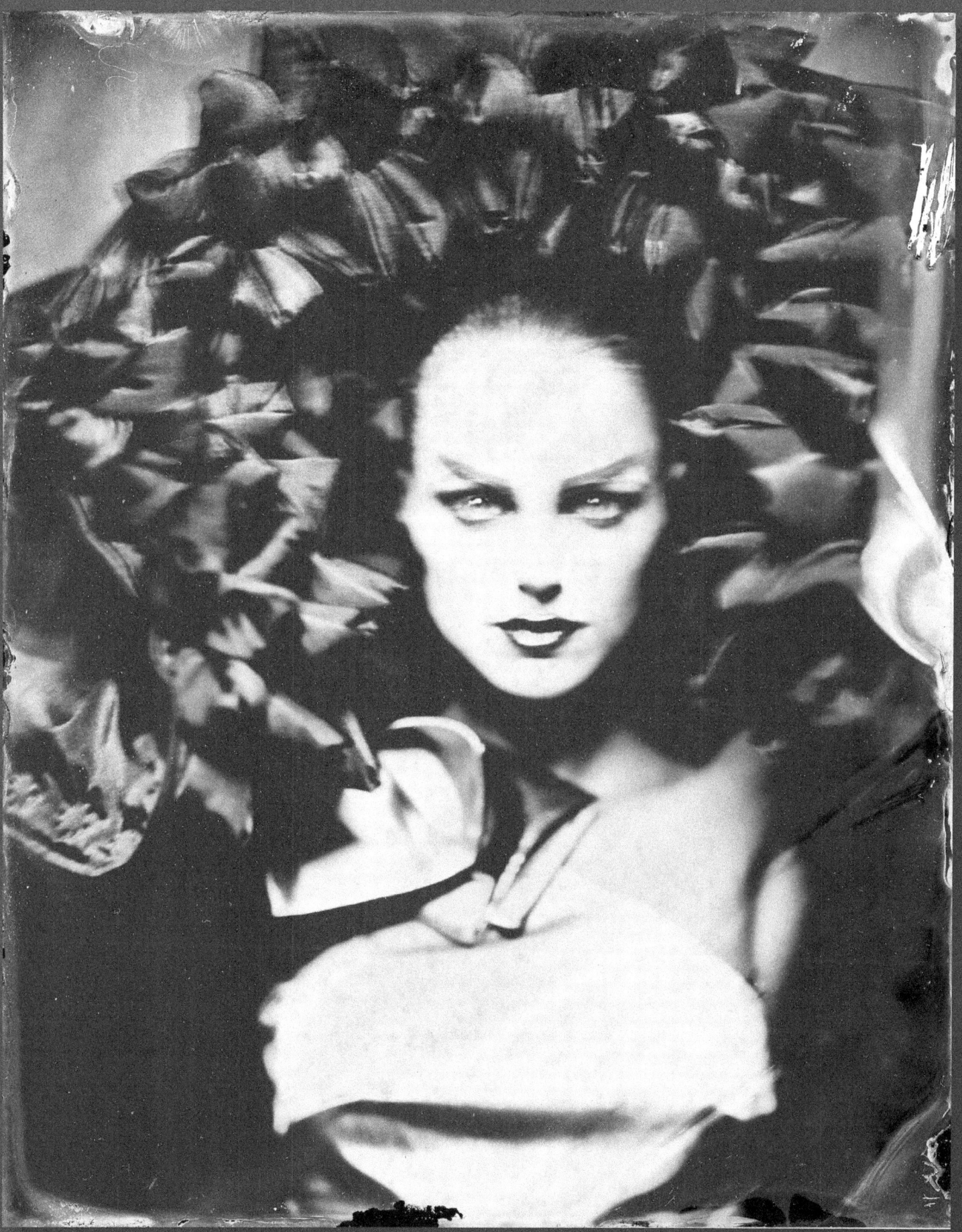

IGOR VASILIADIS

110324-0005

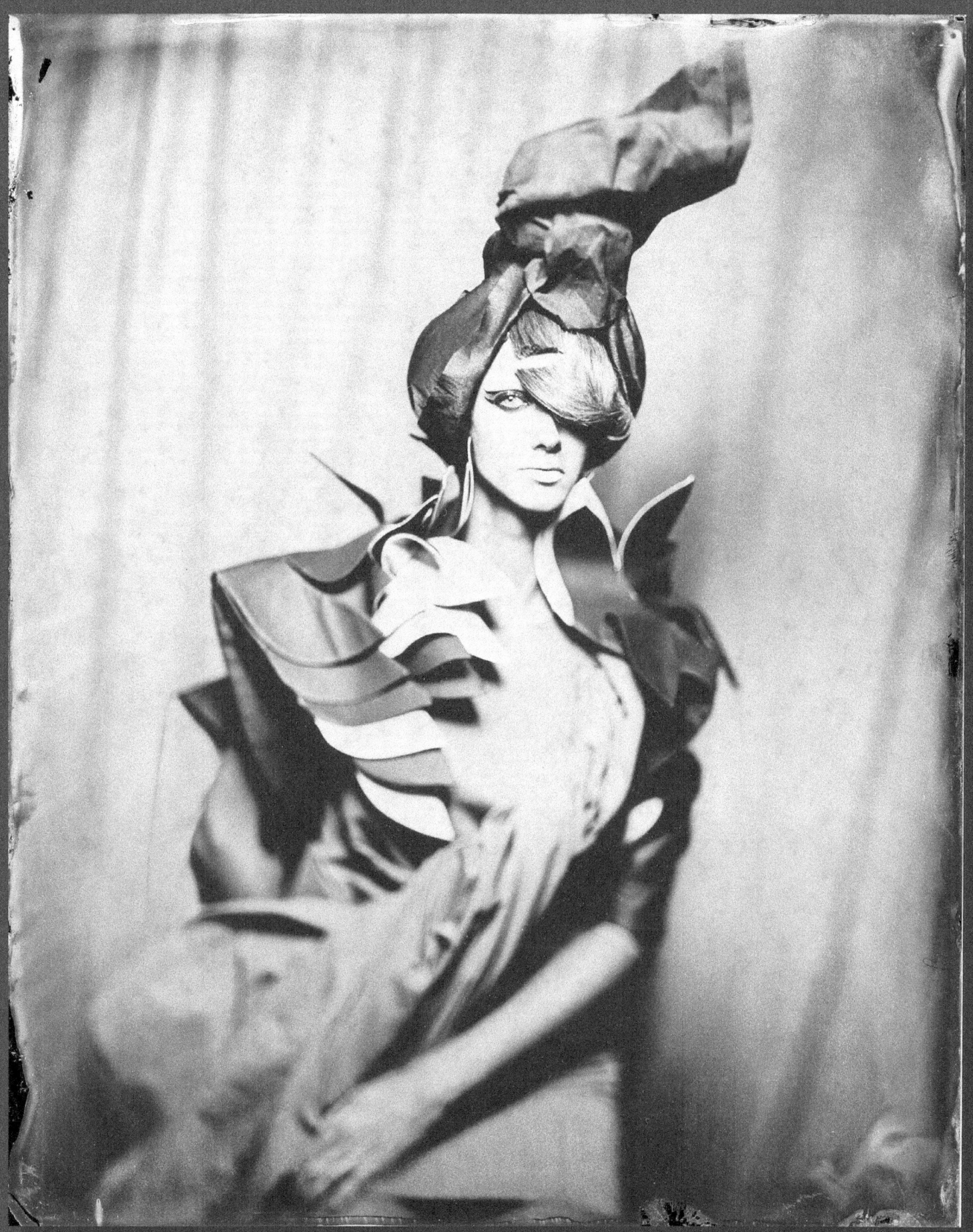

IGOR VASILIADIS

110316-0001

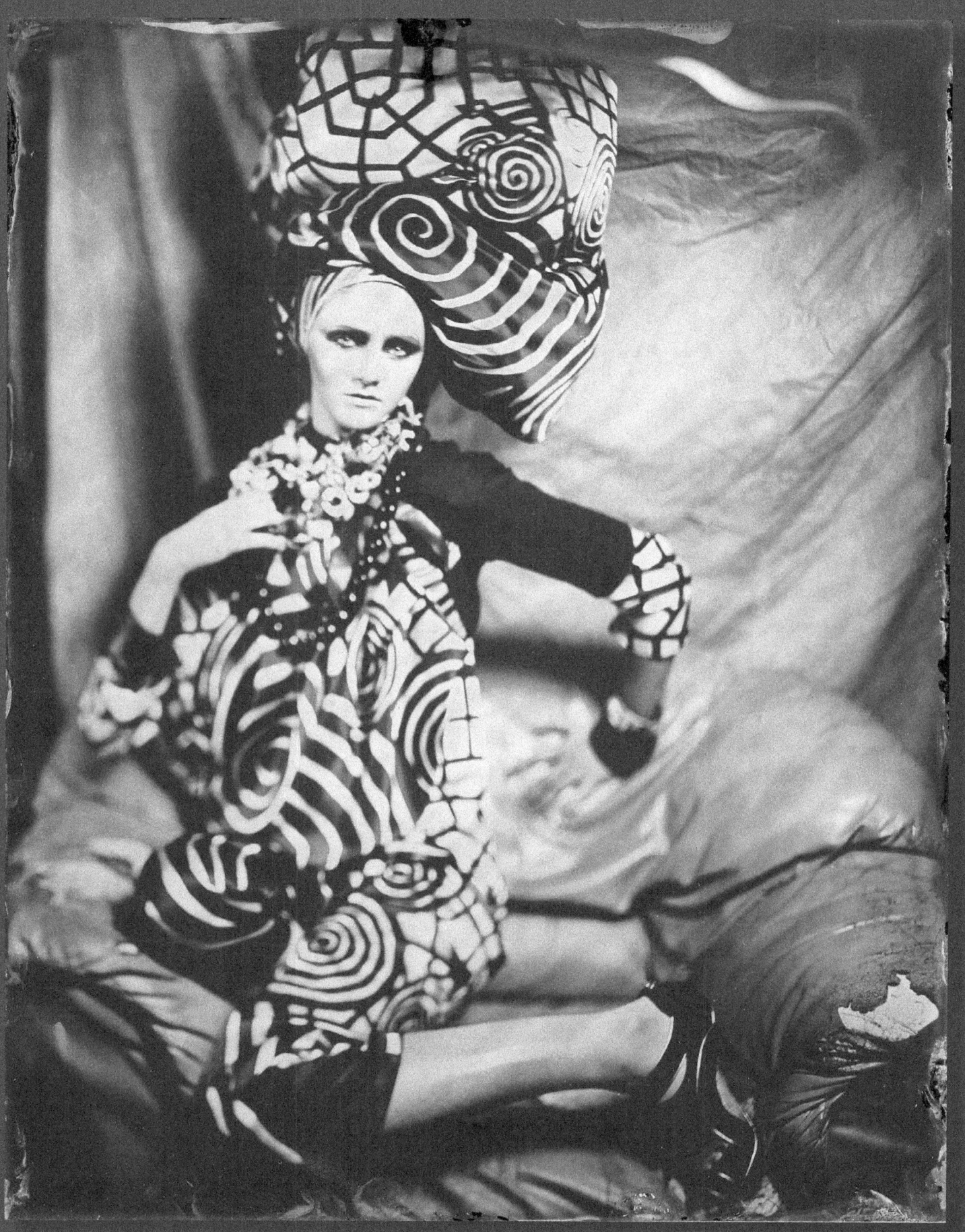

IGOR VASILIADIS

110317-0002

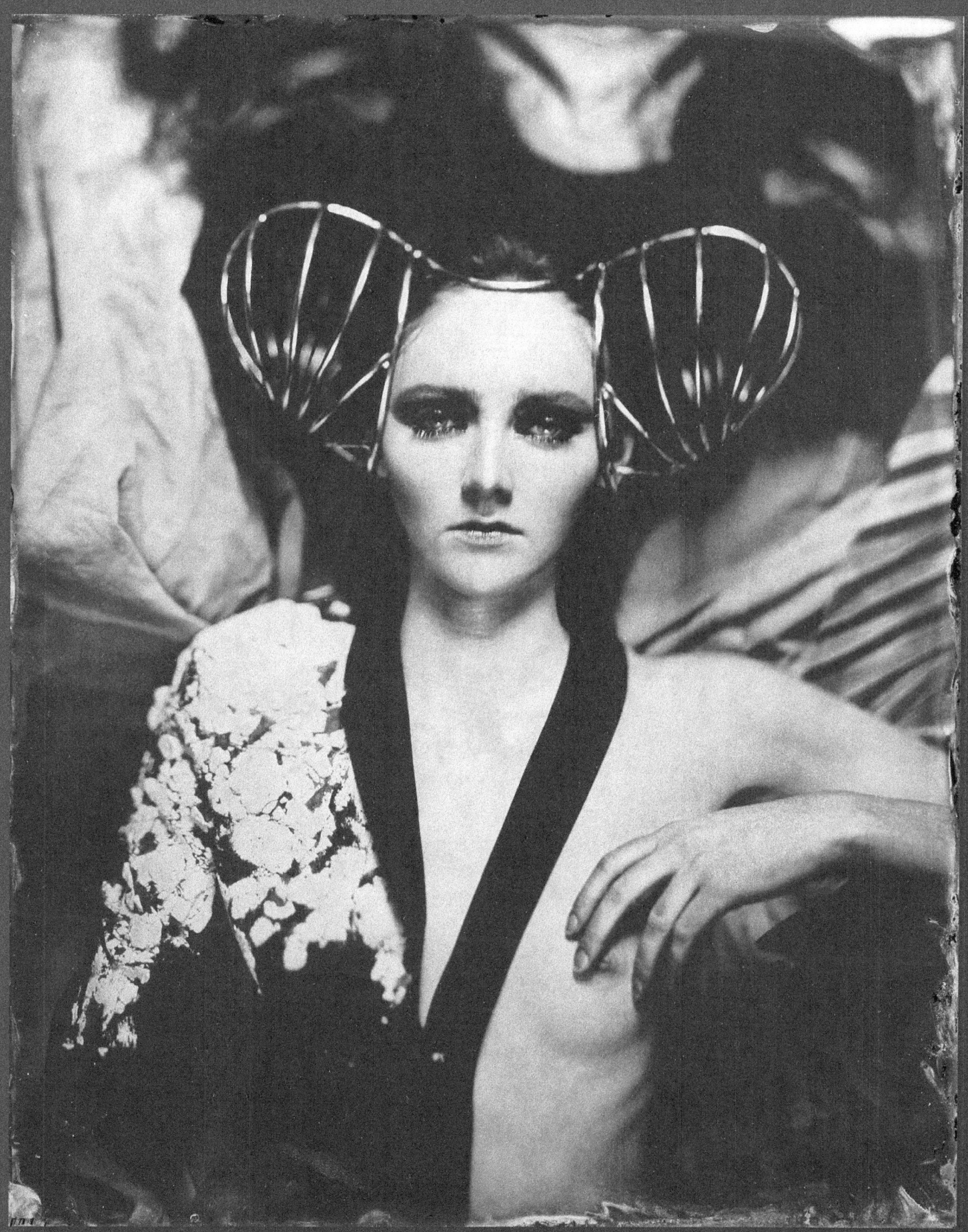

Grace

Terseness

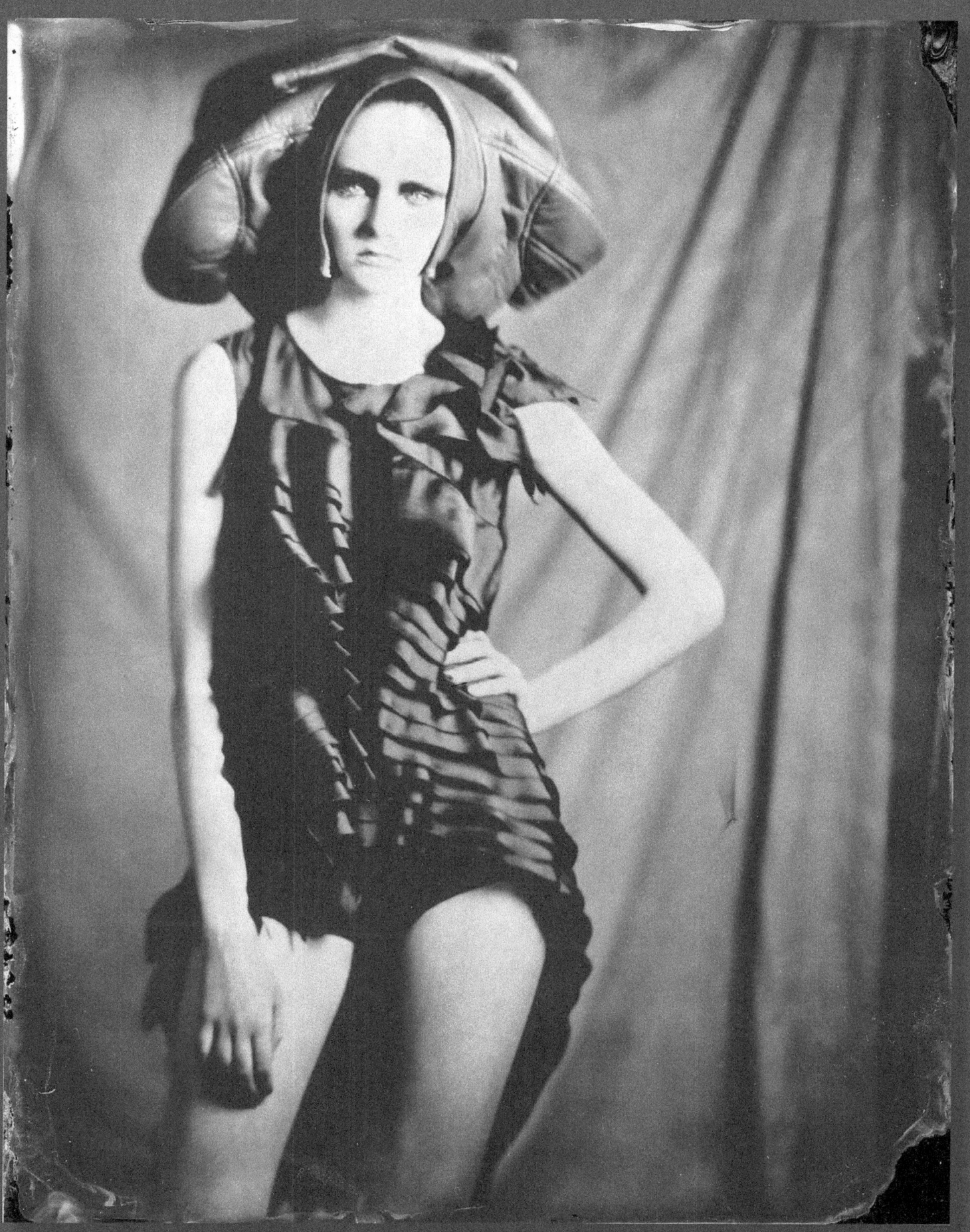

IGOR VASILIADIS

Eccentricity
Individuality

110317-0004

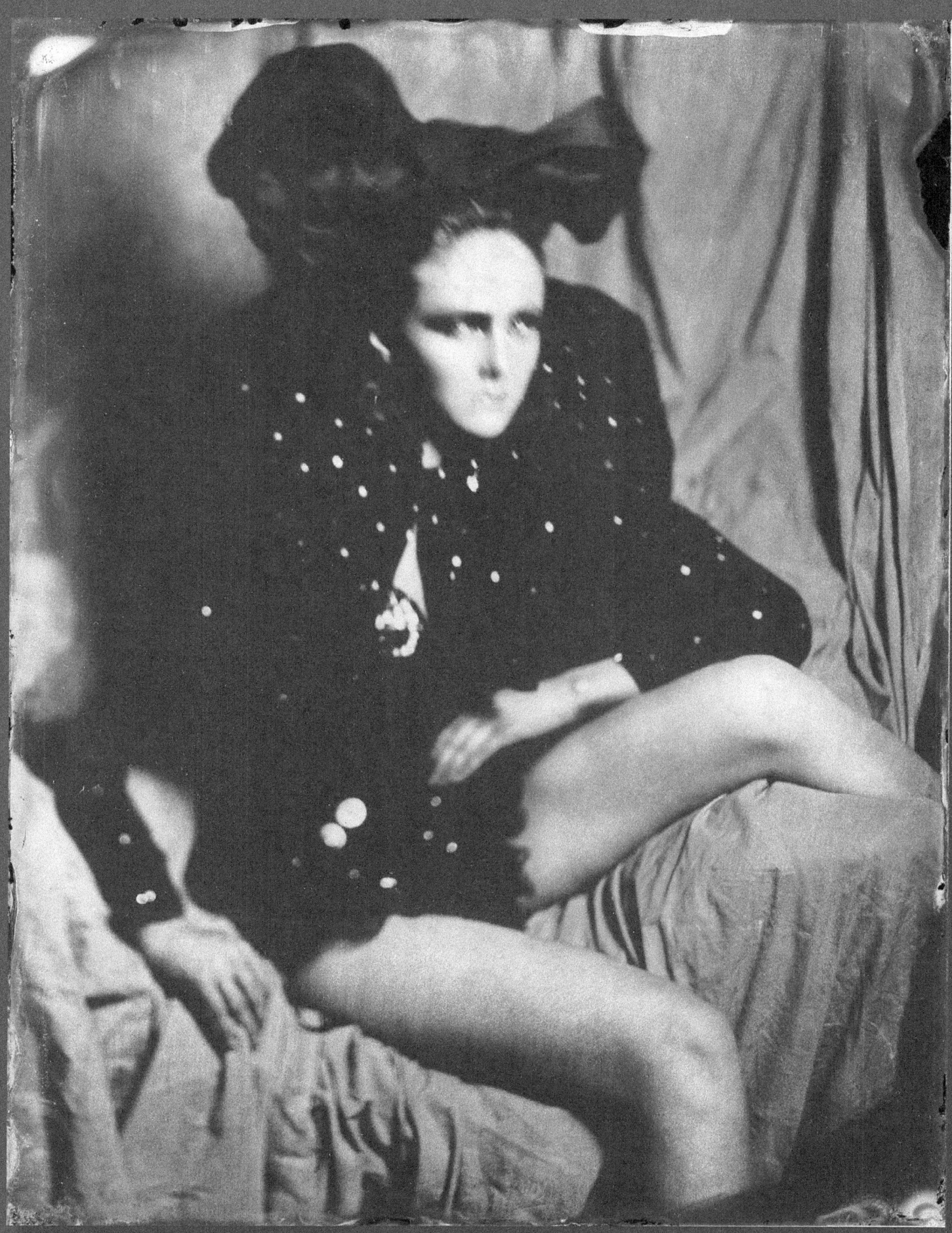

IGOR VASILIADIS

110317-0005

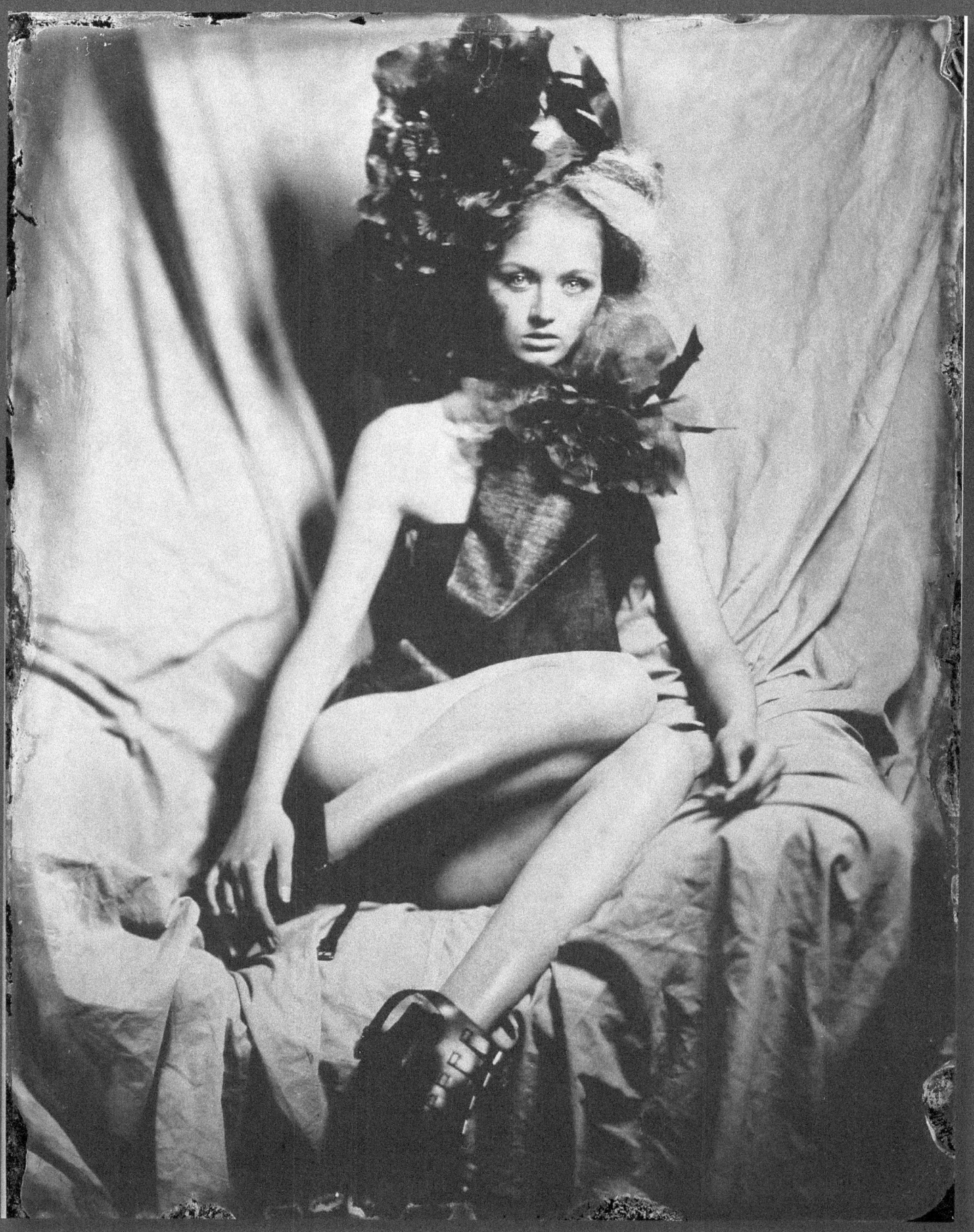

IGOR VASILIADIS

110317-0009

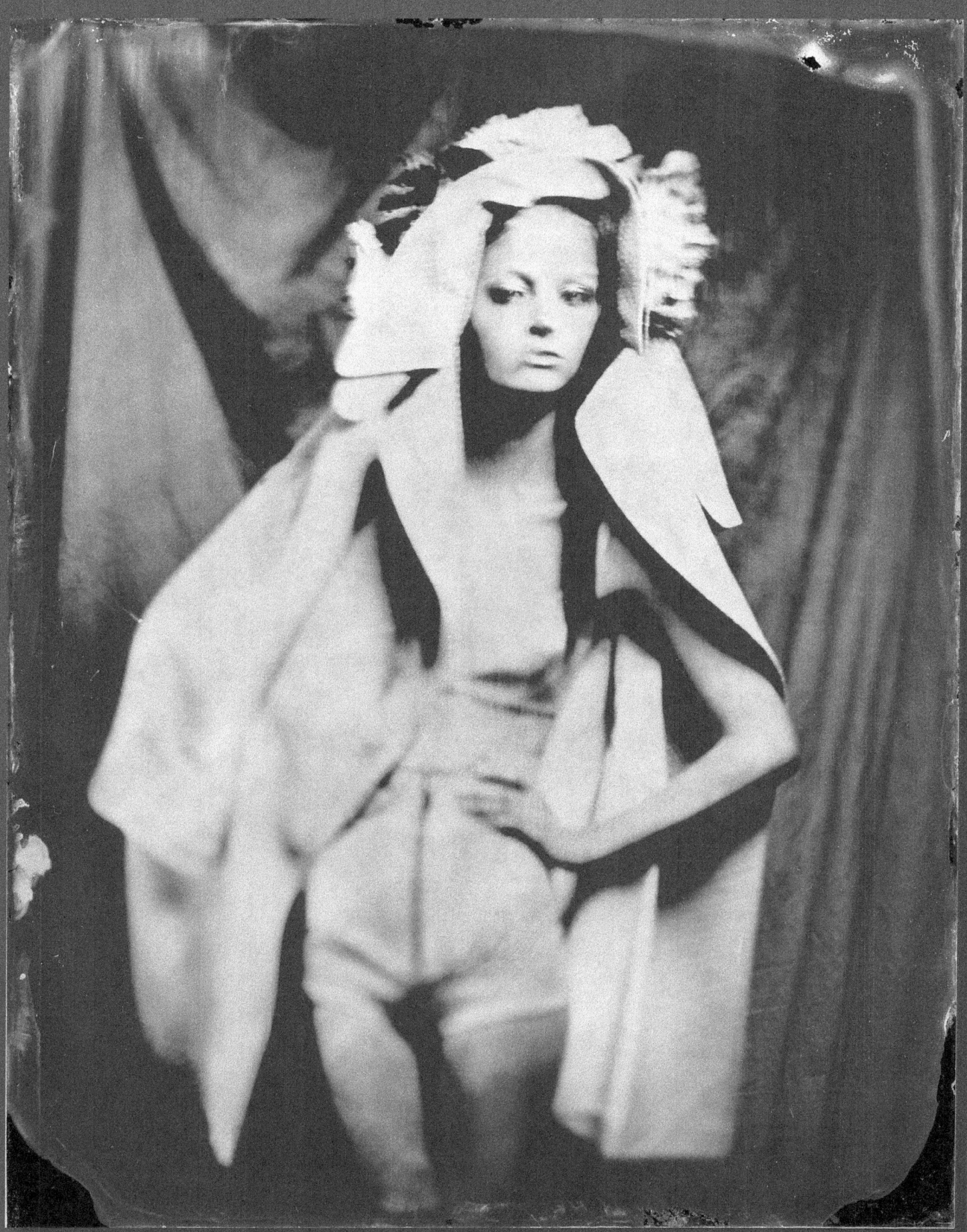

IGOR VASILIADIS

110323-0003

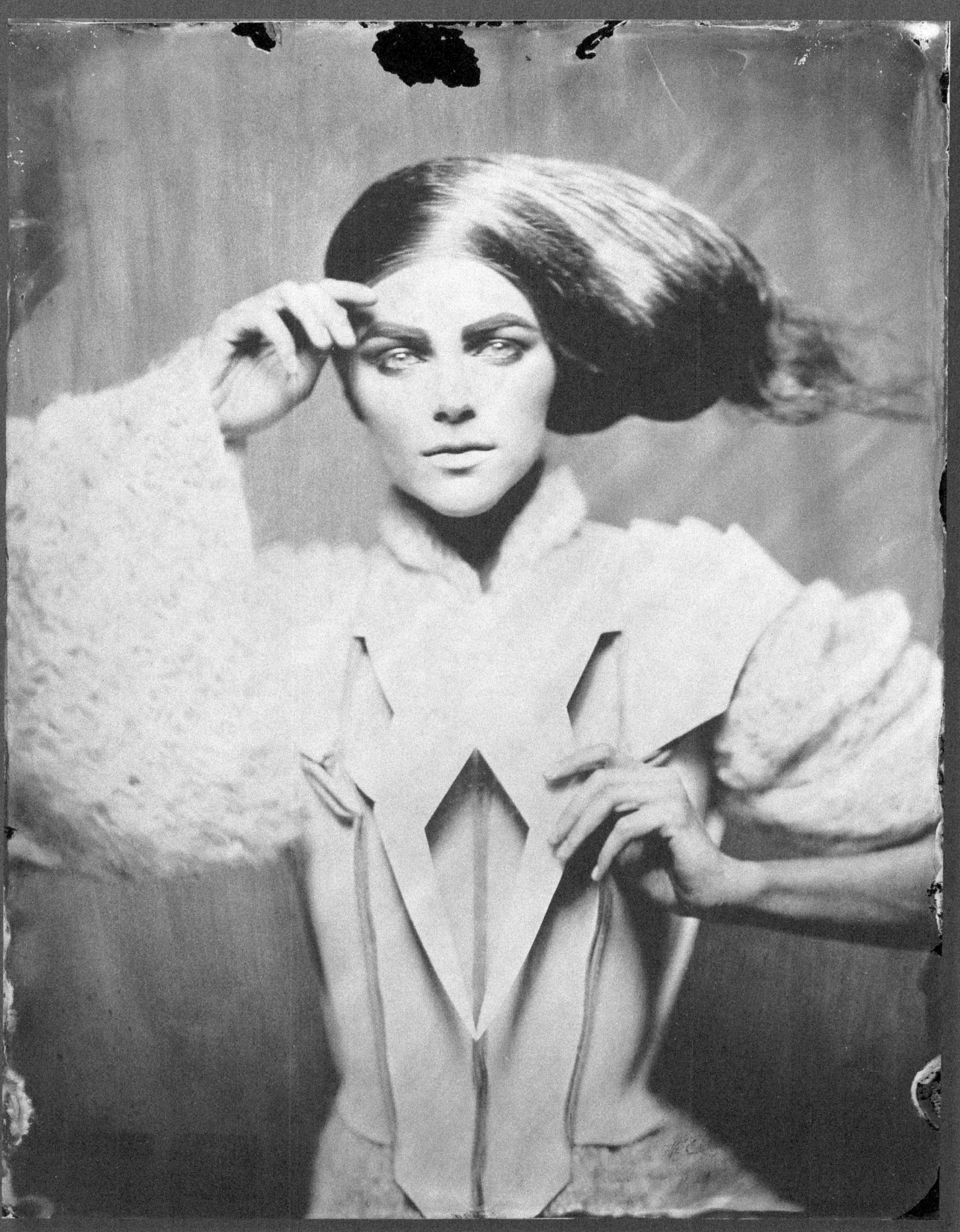

IGOR VASILIADIS

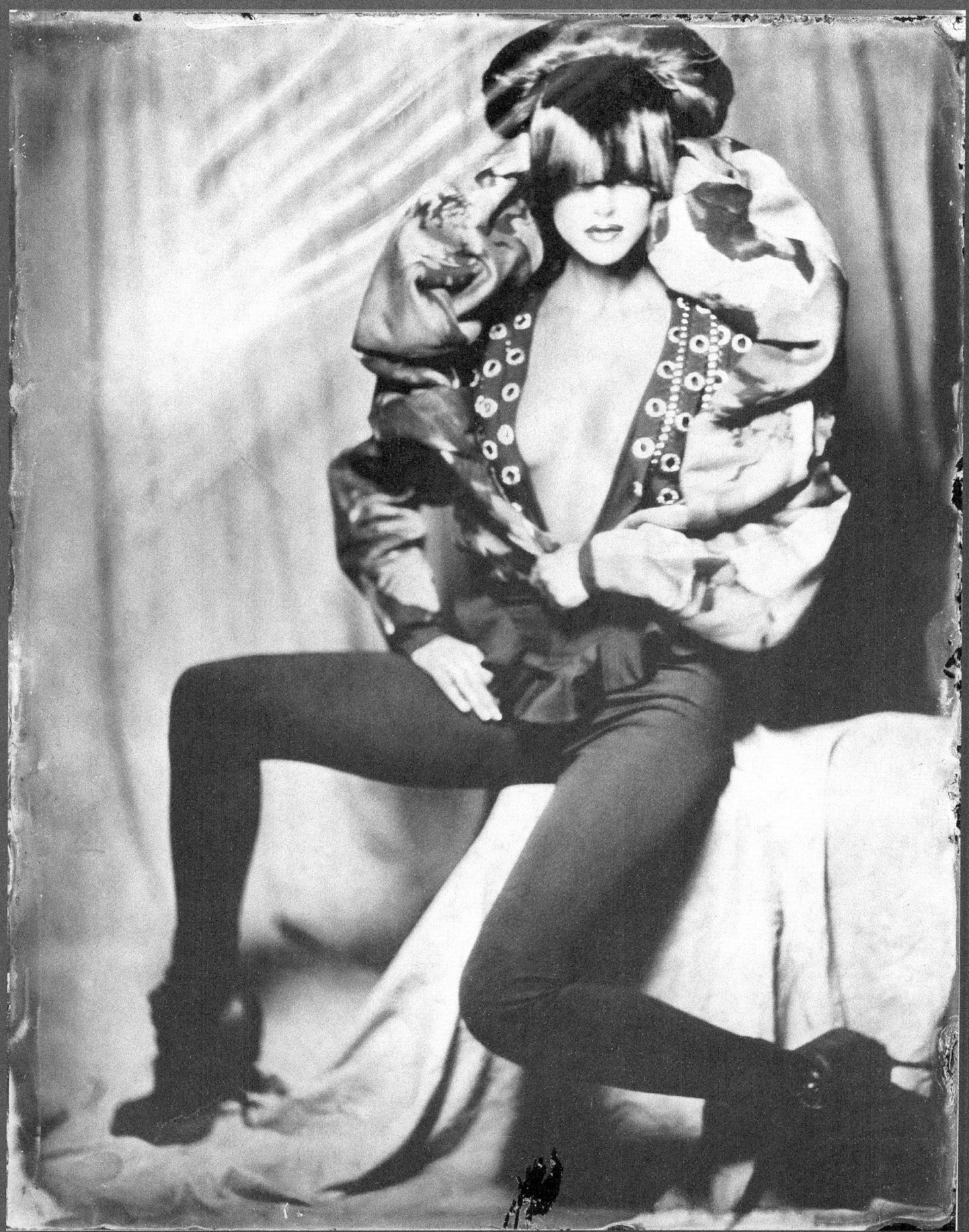

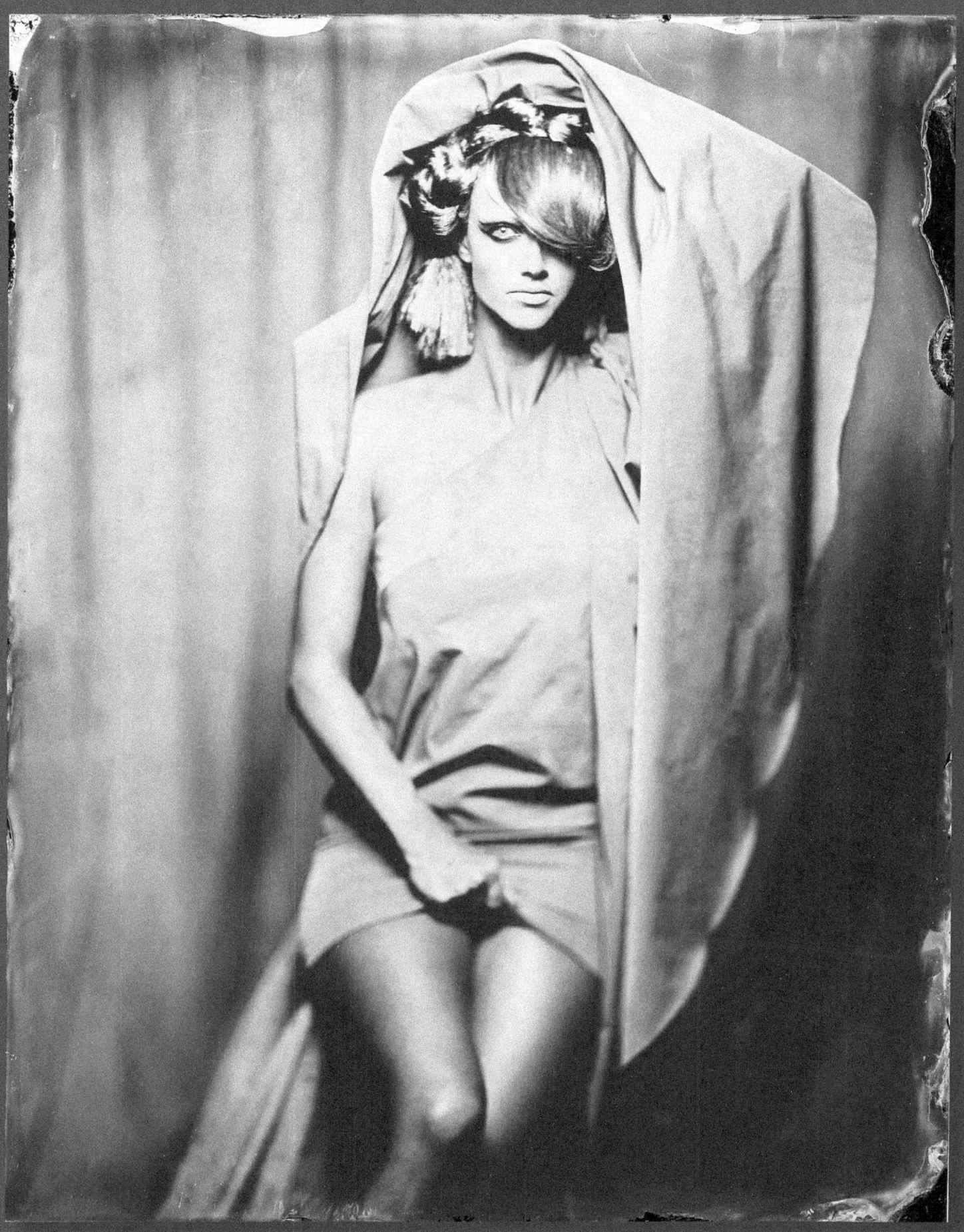

Nobleness

Devotion

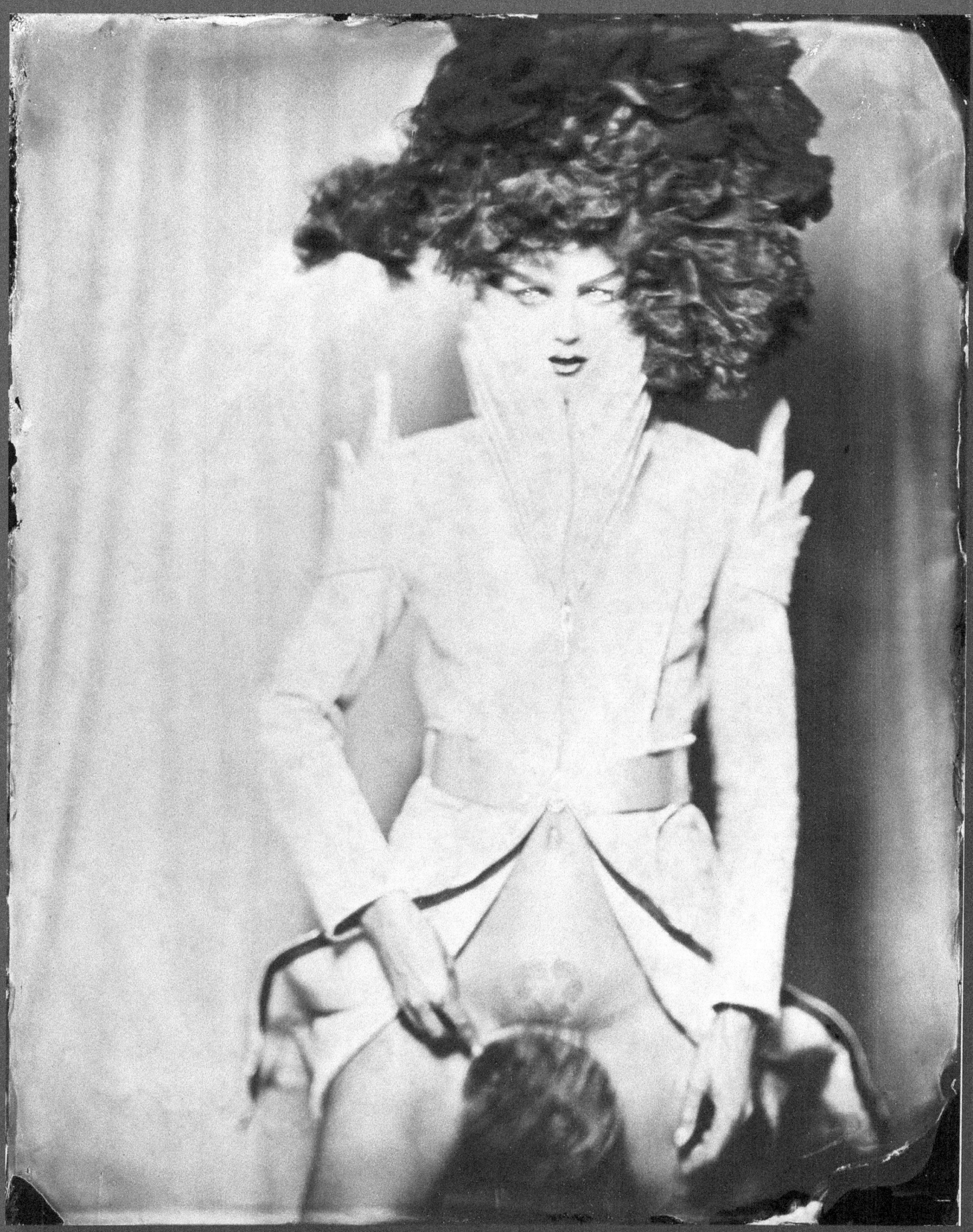

IGOR VASILIADIS

Farewell

Melancholy

110317-0010

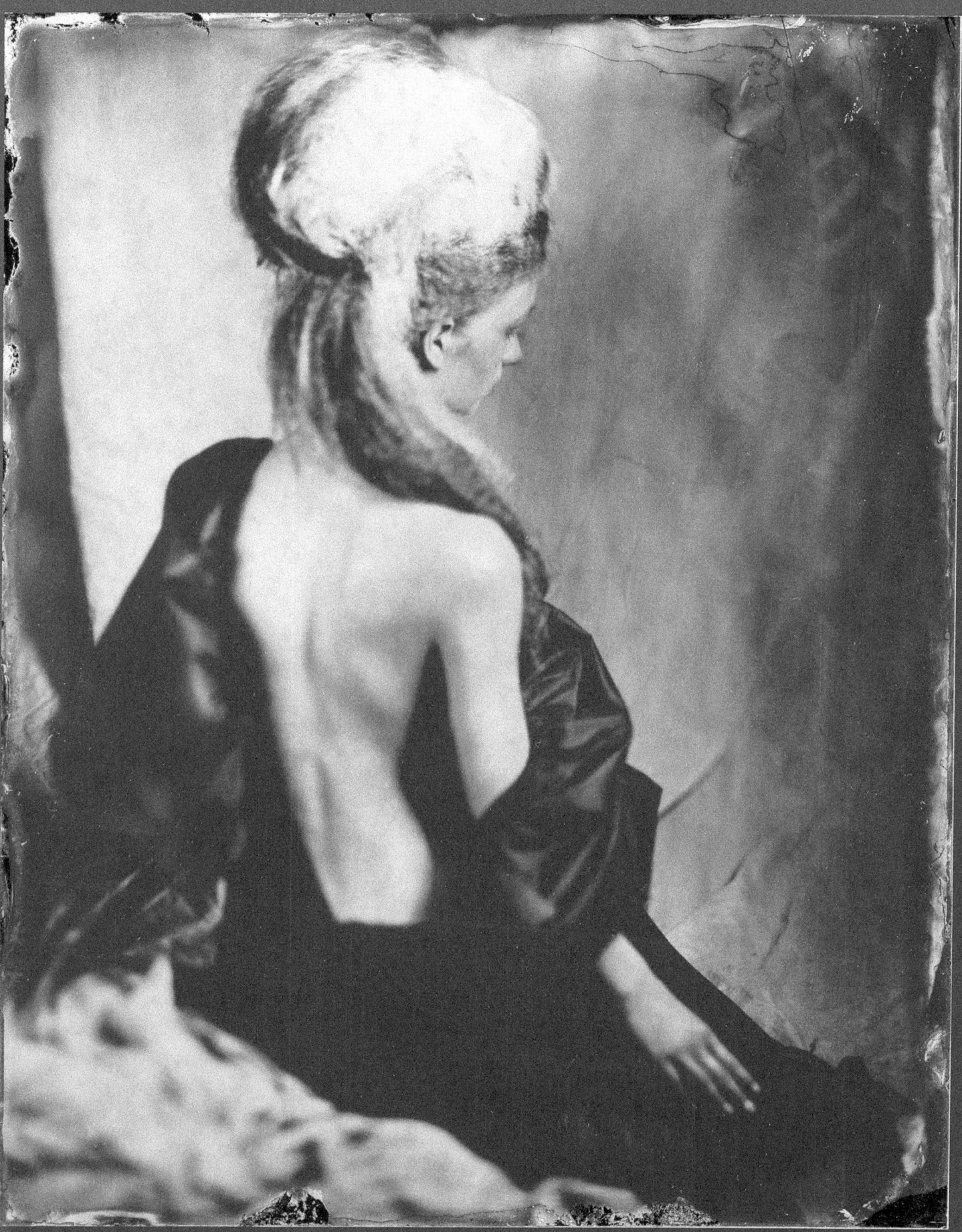

Personal thanks to http://www.artlimited.net Founder Denis Olivier

ISBN   978-1468070514

Printed in USA

www.ingramcontent.com/pod-product-compliance
Lightning Source LLC
Chambersburg PA
CBHW081440170526
45166CB00008B/2260